MARKET RESEARCH MATTERS

TOOLS AND TECHNIQUES FOR ALIGNING YOUR BUSINESS

Robert Duboff

Jim Spaeth

John Wiley & Sons, Inc.

New York • Chichester • Weinheim • Brisbane • Singapore • Toronto

This publication is designed to provide accurate and authoritative information in regard to the subject matter covered. It is sold with the understanding that the publisher is not engaged in rendering legal,
accounting, or other professional services. If legal advice or other expert
assistance is required, the services of a competent professional person
should be sought.

ISBN 0-471-36005-8

Printed in the United States of America.

10 9 8 7 6 5 4 3 2 1

Contents

Contents

Preface

We have written this book to help an industry earn its place at a table to which it has rarely been invited. Market research can and should contribute to setting strategy for businesses. To be included, however, research should not play the traditional role of the rear-view mirror describing the past but rather be the beam in the headlights such that the driver—knowing the power of the vehicle—can more safely steer.

We hit upon this point of view in our roles with the Advertising Research Foundation (ARF), the only association that represents all the marketing elements—communication/advertising agencies, media companies, advertisers, and research providers—that focus on the informational lifeblood of research.

We both love research. Jim, now the full-time president of the ARF, has worked at most of these component parts of the industry—agency, advertiser, and provider—whereas Rob had only worked on the provider side until quite recently. However, Rob (the part-time chairman of the ARF) has felt the potential for researchers in his career. At first, he ran a business called Decision Research (actually a part of a small consulting firm, Temple, Barker & Sloane). Over time, the firm was sold and combined into a rather large strategy consulting firm, Mercer Management Consulting (Mercer). Rob—with the same skill set and belief in research—was now a "management consultant" instead of a "researcher." As such, he has led teams consulting to senior management at such fine companies as America Online (AOL); E*Trade, Hilton Hotels, MicroAge, PPG, and The Walt Disney Company. As a consultant, his views are solicited in a way that those of researchers rarely are. Much of his thinking contained in this book is a product of Mercer teams—particularly interactions with Jon Fay and David McIntosh for a Conference Board Presentation in 1996. These concepts are presented here with the permission of Mercer.

Jim has spent the last 30 years in research, first at Young & Rubicam and then General Foods, where his consistent focus was the support of marketing decision makers—those who had to deal effectively with a future not yet known to us. The second half of his career was spent working with great friends on inventing the future of research, first at Burke Marketing Services, then at Viewfacts, and finally at ASI Market Research before joining the Advertising Research Foundation as president in 1996. Jim has *lived* the transformation of the research profession, from one-off consumer surveys to integrated marketing process models used to steer businesses from day to day. This emerging role for research promises both far greater value to those who use it and far greater rewards to those who provide it—goals worth striving for and the central message of this book.

It is this history that formed the core of the book and the raison d'être for writing it. The ARF has railed for years about the need for researchers to prove their value and continually sought case studies in our belief that the right paradigm existed somewhere and just needed publicity to blossom. However, as we jointly had some responsibility for making this happen at the ARF, we recognized that although research is an integral part of marketing decisions (as documented vividly in the ARF's annual David Ogilvy Research awards for communication campaigns based on research), it is rarely the basis of strategic thrusts in helping businesses plot their future. Hopefully, this book will help businesses and researchers create the case studies for documentation early in the twenty-first century.

For giving us the confidence to launch this book effort, we need to thank the ARF and its board first and foremost. They are great professionals and friends.

In addition, Rob wants to thank his family, particularly Janet Berkeley, a great person and wife; three boys—Josh, Sam, and Brett—and his parents, who provided both strong left- and right-brain instincts. Professionally, former colleagues at Mercer Management Consulting and clients (particularly Victor Millar) provided ideas, stimulation and support. Al Boote was a great mentor at the onset, and Peter Temple and Carl Sloane provided stimulation and a caring environment.

Jim wants to thank his family, his wife Ruth, and his daughters Bess and Amanda for their patience and support. He has had the great pleasure of working with many visionaries of marketing research, including George Williams, Bill Moran, Bill McKenna, Rand Nickerson, and Bill Moult; he hopes that some of the wisdom they have each imparted has found its proper place in this book.

We both sincerely hope this book has an impact and helps businesses plan and strategize better. We also hope researchers will proactively assert themselves, contribute, and prove the value of our craft. Finally, we hope readers will respond. Please e-mail reactions, examples, and so on to us at Jim@thearf.org or Robert.Duboff@ey.com.

■ ORGANIZATION OF THE BOOK

The first chapter lays out the rationale for why businesses should be concerned with the issues addressed in the book. Why is Strategic Anticipation® important?

The next chapter describes in some detail the key research methodologies that form the researching the future tool box. And Chapter 3 suggests how (through processes and tricks of the trade) businesses can implement Strategic Anticipation®.

The remainder of the book focuses on specific topic areas and domains such as customers, competitors, channels, employees, and the like. Each of these chapters, in essence, shows how the thoughts and tools can be applied to that domain. A diagnostic is included to allow you to assess how your business is progressing in each area.

The careful reader (i.e., any one of those who still read in linear fashion end to end) will note some redundancy we've built in to ensure that the grazer-type reader will receive our key themes.

Introduction

No business strategy lasts forever. In fact, you're lucky if it
lasts four quarters. Welcome to the Twenty-First Century.
— Kurt Andersen, *The Turn of the Century*

Businesses that successfully anticipate major marketplace
shifts such as e-commerce, PCs and software, or demand for
bottled water reap rewards of legendary proportions. Few do.
Less dramatic but equally important is the opportunity to
continuously improve customer understanding and marketing, which will grow profits daily. Even in this more pedestrian
pursuit, few businesses demonstrate reliable performance over
time. We believe that business can and should do better, and
this book will tell you how.

The objectives are twofold:

1. Influence and motivate executives to adopt techniques that will enable them to seize opportunities
   that the future offers or, at least, avoid its pitfalls.
2. Establish a new generation of marketing researchers
   eager, able, and recognized as contributors to this
   important process—and the decisions and strategies
   that may emerge.

■ OPERATING IN THE DARK

The first objective may seem too logical, if not obvious, for a
book that will give executives tools that will not only help

them address day-to-day change but also enable them to capitalize on seemingly discontinuous change. However, although virtually all of the evidence suggests that the importance of the process of strategic planning is being recognized, specifically grappling with what might happen differently in the future is not a focal point and is not typically considered critical to the process. For example:

➤ Nary a survey of CEOs or other senior executives has found the need to effectively plan for the future as a top issue. A case in point are the surveys conducted by Mercer Management Consulting. Clients are regularly asked what is paramount on their minds. The responses range from growth to controlling costs, but they rarely revolve around understanding what might happen next.

➤ The Spring 1999 special issue of *Sloan Management Review* featured 13 articles from foremost academic strategic thinkers. There was virtually no mention of marketing research or how it could provide insight into the future.

Actually, most strategies of existing companies—virtually all strategic plan documents—are based on business-as-usual assumptions for the outside world of customers and competitors. And when corporate strategy for the future *is* the topic, marketing researchers are rarely at the table for the discussion.

So, to the extent that senior executives don't mention the need to assess what the future will bring—either from the mistaken belief that there is no way to determine what will happen or from blindness due to short-term performance demands from stakeholders—this book's contents will be eye-opening.

This leads to the second objective: There are tools—established techniques of the marketing research trade—that can be effective in helping companies confront the future they cannot hope to control.

Ironically, such tools are infrequently used. In fact, research by both authors' organizations suggest that few of the techniques described in this book are used by more than 10 percent of the large firms in any given year. Even within those firms that do conduct marketing research, according to a Mercer Management Consulting survey,[1] few CEOs or boards spend even a small fraction of their time perusing data on their own customers, despite the considerable amount of lip service they pay to customer focus. A recent ARF set of one-on-one interviews with senior executives suggested a relatively low level of esteem for what market research provides them.

There are even some executives who fail to use marketing research to gain an understanding of their current relationship with customers, employees, and shareholders. If you are one of these executives or one who uses marketing research only as a lamppost to support already agreed-upon business arguments instead of as a beacon to define future direction, then you might as well stop reading. There is little that we can do for you. Understanding the recent past and present is necessary—though not sufficient—to researching the future. You need a stable foothold and insight into the dynamics of the marketplace from which to be able to peer effectively into the future.

■ THE STATE OF MARKETING RESEARCH

There are various reasons for resistance to marketing research as an aid to strategic planning. Sometimes it is because the marketing research function is staffed with scientists who focus on numbers rather than meaning and hence are buried deep in the corporation. Sometimes it is because the company, concerned about unnecessary expenditures, demands that its marketing researchers minimize costs and not *waste* money on learning. Sometimes it is because the marketing tools can appear to the firm's leadership to be too technically complex and obscure or too slow to have immediate connection to the god of actionability.

But arguments against marketing research all boil down into two basic dimensions: one rational, the other emotional. It is worth discussing these viewpoints about marketing research. Like most widely held perceptions, there is a degree of insight and even truth to be found in them. The trick is to separate the insight from false or unproved assumptions.

➤ Just the Facts, Please

➤ *Rational argument #1:* "There's no way to get the real facts." Although it's true that marketing research does not offer rock-solid facts, it can produce numbers with validity and reliability for specific and limited situations when done properly. Well-thought-out research can provide estimates of how those in the sampled universe will respond if asked the same question. That's the beauty of marketing research—if you follow the laws of probability and the correct process, you will get information within known constraints (e.g., 95 percent assurance that, if asked, between 40 percent and 50 percent of all your customers would be very interested in trying your new product).

➤ *Rational argument #2:* "Customers can't predict the future." Although individual customers (presumably) can't forecast the future, researchers can make accurate estimates based on many customers' expressed needs and desires. Some techniques have been with us for some time; others are brand new. At a minimum, they can produce information that offers better input to decision making than if no marketing research were done at all.

➤ *Rational argument #3:* "Market research is vague and imprecise, if not downright biased." This argument breaks down into several concerns—for example, about the nature of those surveyed or their veracity or the intentions of the sponsors. But these issues can be overcome by a well-designed research approach that is part of a continuing process, one in which there is ongoing information gathering about the target and dialogue between researchers and decision makers.

➤ *Rational argument #4:* "I don't have time for this stuff." These days, time to market is a critical competitive factor, as a great deal of product development must occur simultaneously rather than consecutively. Consequently, it is easy for a harassed executive to decide to eliminate seemingly unessential steps. Yet it is not only shortsighted to think of market research as less than essential—it is, after all, the best way to receive potential customer feedback prior to market launch—but it is also unnecessary: Any tight, focused, short-term market research project can be completed in four to six weeks. If even that time period is considered too onerous, then the researcher should consider using electronic means to reach potential respondents and produce results more quickly. A less polite observation is that there's really no hurry at all for information if the decision maker is committed to rushing to the market with a product for which there is no demand.

➤ Emotional Undercurrents

Emotional arguments are often not clearly articulated, and the decision maker may not even be aware of the root of his or her concern. But the authors have identified two strains of inner thought:

➤ *Emotional argument #1:* "The scientists will take over my job." Some decision makers simply are uncomfortable with cold numbers generated through a process they can't control from respondents who are anonymous, and they refuse to let them determine business decisions. After all, the fun of being a decision maker is making the decisions.

➤ *Emotional argument #2:* "I graduated from school a long time ago." Those who feel this way tend to be command-and-control types who see marketing research as equivalent to report cards and don't want to hear the results, especially if it counters their gut feelings.

Although it would be tough to change the mind-set of the last species of executive, should you harbor one of these other concerns, you should soon realize they are unjustified. As you discover how marketing research paired with financial and other data can hone your decision making for greater success in the near future and enable you to anticipate the potential for discontinuous change and improve decisions over the longer term, you are likely to become an advocate. The decisions are still yours, but the opportunity to base them on facts and strong inferences will be established. Research can't make decisions, but it can help make them better.

■ THE CHALLENGE OF THE FUTURE

J. W. Marriott is credited with observing that "success is never final." This sentiment has never been more apt than now. Every entrepreneur dreams of establishing a giant enterprise that becomes a powerhouse—a Fortune 500 firm. The vast majority of new ventures fail, but historically, if a company achieved that size, it was likely to stay strong. Recent data show, however, that such success, once achieved today, is mighty hard to maintain. The Fortune listing began in 1955, and only a minority of those on that first list (less than two hundred) would still qualify today. And the pace of attrition is quickening. For the first 40 years (1955–1995), the average loss was between 8 to 9 dropping each year. Over the past 4 years, on average, 70 firms have dropped per year (albeit with a slightly different formula being used by the magazine). Mercer Management Consulting research supports this point. Looking back a decade, Mercer has found that only 8 percent of the Fortune 500 firms were "profitable growers" (show above average growth in revenues and profits for their industry) in both five-year periods.[2]

Although it has always been somewhat difficult to stay on top, the task is clearly far more difficult today as the pace of change intensifies. The marketplace displays a growing proliferation of new products and advertisements about them on top of those that already exist. Either because of this increasing choice and competition or as a coincidental trend, loyalty to brands has never been in greater jeopardy. At the same time, layoffs by even the best employers have eroded employee loyalty. We have truly entered the "free agent" era, as *Fast Company* magazine has so aptly put it. This change is so pervasive that as Chris Meyer and Stan Davis point out in their book *Future Wealth,* markets will start rewarding "brain power" in addition to more traditional, tangible forms of wealth.

The result is an ever-changing landscape in which it is hard to stay on top for long. The fate and fortunes of companies change so rapidly now that even Coca-Cola and Disney—two great performers during the past decade—were both called to task the same week (May 3, 1999) in *The Wall Street Journal.* It is harder and harder for consultants, and incidentally, book authors, to cite any company for fear its future will have changed dramatically even before publication, much less 5 to 10 years later.

■ ANSWERS ARE UP FOR GRABS

Strategists have searched for the secret elixir. Here is a brief summary of some of the best:

➤ In the classic *In Search of Excellence,* Tom Peters and Robert Waterman cited 43 companies, including IBM, General Electric, Procter & Gamble, Johnson & Johnson, and Exxon, for their attention to eight qualities: closeness to the customer, a bias for action, autonomy and entrepreneurship, productivity through people, a values-driven organization, corporate focus, lean management, and simultaneous loose-tight management.[3]

► In Arie de Geus's book *The Living Company: Habits for Survival in a Turbulent Environment,* he documents four traits of companies that have lasted centuries: sensitivity to the environment, cohesion and identity, tolerance and decentralization, and conservative financing. Of these, the first—environmental awareness—would seem most applicable to this book's topic.[4]

► In still another book, *Built to Last: Successful Habits of Visionary Companies,* James C. Collins and Jerry I. Porras compare 18 "visionary" picks to a matched control group of "successful-but-second-rank" companies in similar businesses. Thus, Disney is compared with Columbia Pictures; Ford, with GM; and so on. The authors question the myth that visionary businesses start with a great product and are pushed into the future by charismatic leaders. Much more important, and a much more telling line of demarcation, they say, is flexibility as well as having aspirational goals.[5]

► *The Winning Streak Mark II,* by Walter Goldsmith and David Clutterbuck, lists 10 key factors in sustaining high performance in its report of a study of mostly European companies. The most germane balance is "customer care versus counter count"; that is, the successful company "focuses very sharply on who the customers are, why they do business with the company, and how the relationship can be developed to the maximum benefit of both the customers and the company. The lessons are:

—A recognition that the best customer is usually an existing customer;

—A talent for focusing on the customers they really want to keep;

—Building relationships with character; and

—Putting competitive advantage before cost."[6]

With so much direction, why do the giants fade so consistently? The answers vary by company and leader, but undoubtedly they include:

➤ *Arrogance.* Hubris, "the sin of success," can blind leaders into believing that what has worked to date will continue to work.

➤ *Blinders.* Focusing too intently on the present can cause a failure to notice a "point of inflection" (as Andrew Grove calls it) or Value Migration® (coined by Mercer Management Consulting Vice President Adrian Slywotzky), two current terms for discontinuous change.

➤ *Fear.* With a defensive posture rather than an offensive one, businesses can become like sports teams that get the lead and then change their game plan to protect the lead *only* defensively.

Jack Welch offers a summary perspective: "The big companies that get into trouble are those that try to manage their size instead of experimenting with it."[7]

■ THE ADDITION OF STRATEGIC ANTICIPATION®

How can companies, big and small, do better? Our answer lies in a single concept: Strategic Anticipation® (SA®), an apt Mercer term defined as "the ability to continually assess the environment, particularly focusing on targeted customers, and to act on the signals that change is coming." Admittedly, Strategic Anticipation® requires a mind-set shift for most businesses: There can be no sacred cows except that of building shareholder/stakeholder value. GE is an excellent example. Think of its courage at the turn of the last century to turn away from its safe utility core business to become a provider of products and services to that industry. Hewlett-Packard's decision to forsake calculators and 3M's move from mining are other good examples. But more important than turning their backs on the past, these three companies have built systematic methods to ensure continual change. A requirement to always be one of the most profitable in your industry or to set a standard for contributions of new revenue streams each year are institutional strategies that force general managers to stay attentive to customer needs and push for innovation.

The key to the "anticipation" part, of course, can be marketing research. After all, if you reconstruct any successful strategy to determine the basis of the decision, there are only three possibilities:

1. The chief executive officer (CEO) as Plato's philosopher-king, instinctively making the correct decisions, with the ability to pierce through the fogs and shadows of the caves that thwart others.
2. Luck or good fortune.
3. Insights into the marketplace.

The third would seem the likeliest. In war, it's easier if you know the terrain, the weaponry of the opposition, and the skills of your generals. In sports, it's easier if you've scouted the other team and the physical characteristics of the playing field. Likewise, in achieving competitive advantage, it's easier if you know the current environment and the likely actions of all key players, from customers to competitors. As many self-proclaimed philosopher-kings have learned, often what looked like skill was really luck. For awhile, Fred Silverman was king of TV—"the man with the golden gut," a programming genius. His reign was as short as that of Al "Chainsaw" Dunlap, who was a book-writing genius at Scott and something quite short of that at Sunbeam.

Marketers succeed when their decisions lead to profitable growth.

■ PROFITABLE MARKETING DECISIONS

Most decision makers' success is at least partially due to luck, but for some, at least, success is a reflection of the quality of their insight and information. Think about those big decisions you've made. They have been made in the present, using information from the past, to anticipate outcomes in the future. If you had information from the future, it would all be so much easier, though there would still be the issue of judgment. Experience, training, insight, creativity, and even the ability to tap into the unconscious can produce the kinds of judgments that result in profitable growth. The information being used is equally critical. A good judgment based on poor information or no data triggers a business tragedy — "tragedy" because it was preventable.

If your experience, training, insight, and creativity have provided you with excellent business judgment, then you deserve excellent marketing information (unless you are very good with a Ouija board). Anything less is an abuse of your gifts and a dereliction of your duties! What is excellent marketing information? Read on, because that is exactly what this book is about.

Excellent marketing information is the edge that differentiates winners from losers who faced the same opportunity but responded differently. Capturing historical data and applying analytical tools to extract what they have to tell us about the future make up the general process. Understanding why people respond to today's circumstances enables us to know how they will respond to changing future circumstances and the outcomes (opportunities or challenges) that will result.

■ THREE DANGEROUS MYTHS

Why is this news? Wouldn't any prudent manager use the best possible information? Consider these myths many of us live by:

1. I know these things.
2. Things never really change (so simply updating yesterday's plan will be fine).
3. The people with whom I talk all agree with me.

The first myth is built on overconfidence. The second myth is almost comforting—"nothing every really changes" means we already know everything we need. The third myth would seem to support a lazy attitude. ("If I talk to just a few people, I'll know how everyone feels.") We're not even talking about conducting focus groups here but rather casual conversations with one or two customers (or worse, golf cronies).

All three myths are comforting *and* wrong; in fact, they are dangerous. Nevertheless, they represent common thinking.

This book makes the case that better decisions—that is, more profitable marketing decisions—are made when quality information is employed. Furthermore, it outlines the types of decisions made and the types of information available. It describes case histories to demonstrate that this can happen.

It also states that this better information—and even insight—can and should come from marketing researchers. This, too, flies in the face of tradition. As noted, a recent ARF pilot study of CEO interviews (conducted by Dawn Lesh) provided the unsettling news that CEOs essentially distrusted marketing information generated by their research department compared with financial information or even information from their internal Management Information Services department. This finding parallels an earlier study by William Schiemann & Associates, in which senior executives from 205 companies were surveyed. Of those queried in that survey, less than one-third said they would "bet their jobs" on the quality of information they received about their market and customers (versus over 60 percent for quality of financial information and 40 percent for operational information).[8]

In a more generous vein, Dan Dinnell, head of strategic planning for Hilton Hotels, said in an interview with the authors, "Traditional market research has a tough time getting to the unknowns."

Yet even so, marketing research can provide real value by helping to provide the radar that will alert the enterprise to perils—and opportunities—ahead. The techniques mentioned in this book will provide all the tools a researcher and his or her CEO need.

However, tools alone are not enough. (After all, many of these tools have existed for a long time.) Not only does an enterprise need to embrace the possibility of continual change, but also the marketing researcher has to be able to employ the tools and communicate their results effectively. He or she also has to accept responsibility, and be held accountable for his or her findings, to earn a seat at the strategy table. The opportunity and need are there; hopefully, the research community and enterprise leadership are up to the challenge. They had better be. The past is no longer prologue to the future, and the pace of change is approaching "Internet speed" for all industries.

> You can't solve current problems with current thinking.
> Current problems are the result of current thinking.
>
> —Albert Einstein

■ NOTES

1. A Mercer Management Consulting survey of senior executives conducted prior to (and results presented at) an Executive Forum in May 1996.

2. Mercer Growth Team Analysis, 1997.

3. Thomas J. Peters and Robert H. Waterman, Jr., *In Search of Excellence* (New York: Harper & Row, 1982).

4. Arie de Geus, *The Living Company: Habits for Survival in a Turbulent Environment* (Boston: Harvard Business School Press, 1992).

5. James C. Collins and Terry I. Porras, *Built to Last, Successful Habits of Visionary Companies* (New York: HarperCollins, 1999).

6. Walter Goldsmith and David Clutterbuck, *The Winning Streak Mark II* (London: Orion Publishing Group, Ltd., 1997).

7. *The Wall Street Journal,* June 21, 1999.

8. John Lingle, "You Can Get There From Here," in *Case Studies in Strategic Performance Measurement. A Council Report of The Conference Board* (New York: Wm. A. Schieman & Company, 1997).

Why Market Research Matters

> If you change before you have to, by the time the competition catches up to you, you will already be someplace else.
>
> —Sergio Zyman

The tangible rewards that accrue from creating a successful business strategy in an environment of discontinuous change are as unparalleled as the challenge of divining that strategy in the first place. Just look at the market valuations of such companies as Cisco Systems, Intel, Coca-Cola, GE, or Microsoft compared with those of their nearest competitors. Once upon a time, being number one, two, or even three in an industry segment was good enough. Now, as Mercer Management Consulting's research shows, even a silver medalist may not be an economic winner.[1]

Navigating business hyperspace today requires new strategic skills and strategies; it's no longer just about being nimble and agile enough to react to discontinuous change. Lean manufacturing alone won't sustain companies over the longer term, any more than downsizing alone is a winning strategy. Just-in-time responses and just-in-case marketing are insufficient in an era in which it's more important than ever to identify key trends first and then act more quickly than the competition. Our focus in this book is on developing Strategic Anticipation®, which we consider a key core skill to achieving the kind of performance that can lead to quantum growth in revenues and market share, and quantum gains for shareholders.

What's needed to take companies to the next level before the competition gets there is the ability to strategically anticipate what's coming while continuing to efficiently manage the business on a day-to-day basis. A tall order? Not really. Others have done it, and definable skills, techniques, and even models can help businesses grasp and implement this concept. That's the purpose of this book—to help you manage today while thinking about where to steer the organizational ship tomorrow.

Mercer Management Consulting's book *Profit Patterns* (by Slywotzky et al.) touched on this theme when they stated that "reacting to discontinuity is no longer enough. . . . The key skill needed is Strategic Anticipation® and focused, rapid investment in the next generation business design." The authors went on to say that "in the era of polarization, the rewards will go to those who identify patterns early and act on those insights one year sooner than the competition. Being first to establish the trajectory of success translates into being the winner in the polarized environment that follows."[2]

Things have probably not at the leadership level seemed more incomprehensible at any time in recent history. Many of the rules of business have been suspended or overturned by new innovators and technology. One thing is for sure: If a company figures out a new business model before the competition and gets it right, the resulting rewards can be astronomical.

Before we set a trajectory for the moon, let's start with our feet on the ground and take a look at where we might start to build up to something as grand as a leapfrog over the competition.

■ THE PRESENT AS VIEWED FROM THE PAST

Because so much of the future is connected to the past, let's begin by searching for a historical context into which we can place Strategic Anticipation®. The earliest precursors of today's best-of-the-best business leaders may very well have been fortune-tellers.

At one level, Strategic Anticipation® does sound a little like fortune-telling at first. Fortune-telling has enjoyed quite a long history and it could be considered one of the world's oldest professions. Among its most successful practitioners were Nostradamus, Merlin, and if we fast-forward to the nineteenth century, Jules Verne. The first two made fine careers in the fortune-telling business. However, predicting the future accurately is also a dangerous game. There's a little bit of luck and a lot of danger mixed into the equation.

Yogi Berra is quoted as having said, "The future ain't what it used to be." We can see the truth of this statement clearly if we roll the clock back to 1938, when the editors of *Harper's Monthly* predicted what the world would be like in 1988. Some of the items they foresaw are indeed part of daily lives now:

➤ Air conditioning.

➤ Cable TV.

➤ "Electric Pigs" in the kitchen (before you say "What?" think about your garbage disposal).

➤ Direct dialing to countries around the world.

➤ Electronic burglar alarms.

➤ Canned and frozen foods.

➤ Fresh fruits and vegetables all year.

Looking at this list today, you might think that some of these prognostications weren't much of a reach, but they also made some way-out predictions regarding medical advances such as the conquest of death and the production of humans in the laboratory. This may sound pretty far-fetched, but animals have been cloned successfully, and in vitro fertilization is a reality. Biotechnology is advancing at a rapid rate. If things continue at this pace, who knows what dream may become reality next.

Harper's also had some misses and near misses, too—specifically.

➤ *Clocks that keep time by radio signals.* You won't find them in the average home, but if you checked some specialty catalogs, you might find something like these.

➤ *Electronically delivered newspapers.* Although not widely available, *The New York Times* and *The Wall Street Journal* are in fact deliverable via the Internet.

➤ *Chemical toilets.* Not available in homes, but how about airplanes, boats, and space capsules?

➤ *Fruits and vegetables grown in chemical solutions rather than soil.* We are very close with hydroponic gardening.

Even attempts to use science—as the *Literary Digest* magazine tried with its rudimentary polls—does not automatically help, as the magazine learned when it miscalled the Landon-Roosevelt race because its poll was based only on responses from its readers, a very upscale group compared to the rest of the electorate.

■ THE FUTURE VIEWED FROM THE PRESENT

Now let's fast-forward to what some of the futurists of today are talking about. They are worth scanning as idea stimulators.

➤ Faith Popcorn

Faith Popcorn has been anointed the "Nostradamus of Marketing" by *Fortune* magazine. She is particularly adept not at creating trends but at supposedly spotting and tracking them. Ms. Popcorn's 1998 list of things we'll see in the future included the following:

➤ Food engineered with prescription medicine.

➤ At-home surgery.

➤ Virtual post offices.

➤ Personal robots.

➤ Biblical cuisine menu items.

➤ Eye scanner identifiers at banks and grocery stores.

➤ Doctors making house calls.

➤ Satellite monitors that tell parents when the school bus is approaching—to the second—ending those long, cold waits.

➤ Health computer chips that store every individual's health history from cradle to grave.

➤ Paternity leaves as commonplace as maternity leaves.

➤ Virtual fantasy trips: Visit your dream location on the arm of your favorite Hollywood star (as a hologram).

➤ Buying the sets of your favorite sitcom right off the TV.

➤ Wallpaper video screens—roll them out when you want them.

➤ Video post cards—five-second greetings to drop in the mail.

➤ John Naisbitt

John Naisbitt, another leading futurist, has been in the trend-spotting business since his 1982 book *Megatrends* hit the bestseller lists.[3] He's particularly good at spotting big changes on the horizon. One of his more enduring trends was the maintenance of human-to-human contact (dubbed "high touch") amid the technology advances of our age.

High Touch

The acceleration of technological progress has created an urgent need for a counterballast—high-touch experiences. Heart transplants and brain scans have led to a new interest in family doctors and neighborhood clinics; jet airplanes have resulted in more face-to-face meetings. High touch is about human intersection counterbalancing high-tech advances.

What Does It Mean?

High touch recasts the terms of a company's interaction with its customers. German car makers have incorporated into their products the ultimate symbol of high touch: the owner's thumbprint as a car key. Forward-thinking retailers are transforming shopping into an experience of place. Barnes & Noble recognized that people yearn for community and designed its stores to suggest living rooms and home environments.

High touch also plays into corporate structure. Microsoft's Seattle campus, where no building is taller than the trees that surround it, better reflects the high-touch era than the mammoth towers under construction in Asia.

➤ Stan Davis

Stan Davis is a strategy and organizational consultant whom Mr. Naisbitt calls "a master at linking abstract truths and discoveries to specific business applications." He introduced the concepts of mass customization, real-time organization, virtual companies, and the shift from producing manufactured goods to intangible goods.

Stan Davis talks about the "growing customer role in the value chain through self-service," the replacement of mass-produced products by products designed by customers themselves, and the growing value of information content in traditional products, a current example of which would be the scanner at the cash register in your local supermarket picking up valuable information about you and your buying habits from the products you are purchasing.

A sidebar in *Forbes ASAP*, its periodic supplement focused on technology, described some bad predictions made by futurists:

➤ Nicholas Negroponte, cofounder/director of the Massachusetts Institute of Technology (MIT) Media Lab.

—*The prediction:* One billion Internet users and a trillion-dollar economy on the Net by the year 2000.

—*The reality:* Last year, there were only 50.2 million users online, and the *entire* U.S. economy was $8.1 trillion.

➤ Peter Schwartz, cofounder of Global Business Network.

—*The prediction:* E-cash gains acceptance around 1998.

—*The reality:* E-cash remains in the developmental stage because of differing standards and low merchant acceptance.

➤ Alvin Toffler, author of *Future Shock.*

—*The prediction:* "Long before the year 2000, the entire antiquated structure of [college] degrees, majors, and credits will be a shambles."

—*The reality:* Long live the antiquated structure.

➤ Paul Saffo, a director of the Institute for the Future.

—*The prediction:* In February 1996 Saffo predicted the Web would mutate into "something else very quickly and be unrecognizable within 12 months."

—*The reality:* Last time we checked, the Web was still the Web.

➤ Bob Metcalfe, sometime futurist and *InfoWorld* columnist.

—*The prediction:* In 1996, the Internet would catastrophically collapse.

—*The reality:* Metcalfe eats his words—literally. (Chewed his column in front of a packed crowd in 1997.)[4]

The predictions of futurists (only a few of which have been cited here) range from the very general to the very specific. Some seem to be routine incremental thinking, and others look pretty safe. Some read like horoscopes and are so vague that you can pretty much read whatever you want into them, whereas others can be directly linked to today's market.

■ THE PREDICTION BUSINESS IS FULL OF PERIL

When we look at these predictions, it's worth keeping in mind that futurists aren't licensed. The person who cuts your hair has to pass a minimum competency test to obtain a license, but anybody can declare him- or herself a futurist by simply hanging out a shingle. Or as Watts Wacker, the notable futurist from SRI, put it, "It's easy to become a futurist. All you have to do is announce that you are." Significantly, there are far more astrologers today than astronomers.

➤ Big Miss

Nuclear power was once forecast to become too cheap to monitor. Today, in fact, rather than being cheap and widely available, not to mention profitable, nuclear power has become a financial albatross, even threatening the solvency of a number of utilities. New York's Long Island Lighting failed, beginning a state-supported takeover. Power companies in New Hampshire, Washington, and elsewhere around the country are trying to figure out how to get out from under the costs of these bad investments—not to mention the enormous hazardous materials problems.

➤ Another Miss

In 1977, about four years before the PC was invented, Ken Olsen, the founder and then chair of Digital Equipment Corporation, stated that "there is no reason for any individuals to have a computer in their home." Today, about one-half of U.S. households have computers, and the Digital Equipment Company was bought by Compaq, one of the largest manufacturers of personal computers. Of course, Thomas Watson Sr. of IBM once predicted the demand for computers would be about four, but Tom Jr. and IBM persevered to help establish the market for this technology.

➤ Other Misses

We have witnessed many similar botched attempts at innovation in our lifetimes:

- ➤ FedEx's ZapMail (too early for faxing and e-mail).
- ➤ Videotex.
- ➤ Betamax, laser discs, and so on.

Such are the perils of prediction. In reality, however, the risks of predictions can run in two directions. One can lose a fortune by placing a big bet on a trend or technology that doesn't work out, but not placing a bet on something that turns out to be an enormous success can be just as bad. Both of these scenarios are fairly serious and fairly common as well. Perhaps one of the biggest missed opportunities in recent years occurred when H&R Block rejected a proposed deal to purchase America Online (AOL) for the sum of $65 million. The point we are trying to make is that although thinking about the future is a vital, ongoing exercise, it is also:

1. Not easy at all.
2. A practice that requires customized focus (if not market researchers of your own) to have any value because its real benefit is learning more about the factors that drive your business and developing signposts to watch them.

Returning to forecasts, Steven P. Schnaars has studied them and generally observed that most overestimate the impact of specific technologies, particularly at the announcement of an invention. With a co-author, he pointed out: "Popular beliefs are not necessarily accurate beliefs. Over the past twenty-five years there has been a plethora of expectations regarding the emergence of growth markets. More than half of these have turned out to be false leads that have wasted both time and money." They advise people to focus on the "consequences of the change" and not on predicting exactly how big or pervasive the change will be and also provide these tips:

➤ Stress the fundamentals. Define the customers, the benefits, and so on.

➤ Beware of seemingly immutable trends. Even demographic projections are not fulfilled if birth rates change suddenly.

➤ Beware of growth market predictions that are in bed with the technology they are predicated on.

➤ Finally, stay flexible.[5]

■ WINDS OF CHANGE

The winds of change have left no company and no industry unscathed. Even the giants have stumbled. Looking back a little further than the *Fortune* lists, of the 100 largest companies in the U.S. in 1917, only 15 survive today.

In our increasingly technology-based economy that is becoming more and more centered around the Internet, companies are emerging, merging, and disappearing at a faster-than-ever pace. In the energy industry, consumption has grown at the rate of 3 percent. Contrast that to computer memory per person, which has grown at a 67 percent annual rate since the 1960s. The computer industry has personified the creative destruction syndrome of Joseph Schumpeter. Intel, which just made it into the *Fortune* 100 companies in

1987, is in the number 5 slot today, and its market value is greater than the sum of the Big Three auto companies combined.

Turning to the computer-related companies themselves, Microsoft, Computer Associates, Oracle, Compaq, and Cisco have rocketed up the top of the list from nowhere in just the past 15 years. However, companies such as IBM have been up and down the list from a high of $170 billion in market value in 1997 to less than half that, but moving back up today. Digital Equipment, Unisys, and NCR have disappeared off the top 100 list completely.

Would anybody care to guess what the makeup of the *Fortune* or *Forbes* lists will be in 2010? It's certain to have some new names, and doubtless many of those will belong to Internet companies. Although dramatic changes are very unsettling, they also bring with them major opportunities.

■ HISTORY OF WEALTH

By "major opportunities," we mean opportunities to amass a great amount of money. Just take a look at the simple illustration that follows. I'm sure a lot of us can't wait for the latest *Forbes* list of the 400 richest people in the world. Maybe we aren't looking to see if we made it or not, but it sure is interesting to note the sources of that wealth, which have changed over the course of the past 80 years or so. Fortunes are made in times of major change. Examples range from the railroads, the steel industry, the oil business, and newspapers/media giants. Today it's the computer and telecommunications industries that seem to be the crucible of momentous change and opportunity.

As the sources of wealth have changed, the real money seems to have been made by those who could successfully anticipate the next shifts. If you do that well, you could become a billionaire like Bill Gates or Michael Dell or the telecommunications industry moguls, who are the new billionaires of the communications age. The pace of wealth accumulation is increasing at almost the speed of broadband development.

■ BETTING ON THE FUTURE

How do you position yourself to win the big bets as Bill Gates did? There are always a number of options when you place your wagers on the future, but the key to increasing the chances for success are speed, maneuverability, and a mind-set open to change. Both speed and maneuverability can range from low to high. Let's look at some of the possible combinations shown in Figure 1.1.

If you get out of the gate slowly and without a lot of maneuverability, then you can't make midcourse corrections. You're like the proverbial deer in the headlights and could end up as roadkill. In the corporate arena, the large steel makers would be a good example of this. When specialty steelmaker Nucor first appeared and focused on making the lowest-quality steel, the major integrated makers paid little attention. Meanwhile Japanese minimills started taking away other business. Now Nucor is the second-largest steelmaker in the United States. Digital Equipment is another company that failed to see things changing; Howard Johnson's, a venerable franchise at the consumer level, just went along doing the same thing on country highways while the world changed around it and sprouted superhighways.

If you don't wait but try to get out of the gate fast, you may encounter other dangers. You may speed along like a cannonball with high muzzle velocity and get there first. But the question is, where do you get? It's possible you may hit the wrong target without the ability to change course as needed. Corporate graveyards are littered with the corpses of those that suffered this fate (the Apple Newton and FedEx Zap Mail, to name a few). The dangers here are not getting enough information, not acting appropriately, and not being able to adapt to shifting conditions.

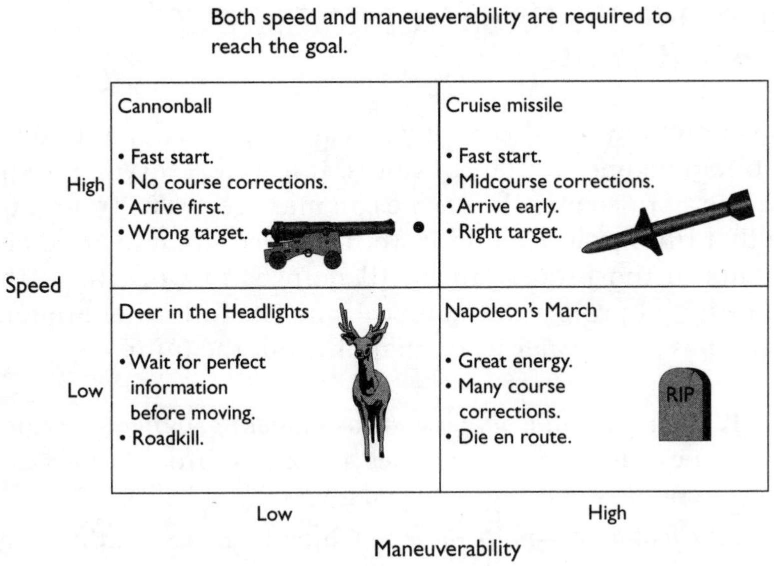

Both speed and maneueverability are required to reach the goal.

	Cannonball	Cruise missile
High	• Fast start. • No course corrections. • Arrive first. • Wrong target.	• Fast start. • Midcourse corrections. • Arrive early. • Right target.
Low	Deer in the Headlights • Wait for perfect information before moving. • Roadkill.	Napoleon's March • Great energy. • Many course corrections. • Die en route.

Speed

Low   High

Maneuverability

Figure 1.1 Betting on the Future.

Source: ©Mercer Management Consulting.

If you move slowly but have the ability to maneuver and make all sorts of corrections, you could end up going around in circles like Napoleon's army slogging its way through Russia. The army may die along the way. A few years ago Sears seemed to be in this category. It had a new strategy every couple of months or so it seemed: "Store of the Future," "Everyday Low Prices," and "Brand Central." Quaker Oats, with the Snapple brand management, would be a more contemporary example, as would Hayes modems. And although the "Softer Side of Sears" stuck for a while, the future for Sears is quite unclear.

Finally, there's the high-speed and highly maneuverable company that's like a cruise missile, the smart weapon that starts fast, makes midcourse corrections in real time, and arrives on target and on time or earlier. Nucor, Microsoft, and Schwab would be good examples of this sort of organization. How did they do it? How can you do it?

■ FACING THE FUTURE USING STRATEGIC ANTICIPATION®

No matter how we slice it, it isn't easy to project or anticipate future outcomes for our business. If it were, everyone would be like a cruise missile. But we can manage a worthy attempt with a little practice and if we introduce some focused elements to the process that will help us to work from the known and project to the unknown. The following are four variables to consider when mapping out the future.

1. *Futures—alternate scenarios modeling.* Objective: Look beyond today's urgencies and assess broad trends that could sweep over your business.
2. *Customers—your buyers.* Objective: Use leading-edge market research techniques to test the demand and need for products and services that don't exist yet or, somewhat easier, to detect shifts in values.
3. *Economics—the cost dynamics of the business.* Objective: determine what will be required to win competitively— massive preemptive investments, development of key capabilities, and an escape plan.
4. *Alignment—unity of purpose.* Objective: ensure that others inside your organization share the vision and pursue it together.

First, look at futures. Notice that we used that noun in the plural, not singular. No one is smart enough to consistently know exactly where the world will be x number of years from now. But maybe we can get smart enough to look at some alternative futures and get our arms around the capabilities they might require. Being smart enough can pay off big time.

Second, know your customers. This isn't simple either, and it may require tricks to help customers anticipate, if not articulate, demands for things that you haven't invented yet. This perspective is where we will spend the most time in the rest of this book.

Third, you must figure out what it is going to take to profit competitively. Just focusing on where customers will have needs in the future is not enough to ensure financial success.

Finally, there is the alignment issue ensuring that others both inside and potentially outside your organization share the vision and pursue it together. It's important to add emphasis here on *inside* and *outside*. There is a popular idea now called *co-opetition* a core part of which is the notion that it is not enough just to bring along the people in your own company but that you must bring along the others who will be affected by your decisions in the real world. Honda Motor is a company that exemplifies this kind of thinking in the way it works with its key suppliers, bringing them on board from the product development stage and keeping them up to speed in the strategic and cooperative race to stay competitive.

➤ Futures

With such big potential payoffs, you'd think everybody would be parlaying the futures activity into big money. However, as Mark Twain put it, "The art of prophecy is very difficult, especially with respect to the future." No one outcome is guaranteed. It's even more difficult when we're talking not just about projecting trends into the future but about adding discontinuous change into the mix. For such a complex environment, we need to think in terms of developing a number of different scenarios. A recent book entitled the *The Alchemy of Growth* sets an appropriate tone about futures, explaining that a company needs three time horizons across which to manage its businesses: extending and defending core businesses, building new businesses, and seeding options for the future.[6] We would add for emphasis that you need to have several different visions for the future because you may have to exit one to embrace another or make a radical jump into your most forward-thinking vision.

To set the stage for futures options, let's focus on discontinuous change—change that happens in discrete bursts rather than along straight, steady lines and that is more intense and certainly more unpredictable than the other kind of change. The before and after are really different in kind, not just degree. The difference between cars that can go 55 miles per hour and those that can go 70 miles per hour is more of the same, a continuous improvement change. But the difference between a car that can go 70 miles per hour and one that can be driven by voice command or on so-called smart highways (where sensors in the road guide the cars) is a discontinuous change. If you have a tank and your enemy has the atom bomb, you are a victim of discontinuous change. When the world changes dramatically, your assumptions need to change just as dramatically.

Discontinuous change means the market is different than it used to be. Products and competitors are different, too. This has happened to the television industry. It was once in competition with radio stations and movie studios, but who is its competition today? The video store. The phone company. The computer company. The online industry. The product may also be changing. Just ask yourself this question: For both television and cable, is the product the content or the pipeline? Why did AT&T buy TCI Cable, the largest cable company, and then Media One, another major cable operator, just a few months later? No one seems to know for sure just yet, but things are surely changing. Discontinuously.

Seeing or actually foreseeing revolutionary change is even harder than just seeing the future. We're talking about the difference between making markets and merely serving markets; the challenge is to create whole new product categories that exploit trends and discontinuities. It could be argued that FedEx created the market for overnight package delivery. CNN created a whole product category with its 24-hour news network. Chrysler invented the minivan. Microsoft and Nucor exploited discontinuities and inflection points in the economy. And companies like Intel and Nike virtually reinvented their business. Running shoes have become fashion. Of the many chipmakers, Intel has become the brand.

So no matter how hard it is to predict, we have to try. Theodore Levitt of Harvard Business School reminds us: "While prediction is always hazardous and seldom very accurate, it is undoubtedly far better than not trying to predict at all. In fact, every product strategy and every business decision inescapably involves making a prediction about the future, about the market and about competitors."

Discontinuous Results = Giant Payoffs

Not only do we have to try, but we have to do it as well as possible. Why? Because if we do it a little bit better, the payoff can be a lot better. This is a world of discontinuous results, too. Just as the logic of straight-line extrapolation no longer applies to prediction, so, too, it no longer applies to outcomes.

So how do we try? Well, the first step is to face the future. Switching analogies, this means developing vision outside of the cockpit and moving our eyes off just what's on the instrument panel. We must be aware of what's going on out there all around us; the crosswinds, downdrafts, tailwinds, and microbursts. These are just as important to a pilot of say a Boeing 777 when making a landing at LaGuardia airport as they are to a pilot of a small single engine craft attempting to land on a windy island strip in the Eastern Caribbean. And they are important when you're making business decisions about the future.

Picking Up on Clues to the Future

What's going on out there may fall into several categories, and there are all sorts of ways to pick up on them.

Broad Social Trends. Information about events that may have an impact on business can be gleaned from something as straightforward as reading the headlines in *The Wall Street Journal.* Information on general trends may be as close as scanning the front pages of publications such as *USA Today* while waiting for your aircraft to get clearance for takeoff. Even events that seem unrelated to business can have implications. *The Wall Street Journal,* for instance, frequently runs stories on page one that don't seem directly related to business, such as a new way of teaching kids to read that is in contrast to the way most of us learned. What's the business connection? Kids, parents, and grandparents purchased $50 software packages and CDs teaching their kids this method, resulting in major sales for companies such as Broderbund and the Learning Company.

Evolution of Economies. Scan globally. Malaysia has become a high-tech fabrication center. India is a source of world-class inexpensive programming. Isolationist thinking is narrow, outmoded thinking. The CatScan division of GE programmers is working on a new product that uploads information to a satellite from which it is then downloaded by programmers in India who take up the work where they leave off. After working through the night, the Indians upload to the satellite, and the U.S. programmers continue the cycle the next morning. So GE's new product development is running 24 hours a day and has a built-in cost advantage as well.

Changing Consumer Expectations and Behaviors. Here again it's a matter of looking at a rich diet of information and making connections. Perhaps the greatest and most rewarding opportunities lie in reading into and capitalizing on developments in the technology field. For example, what long-term trends do you see in the perfection of speech recognition technology? Keep an eye on the trades such as *PC Week* and *Info Week* or Web sites such as ZD Net.

Connecting the Dots

The next step in developing a futures scenario is to bring home the facts and events that we accumulate, which means making connections between seemingly unrelated information. For example, consider the increase in two-income households, improvements in the U.S. distribution infrastructure, in the rise of supermarkets, and military radar research. Put all these things together and you get a major trend: packaged microwaveable foods. Four disparate things came together over a period of years to add a new dimension to the way Americans cook their meals.

Think about implications for your customers, your company, and your stakeholders. Companies don't always do this. In the 1800s, for example, Western Union passed on the opportunity to pay the patent on the Bell Telephone Technology because the company thought it had no value as an investment. And there are a lot more recent horror stories. Barnes & Noble refused to take seriously the change in consumer book-buying habits that allowed a new company to sneak in under their radar screen with a business model that allowed buyers to purchase books without leaving their desks. The convenience model may have replaced the social setting and community model of just a few years earlier.

A good way of bringing this concept home is to challenge yourself to put together consistent scenarios with the emphasis on how trends might come together to produce a new business opportunity, perhaps a truly huge one, being sure to steer clear of straight-line extrapolations that go nowhere. When doing scenario modeling, think big and think unconventionally. We will not get into the details of how best to build scenarios such as these because many excellent books (such as the *Art of the Long View* by Peter Schwartz) do this well.[7]

It's also important to identify the opportunities for new products, new customers, and new channels of distribution. Mutual investment firms such as Putnam and Fidelity noticed that people were living longer, job-hopping among companies, and that with 401(k)s and 403(b)s, companies were shifting the responsibility for investment and retirement planning to individuals. So they identified all sorts of opportunities for selling funds, administering 401(k) and 403(b) plans. Charles Schwab recognized a similar opportunity among investors taking personal charge of their individual retirement plans and started catering to those who invested in no-load mutual funds, thus drawing new customers who then shifted their commission-based equity investment accounts to the firm.

➤ Customer Needs

We've discussed the importance of looking at a number of possible scenarios. But it is not enough to simply have a lot of free-floating futures out there. It's important to prioritize them and think about which ones are most relevant, specifically, which ones are most relevant to your customers. This may not be as easy as it sounds as we shall see. For although customers are undeniably important, demand is undeniably fickle. Once again, this makes prediction difficult. Three key questions to ask yourself about customers are:

1. *If we build it, will they come?* You may think you know what your customers will do next, and you may turn out to be completely wrong! Just because you build it, that doesn't mean the customers will come. They might visit someone else.

Consider some examples, starting with Euro Disney. The Magic Kingdom in Orlando is full of European tourists, yet in Europe, the theme park concept was not an immediate hit. Although it now appears successful, not all such leaps have happy endings. Take videophones and picture phones. What a concept—seeing people and talking on the phone. The technology has been around for nearly a decade; it's now affordable, and it sounds great. But how many people do you know who have one? The Newton computer has come and gone, yet the Newton was followed by the Palm communicator, a tremendous hit that spawned a whole new generation of personal communications devices and software products. Sega dominated the home video game market, and its new system came out at about the same time as Sony's

PlayStation. However, Sony made strategic alliances with games and software developers to keep a strong release of new games coming into the market, because it understood well the customer demand for new product, while Sega pursued a very conservative approach to game development. The result? The Genesis system platform is gone, and Sony now dominates the home video game market.

What do these near misses have in common? They were intelligent ideas developed by smart people. The companies responsible for developing them did their homework, but they somehow didn't get it all right. They certainly didn't correctly interpret what the customer wanted in terms of the product. We have addressed the first problem connected to new product development. Now, the second problem:

2. *If we build it, when will they come?* Paul Simon wrote a song called "Sixty Ways to Leave Your Lover." Maybe we can put it another way: How many ways can you be wrong about consumer demand for your product? Every new product has a time element involved, and you have to get that right, too. Even if your predictions are correct, how long will it be before the customers come and you get a return on your investment? It could be quite awhile.

And the final question:

3. *How many ways can we be wrong?* Just when we thought we were home free, there's the final catch-22. Even if we are right about predicting whether the customer will come if we build it, and even if we are also right about when they will come, we can still get it wrong in a number of ways. We can just totally fail to see what else will happen—or won't happen. For example, after the oil crisis of the 1970s and 1980s, it was predicted that renewable energy resources (such as solar and wind power) would eliminate U.S. dependence on oil. Today, over 20 years later, we import more oil than ever before. Progress in solar energy, our greatest renewable energy resource, has been practically nil, and wind power exists in a very minor way in California. We can also succeed in the prediction part but fail by not noticing the prediction has already happened. Some people thought that radio would lead to a common language, and maybe that is exactly what has happened, though not quite in the form that was expected. But when you travel around the world, MTV is a virtually ubiquitous language. I'd say that has already happened with the Internet. It was predicted that Internet commerce would be here by the year 2000. It is currently estimated that Internet sales will be about $350 billion by the year 2002 and $1 trillion by 2003. These estimates, however, will probably prove conservative.

So how do we avoid these three unhappy outcomes? We believe that development and use of Strategic Anticipation® is an answer. We've noted the difficulties of predicting and the big risks involved even if you get it right. And what do most companies do? From our broad-based consulting and industry experiences, we can state that most firms do nothing (i.e., nothing different from what got them where they are today). They avoid the whole issue of Strategic Anticipation® in the face of discontinuous change by merely making incremental changes as if business would continue as usual.

Fortune 500 firms as well as those that are the biggest and brightest and have the most resources are probably the most cautious. Like most of us, they keep doing over and over again whatever made them successful, that is fine if nothing has changed, but things *are* changing, which is what we are trying to make abundantly clear.

■ **HOW CAN COMPANIES BE SUCCESSFUL IN THE FACE OF DISCONTINUOUS CHANGE?**

By learning how to strategically anticipate, we can avoid many unhappy outcomes—or at least learn to predict with greater reliability. By now you're probably tired of hearing me say it's not easy. So we'll just move on.

As we said earlier, there are three ways to successfully anticipate the future in the face of discontinuous change. The first is to have a resident philosopher-king or -queen who wisely discerns the real meaning of the shapes of the true reality reflected on the cave walls. If you can accomplish that, you are a great leader. In modern times, we might think of Bill Gates in this context, perhaps the planet's greatest living college dropout. And Michael Dell has to be included—another college dropout. Geraldine Laybourne did graduate from college, but she still created a franchise for Nickelodeon. And we still have enough fingers left to count the few others on the business scene. All we can say is if you are lucky enough to have a Bill Gates or a Michael Dell around, lock them in a closet and feed them well. The second way is what we could call plain old luck. But how many major business leaders have told a business magazine editor, "One day I had a hunch and I owe it all—all the riches I've accumulated and made for others—to luck." In reality, there is usually some sort of rationalization. Dumb luck is very hard to sustain.

Now how about the rest of us. What if your crystal ball is cloudy? Would you like to count on a little more than just luck? Is there any other pathway to success? By being a little bit smarter in the futures department, you have a chance at the big payoff.

➤ Going beyond Conventional Forecasting Methods—How Market Research Can Help to Make Strategic Anticipation® Relevant and Successful

Developing the foresight necessary to create and develop new products starts with involving the customer in the forecasting process. However, many conventional forecasting methods are insufficient to the task. That's where market research comes in. Of course, many of you have had experience with market research in your company, but as it's usually practiced, it understandably generates some skepticism. Squeezed into a limited organizational role with little functional management vision and constrained resources, market research can be out of alignment with the organization's overall needs. Yet it can be of great help with Strategic Anticipation® as we will clearly demonstrate later in this book. Here we will briefly point out the drawbacks of regular methods and point out some other techniques that can help.

Getting Customers to Dream

If it were easy to get customers to dream and capture their visions, we'd all be rich. Obviously, it's not, in part because conventional research methods such as qualitative predicting, market trials, focus groups, and even extrapolating from trend lines are laden with problems. For example, customers may not tell you what they are really going to do, especially concerning something that doesn't even exist yet. Market trends and focus groups are limited in what can be generalized from their data, and database analysis is very costly. These techniques may work for testing things that already exist or are straightforward extensions of things that exist, but what can we possibly do regarding new, unforeseen changes?

Getting Customers to Dream in Color

If getting customers to visualize what's ahead is difficult, asking them to do it in descriptive color is far more complex. We suggest five methodologies that do a better-than-average job. As we observed earlier, the real issue is determining the potential futures that relate to your business and your customers. (Note the emphasis on customers because they are and should be the focal point.)

Five Leading-Edge Market Research Techniques That Can Help You Do a Better Job of Anticipating Markets

1. *Information Acceleration*™. This method attempts to improve forecasting under conditions of revolutionary change by trying to show the future to somebody and putting them into different scenarios which might exist. An integral part of information acceleration is to identify tomorrow's most likely strategic environments and then develop a multimedia display that familiarizes the consumer respondent with the potential context in which you'd like to pose questions.

2. *Discrete Choice Analysis* or *Strategic Choice Analysis*® (SCA) involves developing a model and seeing what would happen if certain changes were made. Modeling the economics of these varying environments and offerings helps to make forecasting under conditions of revolutionary change possible. It's a useful way for you to understand what would happen. And if in the future your competitors do something or offer something new, as long as you were smart enough to anticipate it in your questioning, you can try and figure out what would actually happen. It is a virtual marketplace way to figure out what might happen in the future if the marketplace changes.

For example, if we were talking with a traveler about some new services a hotel might offer, everything could sound great until you mentioned the cost. But with SCA, you put things into a full and complete context by asking a customer which hotel she would actually stay in if she were going to city A at time B along with a long list of different amenities with accompanying prices. Include some revolutionary conditions (does the business involve an extended stay? Are clients arriving at all hours?), and you start to see which ones would actually be picked.

3. *Lead User Analysis* is a way of learning from customers who already live in the future. It's another way of forecasting under conditions of revolutionary change. In this case you go to your most sophisticated and leading-edge users. Let's suppose that in your industry, marketing through the Internet or getting information to your customer by means of or putting customer service capabilities on an Intranet might be very important. If you started to study your Internet customers today, the ones who are the most comfortable with the technology, and you watch what they are doing with the assumption that they are lead users and that in the future other people will be doing whatever they are doing, you could learn something useful.

4. *The Delphi Technique* is very compatible with scenario planning. It was first developed by the RAND Corporation after World War II; it is based on the premise that many types of minds are better than fewer and that an iterative process is one of the best ways to figure out what might happen in the future. Members of RAND went to experts in military affairs to ask what they thought was going to happen, what the world events coming out of World War II would be. The data came in and were distributed back to everyone; then they began a structured voting process on the likelihood of each of the possibilities. The results were tabulated, and then everything was sent back to the same people with the understanding, "Here is what people think. Here are the patterns that are emerging." Through this back-and-forth process, patterns did emerge, the outliers began to fall into place, and the expected outcome moved to the most—or at least more—likely scenario.

Delphi is a pretty good technique. Our experience has shown that when we have done it, consumers do a better job of feeding back.

5. *Key Customers Focus.* We have talked a lot about customers. But to whom do you talk? Whom do you use as your sample? Market research can be of major assistance in selecting the right customers. However, a lot of times research money is wasted or some misdirection comes out of market research owing to having used the wrong sample. There is a tendency to sample all customers and all prospects, yet not all of them are of equal value, and neither are they equally able to help figure out what is going to happen in the future. They may be followers rather than leaders.

Always try to pinpoint who your most valuable customers are today and monitor them over time. Maybe they're younger or more active or self-described leaders. But those are the people you want. They count the most.

So how can you tell if there is going to be a change in the marketplace? If you're tracking the right people and you start to see changes, something's happening out there. If you see a drop in your customer satisfaction level and there's also a similar drop for your competitors, that's a pretty good lead indicator that something is going on in your industry. If you start to notice that you and your competitors are both losing customers and you don't know to whom—meaning it's not to each other or to the usual suspects—that's another indicator that something radical is happening in your industry.

➤ Competitive Economics

Because understanding customer needs is key to Strategic Anticipation®, once we've applied research techniques to help determine which customers and which needs to focus on, we also need to look at hard economics: at what the costs are going to be and how to look at those costs in the future. So far we have looked at various futures, and at customers needs, and what they might be. But you should want to know not only what might happen in the future but also what certain futures might cost you. Thinking about future economics is the next part of the story, and we have some techniques we like to use to do that. We'll talk about them briefly here and then develop them more fully, with examples, in later chapters.

Piecing together an economic picture about the future is a little easier if we ask some specific questions around certain issues such as:

➤ *Market demand.* Once we know it, can we claim a profitable share?

➤ *Pricing.* Does the industry react by engaging in ruinous price competition that eats up any of the new demand created by the new opportunities? And if that happens, is there a way to pull out?

➤ *Costs.* How are costs going to grow as we grow? How will costs grow when we pursue new opportunities?

➤ Techniques that Can Help You Formulate Competitive Economic Data

Five Forces Framework

Of the many techniques for looking at traditional industry economics, one of the more well-known ones is Michael Porter's Five Forces Framework.

Competitive analysis helps focus on your industry's current environment by determining who your competitors are. This is the center of the radar screen. From there the focus broadens out to the next circle to consider potential players, substitute products, and the power of suppliers and of buyers to diminish industry profits.

The Five Forces Framework broadens the radar scan by also prompting us to ask:

1. Who are the players—not just the current competitors— in our industry?
2. Who has the power to claim the profits that may be pulled away from our bottom line?
3. Who has the power to claim the profits that may be pulled away from our bottom line by suppliers or customers?
4. What is the structure of the industry? Is it concentrated or fragmented?
5. How does the industry rate overall? Five stars, one star, or in between? And how do we rate ourselves?

Economic Acceleration

Shifting our focus from the present to the future and trying to anticipate strategically requires a whole new set of tougher questions with fewer knowns. For example, instead of just looking at the current players, we need to think about what economic forces will drive competition and profits tomorrow. Instead of looking at existing profit distribution, we must ask how we are going to increase the overall pool of value and how are we going to increase the size of the pie and not just fight over slices.

Barnes & Noble increased the size of the bookbuyer pie by creating accessible locations with 50,000, 100,000, and then 200,000 books in a large, well-lit, socially congenial setting and thus attracted many more people than independent stores with scattered locations and stock of perhaps 10,000 books per store.

In much the same way, we have to shift our focus from the structure of the industry and instead forecast its dynamic evolution. Try to see what the endgame will look like by focusing less on how many firms are operating today and more on finding out how many survivors there will be tomorrow.

Finally we have to look beyond our current status and industry ranking to determine how to pursue future opportunities.

➤ How Economic Acceleration Applies to Specific Supply-and-Demand Issues

Demand Economics

Understanding how comparative economics evolve is an essential part of Strategic Anticipation®. Let's look at a simple example.

Company A and company B are in the same business and facing the same demand curve with the same price/volume relationship. Moving forward, they face the following questions:

1. How can we begin to pivot our demand curve up and the other firm's down (or at least away from them)?

2. How can we move away from price competition so that if a competitor comes in and cuts prices, they won't pick up much volume? This has happened in the word processing field. At one time there were a number of viable products besides Microsoft Word. Over time Microsoft has successfully pivoted its demand curve up enough so that a lot of people probably wouldn't switch from Word even if a competing product from, say, WordPerfect suddenly got much cheaper.

DEMAND ECONOMICS

There are a variety of techniques for controlling the demand curve and moving it in the right direction. The first step is to audit. Next, as you start looking at future trends and connections and forecast what your customers will be thinking, ask yourself, do we think this applies to us? Better yet, how can we create the optimum future?

For example, questions you'd want to answer in evaluating whether or not you want to be the first or early mover into a new area or take a wait-and-see approach include:

➤ Are there going to be high switching costs for customers— or can we create them?

➤ Can we make this an enduring relationship rather than a series of independent transactions?

➤ How important will track record be to future customers?

➤ If we establish the track record and people are happy with our product, how much does that buy us the next time they come back into the market?

➤ How important is compatibility with what other people are using (affiliation effects)? Microsoft Excel accepting Lotus 1-2-3 or Quattro Pro Files is a good example of affiliation. Or think of teenagers and how important it is for them to buy the right sneakers or jeans.

Moving to leadership differentiation, the issues that make a difference are recognition and staying power, third-party support, extended warranty contracts (cars and appliances), and relationships (the Wintel [Microsoft and Intel] duopoly). A word of advice about differentiation and how to get leverage in the marketplace to pull your demand curve away from other folks: Don't do it with features that other clever marketers can copy. Do it with those things that are hard to copy, such as reputation (branding), track record (performance reliability), integrated solutions (neo-IBM), and anything you've built into the product that keeps people locked into it.

Cost Economics

First, let's focus on operating leverage. This is a pretty basic concept that describes, say, a business where you have developed a new product or service. It could be a specialty publication, an on-line service, or anything involving the acquisition of a customer base. The question you face is figuring out how your costs will behave as the business grows. After all, you are going to be pretty successful here, and your business will grow accordingly.

Let's say it's going to cost you $125 to acquire a new customer but only $25 to keep a customer. The theory maintains that after you have filled the pipeline and acquired all your customers, your costs will come way down because the gap between $25 and $125 is considerable. But now let's throw in the issue of turnover, or churn. In reality, you're not going to keep all your customers. In fact, maybe 20 percent a year will defect or fail to renew. What is that going to do to your marketing cost per customer? Again, you have marketing tools to help get a handle on this. What will your growth curve look like? Will you be back where you started? These are important matters if you are putting together the marketing budget. Work out the demand curve at 1.66 percent per month for a 20 percent churn. Once you see what that looks like, create a demand curve for a churn of 2, 3, or perhaps even 4 percent. The interesting thing is that the curve doesn't just flatten out; it kicks back up. This is a very simple model, but the answer to the growth curve won't look so simple.

STRATEGIC LEVERAGE

Another example of cost economics involves strategic leverage more than operating leverage. Specifically, how can you really drive a wedge between your costs and those of your competitors? In the past we thought that the experience curve was the answer: Gain volume, and costs will come down. In reality, a lot of companies found themselves in a world where costs just didn't seem to be coming down. For example, in businesses where the infrastructure required to service the expanding customer base is expanding faster than the economy-of-scale part of the equation (such as Amazon.com or AOL), technology changes (cellular phones and PCs) and customer demands change (processing speed and range of use), and we just can't seem to stabilize things enough so that our costs will go down as they should. Of course, the customer's point of view is probably that they are getting a lot more than they used to—perhaps a faster computer, more super absorbent material in disposable diapers, more customization features (Starbucks coffee), and so forth. Here the question isn't really, "What's our cumulative volume, and why don't our costs go down?" but "What's our cumulative experience, and what is our ability to deliver more and more value to the customer at a lower and lower price?"

STRATEGIES FOR COST LEADERSHIP

In creating a strategy for cost leadership the first thing to understand is the real cost curve and how you can exploit that. Looking at scores of companies, we've found a number of strategies for cost leadership, a whole series of factors that let you understand where you can drive a wedge between your costs and your competitors' costs. Some have to do with timing, getting the experience, or expediting the process. Others, such as the following, have to do with scale or with integration.

DETERMINING PATTERNS OF COMPETITION

Again, looking across a lot of industries, we have seen ample opportunities to drive cost wedges between you and your competitors. First you have to determine what kind of industry you might be operating in the future. If you can find a way to drive in those cost wedges—and that may be a big *if*—you can figure out whether you're going to be a player in an industry where there are few survivors or many survivors and where the profits are high or low.

In fact, Mercer Management Consulting's book *Profit Patterns* describes in detail how to do this.

There are industries that have evolved into each of the four squares in Figure 1.2.

As a point of discussion, do you know which industry has generated more millionaires than any other in the history of the United States? No, it's not multilevel marketing or real estate. Believe it or not, dry cleaning has generated thousands

(Continued)

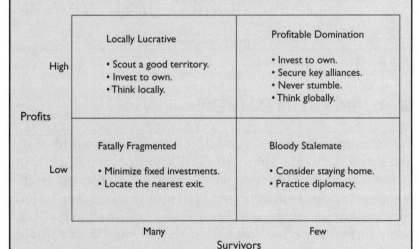

Anticipating the future of competition is, in turn, critical to developing competitive strategy today.

	Many	Few
High	**Locally Lucrative** • Scout a good territory. • Invest to own. • Think locally.	**Profitable Domination** • Invest to own. • Secure key alliances. • Never stumble. • Think globally.
Low	**Fatally Fragmented** • Minimize fixed investments. • Locate the nearest exit.	**Bloody Stalemate** • Consider staying home. • Practice diplomacy.

Profits

Survivors

Figure 1.2 Economic Patterns of Competition.

Source: © Mercer Management Consulting.

(Continued)

of millionaires—probably no billionaires, but a lot of people have made a lot of money that way in this locally lucrative industry. Now take a much sexier-sounding industry such as fancy audio equipment in which a lot of people figured they could make big fortunes. It turns out the economics just weren't there. This continues to be a very fragmented industry; there are many survivors, but profits are low.

Once you understand how an industry is going to evolve, you can figure out how to tackle it. If it's going to be fairly fragmented, then minimize the fixed investment and hope that your competitors come up with a marketing and strategic plan that's dependent on making large fixed investments. In that case you might also want to have an exit plan and stay mobile. If it's going to be a high-profit industry with few survivors, a place we call the Land of Profitable Domination, then you would invest to own and think globally. Here you'd want to set up key alliances and not hesitate.

It may not be rocket science, but anticipating the future of competition is critical to developing competitive strategy today. As we have tried to show, this does involve some acute Strategic Anticipation® around competitive economics issues, and marketing research offers some useful tools to help develop a sensible plan.

■ ALIGNING FOR EXECUTION

Up to now we have been proclaiming a future world of discontinuous change that will be different enough from the present to make Strategic Anticipation® a challenge. In this world it's tough enough to get the right information, to look at the futures, to understand customer needs, and to really get the competitive economics right so you can be a profitable survivor. However, even with these good tools and even after getting this information, you have to do something to mobilize the strategy. More than just crystallizing the vision yourself, you have to make sure that other people do, too, and that they are doing what you all want to be done. In order to pull the whole thing off, you need to align for execution.

There are plenty of tools around to tell you what to align and how to do it—tools for aligning the organization; aligning processes; and aligning culture, systems, communications, and compensation. Surely, if you just get those pieces right and everything aligned, it will all work, and you can move into that profitable survivors quadrant where the multi-millionaires are.

➤ What Do You Align?

When you think about what you will align, the question is, are the conventional tools good enough? We don't think so. You can no longer say, "Let's align the organization and get the people who work here to do the right thing," because it's not enough just to organize your own employees. Aligning all the parts of the organization is a necessary but not altogether sufficient condition to get where you are trying to go in a world of discontinuous change.

For example, Taco Bell decided it wasn't in the cooking business at all but rather in the "give people food quickly" business. So it reorganized its organization and its outlets around these ideas: smaller or nonexistent kitchens, food assemblers rather than cooks, and so forth. You've got to go back and organize your whole value system, all the people who have a stake in the game. People who are a supplier one year may be end users another year and then competitors the next. So what is the product? Who is the customer? If that's going to change, you need to be thinking about aligning all of these people.

At Intel, for example, they don't just want to design better chips; they want to make sure people buy bigger computers and more complex software that chews up enormous amounts of memory. All those players need to be properly aligned to do the right things for Intel to prosper. And they don't all report to Andy Grove. What are the comparable factors in your business?

➤ What Will You Align?

In the world of continuous flux we are positing, you will align your value system, not just your organization; your knowledge system, not just your process; your passion, not just your culture; your business model, not merely your system; and your future vision, not just your communications. You will use wealth-building opportunities, not just compensation plans, to motivate people. You've got to see beyond what you've got to where you want to be and then get the whole package to work for you. Your organization is much more than your company. It's your entire value system. Obviously we don't mean morals here but rather an interconnected set of players whom you influence and at the same time by whom you are influenced and with whom you interact at various steps along the value chain. This includes your business partners, your channel partners, your suppliers, and (absolutely) your customers. And how do your reach these people? That's where the trade press and the investment community and your Web site come in.

For another take on whom you should align, listen to Bill Joy of Sun Microsystems: "The idea behind our Java strategy was that the smartest people in the world don't all work for us. Most of them work for someone else. . . . Innovation moves faster when the people elsewhere are working on the problem with you."

Later we will get into some ways of communicating your view of the challenges ahead. One, for example, is a kind of "think week" program where you take people offsite and have them concentrate in an interactive format on the very things we will discuss throughout this book. The emphasis is to have them look outside the cockpit, as it were, at the crosswinds and tailwinds, not just the instruments in front of them. The theme of Strategic Anticipation® encompasses tenfold change, the kind of yardstick that venture capitalists look for in pay-back before they will even consider a new investment.

■ FROM ALIGNMENT TO ACCELERATION

We have talked about a lot of things so far: some of the issues in organization alignment, future conditioning, using models, and putting people into a setting where they are doing action learning in an interactive way. So there are lots of tools to help get people out of today's job and into tomorrow's value systems. But we really want to move beyond alignment to acceleration.

If there is discontinuous change in this world, there are also discontinuous opportunities. If you do it right, you may actually get more than you bargained for or more than you might have expected in a world without discontinuous change. The challenge is how to do that and how to give people a picture of your perspective. That's what you haven't read yet: how to give you that picture and suggest some of the ways it is possible to be just a bit smarter than the next outfit. That's Strategic Anticipation® in a nutshell, and we will present a lot of practical tools and suggestions for capitalizing on discontinuous change in the coming chapters.

By now we have stressed how hard it is to predict the future. But it's not hopeless; it's not just pure dumb luck or fortune-telling. To summarize, Figure 1.3 lists some of the things we talked about to help you capitalize on discontinuous change. These aren't necessarily magic, but they may make enough of a difference to get you moving to where you need to be.

If you are still reading at this point, then we probably don't have to say why you should care about Strategic Anticipation® and future conditioning. But we will anyway. It's because you want to be among the winners, not the wannabees (Table 1.1) among companies that were pretty similar in results at one point in time. Thinking back to the lists of tools and techniques we have discussed, remember

The first step is to assemble information and insights
not routinely captured in planning and budgeting processes.

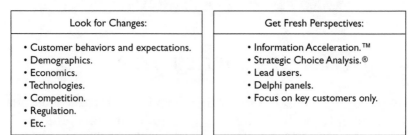

Look for Changes:	Get Fresh Perspectives:
• Customer behaviors and expectations. • Demographics. • Economics. • Technologies. • Competition. • Regulation. • Etc.	• Information Acceleration.™ • Strategic Choice Analysis.® • Lead users. • Delphi panels. • Focus on key customers only.

Figure 1.3 Strategic Anticipation®.

Source: © Mercer Management Consulting.

Table 1.1 Similarities in the Past but Not the Future

	Winners	**Wannabees**
1948	Sears	Wards
1958	UPS	Railway Express Agency
1968	McDonalds	Howard Johnson
1978	Microsoft	Digital Equipment
1988	Starbucks	Chock Full O'Nuts
1998	AOL	Prodigy
2008	You?	You?

that the difference between the winners and the wannabees may not be huge. You don't have to be a genius or perfect. Just be a little smarter and a bit more aware on a few more dimensions and the difference on the results side may be huge. The value of Strategic Anticipation® is that it can help put you in the winners' column.

There is no proprietary data about the future. But there are levels of understanding about the various factors that are going to open up possibilities for industry revelation. Some companies work a lot harder than others to understand these factors at a deep level. The data are there for everybody, but there is an enormous difference in people's abili-

ties to construct imaginative, compelling new opportunities
out of that understanding.

—Gary Hamel

■ NOTES

1. Adrian J. Slywotzky, David J. Morrison, Ted Moser, Kevin A.
Mundt, and James A. Quella, *Profit Patterns* (New York: Times Business Random House, 1999).

2. Ibid.

3. John Naisbitt, *Megatrends, Ten New Directions Transforming
Our Lives* (New York: Warner Books, 1982).

4. *Forbes ASAP,* April 6, 1998.

5. Steven P. Schnaars and Conrad Besenson, "Growth Market
Forecasting Revisited," *California Management Review* 23, no. 4
(1986).

6. Mehrdad Baghai, Stephen Coley, and David White, *The
Alchemy of Growth* (London: Orion Publishing Group, Ltd., 1999).

7. Peter Schwartz, *The Art of The Long View,* (New York: Dou-
bleday, 1991).

Chapter
2

The Tools to Research the Future

Life can best be understood backward, but you have to live it forward.

—Charles Handy

If you accept the need to constantly try to anticipate key changes in the environment and test your business design in light of what might happen then your inquiry must turn to how a business can do this.

There is an old saying at racetracks when someone is trying to decide whether to buy a tout sheet (picks for a fee from a self-styled expert handicapper) that if the tout were really so good at picking, why would he or she waste time selling their picks instead of just betting on them? The point is that it's a great deal easier to sell advice about the future than it is to actually predict accurately. However, lest perfect become the enemy of good enough, the fact that the future is really unpredictable cannot be allowed to stop the process of thinking about what might happen and the consequences of such events.

This is where research tools become vital. Historically, market research has been a fairly trivial pursuit carried out by people way down the organizational chain. Not too many researchers advise CEOs directly.

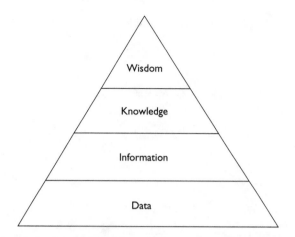

Figure 2.1 The Traditional Management Pyramid.

The traditional pyramid or hierarchy (Figure 2.1) suggests the path for prominence for researchers. The data gatherers support the information packagers and, if they are fortunate, top researchers may be asked for knowledge, if not wisdom (though usually it is marketers or consultants who are asked to make this contribution).

This pyramid itself, however, is far too academic. Figure 2.2 is more apt because it connects data to information to wisdom and the value this can convey to the stockholders. If wisdom doesn't lead to better decisions, then it is worthless. (This doesn't mean that all data gathering must be linked to a pending decision; it simply means that building knowledge and wisdom must be kept within the parameters of what business is likely to encounter.)

Even this improved diagram is inadequate because it lacks the dynamic sense of the marketplace. Today's wisdom is tomorrow's foolishness. Knowing that Americans love big cars had value in the 1960s. Using that outdated wisdom in the 1970s was clearly not wise. Today's wisdom, that an Internet company needs customers more than cash (i.e., profits), will undoubtedly be tomorrow's folly (perhaps even by the time this book is published).

Thus, the more appropriate drawing is something like Figure 2.3, in which hypotheses about the future are used to

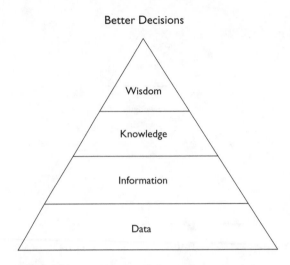

Figure 2.2 Wisdom Leads to Better Decisions.

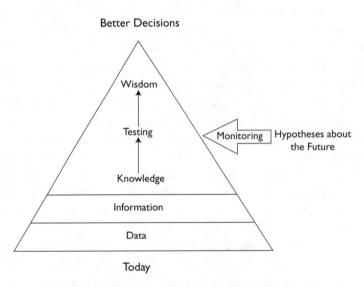

Figure 2.3 Hypotheses Challenge Knowledge.

challenge today's knowledge and, through testing, lead to wisdom with a longer shelf life.

It is from and with this perspective that the tools come in handy. First and foremost, researching the future is not helpful if the pyramid is not built. The business that does not understand today's world cannot hope to cope with tomorrow's; thus, the first requirement is a firm grasp of reality and its drivers.

A key underlying assumption to future research involves *buyer values*—a term used extensively by Michael Porter in his 1980s writing. As the concept of buyer values evolved in work guided by Victor E. Millar (co-author of a seminal *Harvard Business Review* article with Porter and the genuine father of what is now Andersen Consulting), the idea is to understand who makes the purchase decision [not a trivial exercise] and then determine the true drivers of that decision [i.e., selection criteria]. The theory—so far borne out in the work for Millar—is that the buyer values that prompt purchases do not change from day to day or even year to year. For example, if CFOs pick an audit firm to certify their financial statements based on efficiency (as they do), then the Big Five accounting firms should not invest in bells and whistles for their basic audit services but rather should work to streamline processes. They also should not lowball to buy business assuming they will earn profits back in later years because if clients value efficiency most, they can be expected to continuously monitor efficiency. This last lesson is not yet fully understood by all the Big Five, but the need to be efficient is. At the same time, Arthur Andersen and Ernst & Young (among others) have cleverly developed other services lines to augment the audit. For example, Ernst & Young has renamed the audit line of business "Audit Advisory Business Services."

Understanding buyer values can lead to major strategy decisions—particularly around investment and branding to meet and market to customer needs. If the client values the attribute, it is worth investing to improve and/or market that attribute—if the client doesn't, then the investment is likely to be wasted (somewhat akin to spitting in the wind).

For example, BMW (and other German auto makers) kept investing and publicizing their workmanship and features in the late 1980s and 1990s when their competitors (particularly Lexus) understood that customers valued convenience (e.g., loaner cars and emergency pickups) more than high performance, which was a secondary value. Similarly, the U.S. auto makers missed the primary value of fuel efficiency in the 1970s and allowed the Japanese to penetrate the U.S. car market.

Yet another good example of the power of understanding buyer values comes from the Big Five. As Andersen discovered the need for efficiency in audit, it also learned that buyers of its consulting (dominantly information technology [IT], which was called information services [IS] at the time) were different. First, there were different people (management information system [MIS] directors or chief information officers [CIOs], not chief financial officers [CFOs]) and second, these buyers didn't really care about efficiency per se. They needed to be able to rely on the outside firm (in essence, they were choosing reliable effectiveness over efficiency). In fact, they demanded that their consultants know the latest and greatest tools so that investment was required. Furthermore, they naturally wanted a track record to be able to infer reliability. Thus, there was a very different set of needs with very different implications from the audit business.

It was this type of research findings about the future that helped prompt the decision to separate the Andersens, with a different brand and strategy for Andersen Consulting than for Arthur Andersen.

Several additional points need to be made:

➤ Given the strategic importance of true buyer value research, it needs to be done carefully (read "with no costs spared"). Typically, extensive qualitative work is needed to develop effective vernacular and hypotheses. Working with internal sales, marketing and service people are also essential.

➤ As noted, a key success factor is learning who the real buyer is (whether in the household for a consumer market or within a business for business-to-business).

➤ As in any other research, changes must be monitored. Because buyer values do not shift every month, an annual update is appropriate, and it should be focused on whether change is evident. This can be qualitative such that finding no evidence triggers no more effort that year and vice versa.

A best practice in this regard—and in others—is Ernst & Young's Value Scoreboard. The practice is to meet with clients at the onset of an engagement to fully understand and document the value they expect to derive from their work with the firm. This can include specific metrics. Obviously, this is a terrific way to ensure that Ernst & Young focuses on the right activities and teams effectively with and satisfies its clients. In the aggregate, it's a great method to assess the stability or change in client/buyer values.

➤ Finally, buyer values work must incorporate both rational and emotional values. Simply having the right features and price does not guarantee either sales or satisfaction. Conversely, as Marlboro learned a few years ago, even the best emotional linkages are not sufficient if the price gets too high.

Currently, Barnes & Noble is grappling with this in the on-line world. Its early advertising emphasized its advantage in the number of titles it offered compared with Amazon.com. This didn't work because the ease and convenience of buying on-line from Amazon.com as well as the "cool" factor are the key values. On the Internet, as Geoffrey Moore points out in the revised introduction to his excellent book *Inside the Tornado,* it is necessary to provide both superior product and service, whereas in the off-line world, one will often suffice.[1] (Barnes & Noble is now addressing this by renaming its on-line site, etc.).

Other typical research methodologies can and should augment buyer value studies.

First, ensure (through one-on-one interviews, focus groups, or surveys) that the business has a firm grasp on its key channel players' buyer values as well as those of employees. As will be described later in this book, without effective channels and employees, even the best customer-focused strategies fail.

Second is environmental scanning. With the glut of information and the Internet, there is now so much data available that the challenge is no longer uncovering it but rather figuring out how not to be overwhelmed. If your business knows the drivers of its success, then you can determine where to direct focus and from where to base peripheral vision. Generally speaking, most for-hire services (e.g., the Omnibus studies tracking values and so on) and most for-hire-futurists are not worth the investment. Having your own people focusing on what your business needs to monitor will work better.

Third, the business needs to know the drivers of its economics. Relatively simple statistical techniques (e.g., regression) can delineate which variables (attitudes and reported or actual behaviors) have the most impact on overall profitability. For example, let's suppose that a business has successfully pursued a segmentation study and knows which customer segment(s) to target for the near future. Let's further suppose that past study has shown that simple satisfaction (e.g., a 5 on a 5-point scale) predicts loyalty and increased spending. This is not always the case. Much research has shown that reported satisfaction does not necessarily mean that a satisfied customer will either stay a customer or spend more. Thus, each business should conduct a longitudinal study to assess whether these relationships occur or not. At a minimum, it is best to assume that only those customers responding at the highest category of satisfaction are truly satisfied.

In the assumed case, whose satisfaction is a good predictor that a profitable customer will remain one, then a regression analysis will inform the business as to which variables truly influence profitability. Thus, in the Big Five example, suppose overall satisfaction were found to derive most from these three questions elsewhere in the survey:

> ➤ Respondents who were very satisfied with the technology of the consulting firm.

> ➤ Respondents who were very satisfied with the experience of the lead/senior consultant.

> ➤ Respondents who were CIOs (as opposed to CEOs, CFOs, etc.).

Knowing these drivers would influence how the consulting firm would invest, train its people, and target its efforts and could also dramatically influence its marketing. (Suppose that Andersen learned that being viewed as innovative was critical; this could have led to its very creative advertising over the years.)

Another building block of research for the future is the traditional segmentation study—research that tries to group customers by what a computer program determines are key linkages in attitudes, (reported) behaviors, and (usually reported) demographics. The tool itself is interesting but not helpful if it is not attached to economics. Many of the first segmentation studies were conducted decades ago by ad agencies for their clients (who generally had only nascent research departments). These studies focused on psychographics (i.e., attitudes/descriptions of one's self), not behaviors. Most were a waste of money because they were not useful (i.e., there was no linkage to demographics or how to reach people, just how to appeal to groups). The best use was probably by Burger King, which developed its "Have It Your Way" campaign to appeal to that psychological group—a small one but one of the only segments willing to go with a nonleading brand.

In any event, in today's world, the various segments of customers need to be analyzed by profitability and for lifetime value to be useful. (Segmentation based on attitudes can only lead to targeting unprofitable customers, even if they are plentiful.)

Yet another tool is won/loss analysis, so named by a long-term Mercer Management Consulting partner, Eric Almquist. This simple tool is a program of blind interviews with key decision makers after they've just selected a consultant, hardware vendor, stockbroker, CEO, or whatever. The interviewer (without disclosing the client identity) asks about the process and about each company or brand considered. The results pinpoint the true levers that make a difference.

Even conventional research tools aimed at the future can be successful if pursued carefully. In the 1980s, a cable TV network was investigating the viability of a cultural pay cable network on a premium basis. Research predicted that 20 percent of cable households would pay for such a service, which would make it highly profitable.

The new division head simply didn't believe these numbers. He sent the researchers back for a more thoughtful study designed to get closer to the truth. The earlier research tool was copied but extended with additional questions. The new study replicated the 20 percent finding of stated intention, but the additional questions brought forth some sobering truths:

➤ Most of those who were interested in the service would not pay $10 per month extra for it. (The initial survey had not stated a price. It had simply described the service as "a premium channel like HBO.")

➤ Most of those surveyed did not currently have a premium channel. (The initial survey did not discriminate between those who were already predisposed to pay for HBO and those who were not so disposed.)

➤ Most of the respondents did not currently spend their time on the activities (such as museum tours or operas) that the channel was designed to feature. Only Broadway shows, which would not be on air, seemed to generate much interest.

➤ Only a very few respondents indicated that they would actually sign up for this service.

Armed with the new data, the executive confidently went ahead to kill the concept.

Many other conventional uses of research could be cited, but the major points of inquiry are twofold. First, research must learn what has the most impact on the most important customers (or targets or channels or employees). Secondly, to focus on the future, the inquiry must always be searching for trends. This means analyzing every survey or study against what is already known or learned.

These are two crucial aspects to this. The first is obvious—notice changes, no matter how small, and study these in depth. If satisfaction is down for your business, is it up for anyone? Who? If its down for everybody, why? Is there a new competitor or a new standard? The second part of the inquiry is to search for unmet needs or inconsistencies, particularly if they are growing. With regard to the former, most people can't articulate an unmet need as such, but they can tell you what they don't like now. For example, no consumer could have been expected to describe his desire for a mouse to facilitate computer use before Apple invented the mouse, but he might well have complained about problems in manipulating his PC.

Federal Express's basic business innovation is often cited as the type of successful business strategy that research could never have predicted because normal respondents could not have answered about what they could not imagine. However, we disagree with this premise because research has been able to anticipate reactions to spreadsheets (positive) and many pilot TV shows (negative). Although this issue is controversial and open to debate, the broader perspective of research for the future makes an even clearer, less debatable case. Clearly an enormous number of businesspeople were able to express the desire to get hard copies of materials to people more quickly and inexpensively than was easily available (even if they couldn't recognize that they had "positively, absolutely" had to have it).

In addition, once the idea was hatched (and research to test it is not part of the mythology of the Federal Express launch), Federal Express reportedly did use research to help the effective marketing of the concept—particularly in regard to the advertising.

Subsequently, Federal Express used conjoint analysis to suggest refinements. With options of delivery time and costs traded off with other enhancements, Federal Express learned a few years ago that superior tracking of shipments would yield more bottom-line benefit than discount or delivery earlier in the morning.[2]

Inconsistency examination is another way to detect a change coming or an opportunity to exploit. Low-fat food products are a result of this type of thinking. Consumers want to lose weight but the percentage of overweight adults grows, as does consumption of desserts. This is a continuing opportunity (because somehow low-fat food consumption grows along the two preexisting measures).

Pringles, from Procter & Gamble, is often cited as an example of this type of thinking as it provides chips of uniform quality that aren't crushed in the package, thus solving what was heretofore a problem for some consumers.

Beyond these inferential techniques is the "history that has already happened" approach, coined, again, by Adrian Slywotzky. This discipline requires a trend-line look at changes to pinpoint what the impact would be if this history were to continue. All the news this year about how the traditional Big Three television networks are experiencing problems was no surprise to anyone looking at the trend lines of cable viewing vis à vis these three networks (much less the two to three new noncable networks joining the competitive array). Clearly the situation is going to worsen. As more and more people spend more and more time in front of computer screens, ultimately TV (including cable) viewing time will erode further.

An instructive market to consider is consumer long-distance telephone in the United States, a market dominated by three companies (really by one company with two niche players). At one time, this was a very profitable business and even a decade ago was a very good business for all three.

To the discredit of AT&T, MCI, and Sprint, they spoiled their own profit zones. They all recognized threats coming (deregulation issues, for example), and all reacted to the lack of customer exit barriers. Thus began the wars of discounting, eroding profits before their time as the three essentially swapped customers by raising marketing costs and decreasing prices. Customers would regularly receive bribes in the mail (e.g., a check for $100 cashable if they switched). (Interestingly, none really embraced customer relationship management by religiously selecting customers who might be both loyal and profitable and relentlessly communicating with and customizing for them and only them. This requires a recognition that you are in a niche business, not a mass market, a recognition neither MCI nor Sprint accepted.)

By now, each of these business has adapted and deserves credit for this (although maybe only the threat of Internet telephony spurred change). AT&T, under Michael Armstrong at least, has moved swiftly to transform its assets such that it really is no longer a long-distance telephone company. MCI (by being acquired) is now focusing on the business market. Sprint is still recognized as a long-distance company but already, as with MCI, much of its revenue and profit come from carrying data—much of this over the Internet—than voice. And Sprint's future is clearly focused on a comprehensive offer to consumers—and businesses—of which long-distance voice is only a small part. Although movement has occurred, the loss in market value for these companies is far more than might have happened with more research for the future to pinpoint the impending shrinkage of the long-distance profit zones even sooner.

Similarly, the airline industry has not reacted as quickly as might have been possible in the face of declining profitability.

Today—with Internet speed—history occurs and passes ever faster. After decades of establishing their reputations, Sotheby's and Christie's are threatened by eBay and its cohorts. This is a provable threat that Sotheby's ignored for awhile (before allying with Amazon.com) and Christie's contrives to ignore. The history has happened although as can be the case with a late game on the West Coast, those of us in the East may not yet be aware of the score.

Demographics have that same inexorable nature. There is a growing number of people over the age of 65 in the United States—soon to be far more than ever before. We can't predict all the ramifications of this, but we can predict that some businesses will still be surprised by the change in market composition despite its obvious imminence.

Although there are doubtless numerous other research techniques that are helpful for making better short-term decisions, hopefully those described already demonstrate the value of using research tools to peer into the future.

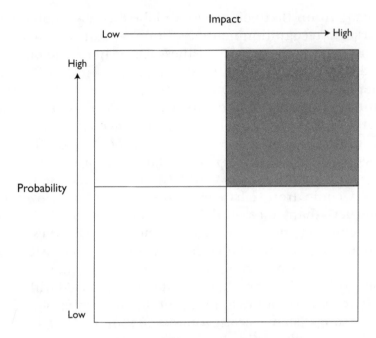

Figure 2.4 Focusing Matrix.

To summarize, amid continuous flux, if not change, it is imperative to have a continuing process that:

➤ Identifies the current driver(s) of business success for the company.

➤ Assesses all the factors that could change these driver(s).

➤ Analyzes each of the factors in a simple matrix with axes of probability and impact (Figure 2.4).

➤ Details for those with the highest likeliness/highest impact what the implications on the business would be.

➤ Figures out potential milestones that will signal whether or not the factor is more or less likely.

Now we can turn to tools that are designed more directly for looking into the future, though all can provide extremely useful insight for short-term decisions, too.

Two major techniques can be employed to provide your business with the time for Strategic Anticipation® actions. Each has been around for decades, but few companies have effectively employed either.

The *lead user* methodology is associated with Dr. Eric von Hippel of MIT. The premise is a simple one: Some users of every product or service will adapt it in use to meet their needs. To the extent that they are typical, if not visionary or role models, their usage techniques can be profitably adapted by the marketer of the product or service itself to capture the value of this user innovation. Thus, as the battle emerged for Beta versus VHS formats in videocassette recorders (VCRs), the latter was better designed for usage by allowing replay of shows and playing of movies or other tapes. The various blue jeans variations (preshrunk, prewhitened, preripped even) were all methods by which manufacturers built in features that lead users (cool kids) developed on their own and other kids wanted to follow. The very success-ful launch of *ESPN—the Magazine* was attributed by its pub-lisher, John Skipper, to cool leaders in schools who chose the design. Gatorade is another key lead user–developed prod-uct, formulated and tested among college football players at a leading so-called football factory in Florida.

There are several variations on the "follow your lead user" theme, but all are based on a key premise: It is folly to study, if not follow, all your customers. You need to deaver-age and focus only on those most likely to provide you with a profitable future. Focusing on the few (albeit even in a qualitative way) provides better guidance than the most ele-gant mass quantitative survey that by definition emphasizes the average.

Thus, a study of lead users should focus on those with high profitable lifetime value who are influencers of others like them. Understanding how they use your products and services combined with insight into their unmet needs con-nected to or surrounding the benefits for which they use your product and service is key. von Hippel adds yet another wrinkle in suggesting an alternative focus on those with the most acute need for the product and service because they have the most incentive to successfully employ it. The point is to focus and study your core future customers. Fletcher Organs has credited this technique for helping it to recognize that its profitable users are generally over age 60 and are attracted to the social aspects of the product. They redesigned their business accordingly and so far have prospered.

The second technique also has a powerful core with many possible variations. The premise of the Delphi technique is that a group of informed participants can be used in an iterative panel to provide insight into the likelihood of alternative perspectives (scenarios) for the future. (In a way, a Board of Directors can be viewed as a Delphi panel.)

The Delphi archetype was designed by the RAND Corporation at the conclusion of World War II. The idea was to tap into the wisdom of a wide range of experts to assess what global trends might occur. The panel was asked to rate the likelihood of each trend, and the results were tabulated and circulated. Then the participants were asked to vote again in light of what their peers had responded in the first instance.

The conventional analysis is that if consensus grows, the sponsor can feel more certain about those trends; to the extent consensus ebbs, there is clearly less certainty about direction.

The keys to a successful panel are twofold:

➤ The richness of the scenarios or potential trends being assessed.
  —Are they provocative?
  —Are they inclusive enough?
➤ The power of the panel.
  —Is it diffuse enough?
  —Is there depth of insight?

A recent Delphi conducted among lead users of TV showed the reluctance to pay extra for digital TV, thus changing business models for the technology.

The best client Delphi conducted by Mercer was a three-ring circus approach with three separate panels: one with conventional experts, another with lead-user consumers, and the third with a diverse group within the client organization. The research effort extended for about a year with three rounds of response.

The most value came from the consumer group. Their insight helped this client avoid a multimillion dollar investment in vidiotex. There was also real insight from a face-to-face group meeting held with the expert panel. Although Delphi historically is a pencil-and-paper exercise conducted in isolation by panel members, pulling people together at the end provided a great way to learn even more about the issues and earlier answers.

In any technique, the need is to go beyond identification and use the Strategic Anticipation® process to map out various economic scenarios (including how the underlying economics of the industry could be transformed) and the potential alignment and organization changes each factor could mandate.

The major conclusion of any of these efforts should be an attempt to prepare for the future by thinking about what might happen and how your business can best prepare for contingencies. It is impossible to predict the future, but it is possible to predict the three or four futures that are most likely and to embed signal points along the way to understand which one(s) are approaching or not. It is also possible to develop your business designs to take advantage of the likeliest scenarios with flexibility to shift in the face of a strong new breeze. Not only is it possible, it is necessary if you want to be one of the reinventors who outlives your competitive set in yesterday and today's design.

Life can best be understood backward but you have to live it forward. You can only do that by stepping into uncertainty, and then by trying within that uncertainty, to create your own islands of security.

—Charles Handy

Indicators tend to direct your attention toward what they are measuring. It is like riding a bicycle; you will probably steer it where you are looking.

—Andrew Grove

THE LAMPPOSTS

Although lampposts are a relic of the past, they still play a vibrant role in two classic descriptions of research limitations.

The first is the drunk who is observed frantically looking for something under a lamppost. When asked, he explains he's looking for his car keys. When asked how he might have dropped them there away from the cars and the bar, he replies he's looking there because the light is so much better than elsewhere!

How often are decisions made based on the best available data—information that may be dated or not focused on the right respondents? Too often. Bad data are worse than none at all because they provide a verisimilitude of rationality. Furthermore, everyone is aware of the caveats at the time, but like the smile of the Cheshire cat, memories of a number or two can often remain to haunt the researcher who provided the strong impetus for a wrong decision.

This, in turn, leads to the second description: using the lamppost for support instead of looking where the lamp sheds light. Research should provide insight and then help for decision making, but the numbers alone should not lead to decisions unless all the other factors are really even.

■ NOTES

1. Geoffrey A. Moore, *Inside the Tornado* (New York: Harper-Collins, 1999).

2. Cited in Gerald Sentell, *Creating Change-Capable Cultures.* (Pressmark International, 1999).

Chapter 3

How to Implement Strategic Anticipation®

Even if you're on the right track, if you're not moving, the train runs you over.

—Will Rogers

What separates the winners from the losers in business is often not a great deal (beyond the economic boom to the former). However, the outcomes in arriving at the strategic decision that sets one organization on the road to success and another down the road to oblivion are determined by many small but significant tactical moves that were made along the way.

The main challenge of management is to want to learn to anticipate strategically and then to do so correctly, of course. In the previous chapters we provided a broad view of the theory behind Strategic Anticipation®, acknowledging how difficult it is to master and explaining the tools that can be used.

This chapter focuses on a methodical approach to Strategic Anticipation®. With work we can orient our thinking into turning what seems at first like a difficult task into one that can eventually become a fairly established routine. If the board, the CEO, or senior executive management suddenly decrees that from this point forward, the business's fate depends on seeing what's coming on the horizon before it appears, then the organization will have to come up with a way to get there. This approach gets us into the Strategic Anticipation® mind-set, and this is how a robust business should proceed.

The art and act of Strategic Anticipation® has several elements:

➤ Researching the future (the main focus of this book).

➤ Using the information and insight to analyze today's business to prepare a business design for tomorrow (the strategy part).

➤ Acting in anticipation (the moves made to execute the model).

➤ Continually doing all three of the above.

To embark on the research part, in turn, requires the following four phases of implementation.

■ RESEARCH NEEDS A BUDGET

These tools are not cheap, and they shed only scant light on providing profits next quarter. Once you (or your research department) have developed an estimate for the annual work, the key is to sell the business leadership on the value and to develop allies in the needed disciplines (finance, planning, etc.).

Strategic Anticipation® is, naturally, best sold to the head of the business—the one responsible for strategy. (It can be done without his or her support, but then it dissolves into an academic exercise.) If that isn't you, support can be garnered in a number of ways:

➤ Propose research for the future (or Strategic Anticipation®) as the key content for the annual management retreat. This is a great topic for an off-site location.

➤ Hook the process into key projects of interest to the leader (e.g., a postmortem of a failed new product, a new Internet initiative, etc.).

➤ Convince leaders and decision makers to visit retired executives from other businesses that missed opportunities.

➤ Most simply, convince those responsible for producing the sterile annual strategic plan to incorporate research for the future into the process this year—if only to reinvigorate the strategy team.

➤ Clever Mercer Management Consulting consultants (credit goes to Vice President Jon Fay for this as well as a great deal of the other thinking behind the initial chapters in this book) once created the annual report of the future and put together two versions—one showing a somber CEO with results to match, the other depicting a jubilant leader who had steered the business clear of the icebergs that sank today's competition. This expedited the client's interest in the topic.

➤ Even better, have top management read this book!

The beauty of researching the future is that, once established, it takes on a fruitful life of its own. Many of the tools described (particularly the Delphi, with its rounds of research) are by their nature self-recurring and are therefore amenable to an annual cycle.

■ UNDERSTAND THE PRESENT

Before launching the tools to focus on the future, as noted in Chapter 2, it is necessary to make sure that the dynamics of the business today is really and fully understood. Specifically, this requires at least rock-solid knowledge of:

➤ Customer segment profitability.
  —Which customers are profitable?

➤ Buyers values of these profitable customers.

—What drives them to buy from you in the first place? What drives them to keep buying or buy more?

—What service characteristics have an impact on strengthening or weakening their loyalty?

➤ Employee issues.

—What is the profile of a valuable employee?

—What are the drivers that influenced them to join you and keep them loyal?

—What experiences cause valuable employees to leave or make them more loyal?

➤ Trend lines for all the above topics.

This knowledge should be encapsulated in a book organized to show what is known and what needs to be learned (and soon). Because a big part of preparing for the future we cannot imagine is to systematically look at the big, relevant changes that might occur, such a book should include a summary of these key factors.

Socially we know the world is changing in substantial ways. Democracy exists in many parts of the world. Communism has failed. Information can flow freely across borders in every part of the world with the arrival of the Internet. Power, which was formerly in the hands of the government or under central control, is now devolving to the people. The same trend is evident in corporations where control that was hierarchical is diffusing into control at the point where the rubber meets the road.

Demographics are astounding. The present population of the earth is over 6 billion people; by 2100, it's estimated to grow to 12.5 billion. It took millions of years to reach 6 billion people, and it will take only 100 years to double that. How does this impact the future of your business?

Knowledge and education are widely available. Economic democracy is a fact. The individual and what's in his or her head is more valuable than muscle power. Brainpower is in.

Technology is racing ahead, and new developments are taking place at ever-increasing rates of speed. The life cycle of a new-generation high-tech product is now less than one year. In your thinking and planning for new product development, do you take early obsolescence into account?

Leisure, recreation, and entertainment now comprise 50 percent of the gross national product (GNP). Companies need to think in terms of positioning themselves to provide infotainment owing to a convergence of information and entertainment. What other convergence forces could affect your industry? For example, what will the convergence of electronic smart cards and cash do to the automated teller machine (ATM) business or the convergence of the above and the Internet do to brick-and-mortar banking?

Clearly, entertainment is vital, whether as a means of making an Internet service more valuable for its "stickiness" or as a part of off-line experiences, even in nontraditional settings such as stores and hotels (as elaborated further in *The Experience Economy* by B. Joseph Pine II and James H. Gilmore).[1]

This is all big-picture stuff. So let's take a look at an example of how a knowledge book could be constructed about the Internet. After all, every organization needs to consider how the Internet will affect its business. And there is some pretty solid research already out there that is tracking trends and developments that help us to predict the impact of the Internet in our current planning.

Internet users are expected to balloon from about 100 million now to 1 billion people by 2002 and Internet sales, which stood at around $10 billion in 1998, are forecast to reach $1 trillion dollars by 2003. This kind of doubling and redoubling will certainly have an impact on almost every business. In putting together the knowledge book about the Internet, we would want to determine:

➤ Which customers of ours are using the Internet?
  —Are they profitable ones?
  —What patterns of growth have emerged?

> ➤ What are the reactions—positive and negative—to our use of the Internet (assuming you're using it)?

> —Which customers have had reactions?

> —How has usage grown?

> —What is the profitability associated with its use? If it is not currently profitable, why?

> ➤ Who among our competitors has gained market share via the Internet?

Although the issues vary from business to business, the need for trend analysis of the Internet and capturing the information is universal given the pace of change and growth, even if it is not totally understood yet. Last year Ethan Allen reported that it was selling furniture on the Internet. Furniture is normally not an item that a consumer would want to buy without sitting in it or laying on it or handling it first, but computer graphics technology has advanced sufficiently on the Internet to allow buyers to get over the hurdle and buy. These buyers would certainly be lead users to survey if you were selling furniture items.

For most businesses, the growth of the Internet is ideal as a lead-user metric. Whether your customers are consumers or companies, careful monitoring of their Internet usage and activities is essential. These lead users could be connected to your business expressly with chat sites or through bulletin boards. This is a great way to gather information and insight while tightening the relationship with groups of customers. Some companies offer free products in return for detailed information about their customers that will help them to understand their clientele better and help them market better in the future.

A key focus of inquiry with these early adopters will be their unmet needs and frustrations. At the same time, conventional lead-user observation will provide insight into the type of activities that could or should be bundled because these users find ways to do them together or in sequence. By now every company has recognized the importance of the Internet. Jack Welch, CEO of General Electric, declared that every GE business unit must utilize the Internet back in 1999. Larry Bossidy at Allied Signal said the same thing for his company. You don't have to be a visionary genius to recognize its impact, but plenty of businesses still aren't doing what GE and Allied Signal have done. They're the ones who won't be among the *Fortune* 500 in 2005. (They might even be bought by an Internet company.)

Regardless of the knowledge book's scope and format, it is vital to the research agenda: What does the business need to know about the future to assess how life might change regarding profitable customers, valuable employees and the drivers? That should be the focus of the inquiry.

■ DELINEATING OPPORTUNITIES AND THREATS

To make the process more than academic, the research/strategy team needs to pose issues in such a way as to facilitate decision making about whether new strategies or business designs are needed. This can be done through scenarios (probably the best way), but there are other techniques. To the extent that the business has a few initiatives on the drawing board, the implications of the research (pro or con) could be drawn for each one. It is worth noting that researchers typically ignore economic reality. For example, much new product research ends with estimates of penetration or market share. Often there is conjoint analysis, which details how to maximize resources/share by modifying the product. However, neither author has ever seen research of this nature in which the research details the cost implications of the modifications such that the conjoint report recommended how to optimize profits rather than maximize sales. And neither does the typical research report detail how marketing costs might be impacted by a more complex product. Only a very sophisticated conjoint, such as Strategic Choice Analysis®, can project the impact of competitive reactions to a product.

Another alternative is for research to own the customer asset. The basic idea to measure the value of the customer base either by counting the number of profitable customers or the "share of wallet" of such customers or the number of such customers with pertinent attitudes or the lifetime value of these customers—or all customers—or whatever other measures make sense. This assessment can then be used to measure the health of the business. The research for the future can then be focused on threats or opportunities to this asset.

■ PUSH FOR ACTION

This, of course, is beyond the control of the research itself or the researcher. However, the whole thrust of the research effort should be on anticipating what you can do, not just learning. To date, our observation is that research has not produced enough stimulus to action (and may not even have produced enough learning). As Henry Mintzberg, one of the major thinkers about strategic planning, has written: "Given that hard information tends to be limited, aggregated and sometimes unreliable, it should come as no surprise that managers generally exhibit a bias toward soft information."[2] Thus, the first challenge for researchers is to produce more relevant "hard information"; the second is to use it effectively to improve decisions focused on the future.

Two experts at mastering the futures game sound additional, yet consistent notes:

> ➤ Warren Buffet: "Forecasts usually tell us more of the forecaster than of the future."

> ➤ Jack Welch: "Too often we measure everything and understand nothing."

If researchers can meet these challenges and provide information, knowledge, and wisdom about today's world, then they may be able to produce research on the future that will influence those in positions of power. Hopefully, the tools described previously will help.

Unfortunately, this is not enough to ensure that appropriate actions will occur. The *Economist* posed the question, why do companies stop growing? A corporate executive board study provided the answer: "The most common weakness was complacency."

Generally, refusal to consider a future different from today stems from either rational (left brain) or emotional (right brain) sources. The former can be dealt with fairly easily by the arguments and data in this book and in other books (e.g., *Built to Last, In Search of Excellence*) if only because so few businesses still look excellent, a decade or two later (see page 88). It is the emotional side that is so difficult to influence. An analogy to frogs is apt: Supposedly, if one puts a frog into boiling water, it will immediately spring out. However, if the frog is put in standing water that is slowly put to boil, the frog will not leap and will die. (Although *Fast Company* states that this tale is not biologically correct, the illustration is still useful.) In good times, when one is prospering and beating competition, it is difficult to even think about change.

Michael Eisner openly described another aspect of this phenomenon in an interview with Charlie Rose (as reported by *Forbes* on July 5, 1999): "The people at Disney have never lived through any crisis, but I worry about what happens when there is a real crisis. We have not been trained for that kind of world." In a similar vein, people who lived through the Depression formed indelible views and habits regarding financial security.

A related problem is perceptual. At Xerox in the 1960s, all problems were viewed through the prism of copiers (just as IBM saw everything through mainframes). Thus, Xerox missed the stunning implications of its PARC's "invention" of the PC (just as IBM lost economic value to Microsoft and Intel when the PC market development occurred). Ken Olsen at DEC had blinders on such that he never saw the need for PCs until it was too late (and his minicomputers' stronghold became almost worthless).

Several ideas and tactics can create a willingness to act on the part of leadership.

■ LEARN FROM THE GREATS

As the books cited in the introduction all point out, many of the market leaders and innovators have characteristics in common; we'd suggest the key ingredient is continual search for aggressive, forward-looking, highly focused strategies for creating future value for customers and shareholders. And they may have a mix of the philosopher-king and a little luck thrown in for good measure.

On the other hand, we also have to remember that singling out the great companies is a little like nominating the mutual fund manager of the year. There aren't very many repeats—or at least there aren't many repeaters year in and year out. Of the original Dow Jones Industrial Stock Average formed in the late 1800s, only General Electric is still on the list, though it was dropped for just a bit. What can be concluded from that? In General Electric's case, it went from being a utility company to a company that sold to utilities and has switched its business design a number of times. Today it has a dominant position in such disparate businesses as jet engines, financial services, and consumer appliances. And even the leadership style of its CEO has changed. "Neutron Jack" Welch has changed from a hard-nosed, numbers-oriented executive into a genuinely caring leader who is very supportive of his people. General Electric is so flexible that it sometimes adopts what others have given up as obsolete. For example, total quality had been declared dead for years when GE established a black-belt quality initiative of its own. GE also adopted the Six Sigma measurement approach many years after it became popular at companies like Motorola. This gives new meaning to the saying "something old, something new, something borrowed."

For our part, we can take some pointers from studying the market greats and at least identifying what specifically they did to see beyond the horizon and capture, reinvent, or consolidate market share.

Wal-Mart reinvented the distribution channel value chain by introducing electronic data communication into the inventory equation and then made it mandatory that all of its suppliers go electronic. It reduced inventory, costs, and warehousing, and most important, provided just what was needed, when needed, to each store, revolutionizing discount retailing in the process.

Hilton Hotels came out of the terrible recession that rocked the hospitality industry in the 1990s to forge a new, aggressive growth strategy that more effectively leveraged the Hilton brand while at the same time reengineering business practices to regain a leadership position. To put the new corporate strategy into practice under the leadership of Dieter Huchestein, Hilton aligned its processes, people, and technology using the balanced scorecard developed by Robert Kaplan of the Harvard Business School and David Norton, president of Renaissance Strategy Group. Its quantitative and nonquantitative measures give the company a snapshot of the critical factors that create value for all its constituencies—customers, team members, owners/shareholders, strategic partners/vendors, and communities in which its properties are located. Built into the system (which utilizes simple color-coded signals) is a self-correcting feature that aids in learning and incorporating shifts in buyer values.

Iowa Beef Processors (IBP) made a core change in the meat industry's business processes—the standard method by which beef carcasses moved from the slaughterhouse to the butcher to the retailer. They put the butcher into the slaughterhouse, trimming carcasses on site, and shipped boxed beef to the retailer ready to be displayed. IBP is now the largest beef processor in the country.

Charles Schwab has also redesigned its business several times. Each time the redesign was based on a different set of customer priorities. Schwab changed its customer orientation from do-it-yourself investors to financial planners to mutual funds and their investors as it changed its business design. It morphed from a discount broker to provider of back-office services to a provider of all mutual funds to address the priorities of these different customers. This company has done the impossible—moving its business design and its brand reputation—from no-frills anti-advisor to include advisement itself.

Dell Computer, the leader in direct sales of desktop computers, differentiates itself in a basically me-too industry in which products share many of the same components by combining field sales reps for high-margin, large corporate client acquisition and telesales reps and the Internet to service and retain customers. They pioneered the direct selling of desktop computers to individual customers, building each computer to order and getting paid for it in advance of shipment, thereby eliminating the distributor and wholesale, passing on savings to the consumer, and stealing market share from its competitors, which dealt with resellers and retailers through distributors. Dell has now established its own portal to further improve on its relationship with customers. It concentrates on computer-savvy individuals and corporations that are its core customer base and is currently expanding its business offerings on-line. Michael Dell says, "It's easy to say what you're going to do. The hard thing is figuring out what you're not going to do."

Intel dominated the desktop computer-chip market in a commodity business. Intel turned itself into a preferred brand name, thus stealing market share from its competitors with its brilliant "Intel inside" initiative and funky advertising, quite distinct from that of other technical/engineering brands. Andrew Grove's philosophy: "Only the paranoid survive."

The World Wrestling Federation (WWF) discovered that its fans wanted innovation and change. Consequently, they now boldly rotate characters with new ideas all the time. For instance, Hulk Hogan used to be the golden boy; he was a cult hero for years. He was allowed to move to a rival league (owned by Ted Turner) as were other stars. The whole wrestling game has become glitzy entertainment, and the WWF shows have top market share in their time slots. If you are Tiffany's or Sotheby's or Dewar's, you may want to project stability. But Vince McMahon, owner of the WWF, understands the wants and needs of his audience, the 12- to 25-year-olds. They want to see something new on a regular basis. So rather than hanging on too long or overpaying the stars he created, McMahon lets them go.

Sports Illustrated wanted to appeal to both boys and girls when it launched *Sports Illustrated for Kids* as a way to help get kids into reading, if not also to get more kids interested in sports and reading about them. Like the WWF, it used research to understand the present so as to succeed in the future. The research (conducted by Maureen Berman, a very talented qualitative researcher) indicated a name (among other findings) that was attractive—if not cool—for both genders at the targeted age level.

There are some common denominators in all these businesses. First, they don't seem to stand still. They are constantly scanning the environment to spot changes or trends that might affect their business. Second, they have an open architecture and are predisposed to adapt. And third, they are willing to change or even scrap their business model. These characteristics make the great organizations much less vulnerable to strategic attack or obsolescence. There's an old saying that it is hard to hit a moving target.

■ ACKNOWLEDGE THAT THE FUTURE WILL BE DIFFERENT

That the future will differ from the present is a simple proposition, and yet many managers practically refuse to think about the future differently from today. Arie de Geus, a seasoned industry veteran who headed up the Group Planning function at Royal Dutch/Shell, observed and forwarded much of the early work in scenario planning and in the decision-making processes of huge corporations there. He discussed this experience in his book *The Living Company*. de Geus wrote about the failure of managers to anticipate change and wondered "why so many companies are seemingly so blind and deaf to what is happening around them"? One key conclusion was that we can see only what we have already experienced, that learning becomes institutionalized. In other words, if you have spent years in the railroad business, it's hard to think outside that experience. And if your business is built around locomotives, then you instinctively feel that there have always been locomotives, "we'll always need locomotives, so we must populate our company with people who run locomotives." Detroit was like this in the 1960s when the VW Beetle appeared, followed later by inexpensive, fuel-efficient Japanese cars in the 1970s and 1980s. Motown executives assumed that there would always be cheap gas. They knew best what the U.S. consumer wanted in a car; just because people were seen driving these little econocars, it didn't represent a relevant trend among the buying public at large. They failed to acknowledge a change in preferences in the market and lost enormous share among folks who wanted a little four-cylinder economy car.

Another theory of de Geus's is that we can see only what is relevant to our view of the future. He bases this on the work of David Ingvar, head of the neurobiology department at the University of Lund in Sweden, who maintains that the human brain is so intelligent that it knows the past has only a limited meaning and so colors the past to live more comfortably with the memories. Lund says the human brain doesn't engage in prediction; it engages in possible futures as in "if that happens, then I will take this action." de Geus calls these "time paths" into an anticipated future. When you head home each night, you aren't wondering whether your car is still at the train station or if it has a flat tire or if you got a parking ticket because you didn't have enough quarters for the meter, but your brain has already registered these possibilities and is half-prepared for the action you will take if that happens. The problem is that companies have very few time paths stored in memory, and so they have a collectively bad perception of relevant futures.

Perhaps the most difficult hurdle of all is one of the last he addresses: If we actually could predict the future, what could we do about it? Although managers seek out information about the future and pay dearly for it, they often don't act on it because they have to convince themselves of the truth of the prediction and then convince others to believe in it. Finally, they all have to agree on what it means. Put it all together and you have a barrier to action. As part of the solution, he proposes that companies need more interaction, more play and learning, and broader representation on their board of directors.

One of the ways that Shell made better decisions was to build a model that identifies emerging issues before they happen. Because vital issues may emerge from who knows where, it is important to scan the environment for all sorts of possible developments in the social, demographic, political, economic, and technological areas.

So how do we avoid obsolescence and get our strategic thinking attuned to revolutionary change? It takes a little practice, but there are some ways of addressing the future that can help.

➤ Scenario Modeling—Think the Unthinkable

Creating a set of scenarios for the future of the business should be more than a mental exercise in brainstorming or postulating hypotheticals. Speculating on a number of possible futures that may occur (although none are guaranteed in any way) at least puts the organization in the position of having thought about market forces or trends and how they might play out in the future. This allows time to think and develop mental models. It reduces the risk of being taken by complete surprise, as the leaders will have already imagined a path of action in response to any number of future scenarios. While at Royal Dutch/Shell, Arie de Geus postulated a world of high-priced oil and the company invested in the infrastructure necessary to supply it to market. In the 1970s and 1980s, that was very realistic because it had happened before. However, postulating a world of $10-a-barrel oil might have been unimaginable to executives. "There's an emotional *haze* that's very difficult to pierce. That *haze* is what we pray for the future to be," he said.[3]

Sometimes the future is unthinkable. To use Shell Transport as an example again, it had built the world's largest fleet of supertankers to carry oil from the Middle East. After the oil crisis, the push was on to develop alternate supplies, leading to new discoveries in Alaska. Now the transport time for transshipment of oil was 48 hours via pipeline versus three weeks around the Cape of Good Hope, and suddenly the need for the 200,000-ton tanker went away. Unthinkable? The lesson in all this is that when doing scenario planning, think the unthinkable.[4]

One lesson from the *Titanic:* Never assume that nothing can go wrong. That supposedly unsinkable ship with too few lifeboats and an orchestra instead of a telescope is the poster boat for Strategic Anticipation®.

Remember to stretch your thinking in scenario planning as the *Harper's Monthly* editors did when imagining what things would be like 50 years ahead. What's it going to be like in 2050? You have a blank canvas on which to paint!

Finally, when thinking about where you or your business could be, make it palpable. Put words to it and describe it in as much detail as possible.

Scenario planning should include such obvious things as Internet connectivity everywhere and convergence—for example, PCs and TVs could become one appliance as opposed to TVs remaining the dominant entertainment medium and PCs remaining primarily an interactive information source. The point of scenario exercises is to provide sufficient time for an enterprise to think and to act as change unfolds before it's too late. It also helps a company to avoid being stranded without a plan of action. Think about what might happen, prepare for the more likely alternatives, and constantly search for signposts of what might happen, and try to plot when it might happen.

➤ Anticipate Future Demand

No matter how right we may think we are, the realization might be different from our prediction. Table 3.1 offers a look back at some predictions that didn't quite pan out.

Market research and market planning can help here. When considering products, remember the stages of product life cycle. There's the initial stage, when a new product is released into the market, which is equivalent to the incubation stage in a business. Sales tend to crawl at a slow pace, and growth comes slowly. If the product catches on, we move into the growth phase. Demand accelerates, and the market expands rapidly. This is equivalent to the momentum phase in the life cycle of a business. The next phase is the maturity or stability phase, when demand levels off and sales grow at a moderate or replacement rate. Last of all is the declining stage, when the product or business begins to lose its appeal and sales start to head south.[5]

The hard fact of these cycles is that even if you get it right for awhile, it's hard to sustain success over time. First look at the qualitative judgment of two consultants who labeled their "best and brightest" as "excellent." Robert Waterman and Tom Peters listed 22 companies back in 1982 (Table 3.2).

Table 3.1 Prediction versus Reality

Prediction	Reality
Private computer networks will dominate.	The Internet dominates.
Solar and wind power resources will eliminate our dependence on foreign oil.	We import more oil than ever.
Esperanto will become the universal language.	English is pretty much spoken worldwide.
CB radios will be in every household.	CBs fizzled out.
Mainframes and minicomputers will dominate.	PCs rule.

Table 3.2 Companies Cited in *In Search of Excellence*

3M	Data General	Intel	Proctor & Gamble
Allen Bradley (Rockwell)	DEC	Johnson & Johnson	Raychem
	Delta		
Amdahl	Disney	Kmart	Revlon
Atari	Dow	Kodak	Schlumburger
Avon	DuPont	Levi Strauss	Standard Oil Amoco
Bechtel	Emerson	Marriott	
Boeing	Fluor	Mars	Texas Instruments
Bristol-Myers	Frito-Lay	Maytag	
Caterpillar	Hewlett-Packard	McDonalds	Tupperware (Dart)
Cheseborough-Pond's		Merck	
	Hughes (GM)	National Semi-conductor	Wal-Mart
Dana	IBM		Wang

Adapted from Thomas J. Peters and Robert H. Waterman, Jr., *In Search of Excellence* (New York: Harper & Row, 1982).

Looking at the list today reinforces the difficulty of sustaining top performance.[6]

➤ Changing Customer Priorities

The key focus should always be on customer needs, or better put, their priorities. When these change, value migrates. Sometimes the priorities change on their own. People wanted to be healthy before food manufacturers were ready: Distrust for authority in the 1960s and 1970s hurt established brands. Competition had nothing to do with it; politics and presidents did. However, more often than not, a business innovator creates a value shift—Federal Express, Wal-Mart, Southwest Airlines, Starbucks, Amazon.com, eBay, and so on. These innovations, it is said, cannot be predicted by research. Our response: Some can, some can't. However, regardless of this, a solid research for the future program provides the ability to decide on how to proceed. Wal-Mart's assault on department stores may have been a startling surprise in 1962 when its first store opened. But the secret was out by 1970. The problem was that most retailers felt that Wal-Mart didn't compete with them until it was too late. Maybe Wal-Mart doesn't literally compete with Sears or Tiffany, but its business design helped shift consumer priorities. Research for the future through lead users or through the Delphi technique could have identified the Wal-Mart threat very early. Just good, solid buyer value tracking would have picked it up early. A good example of strategic reaction is United Parcel Service (UPS). Maybe no one could have foreseen what FedEx's impact would be, but UPS quickly grasped the significance and recouped its balance.

Solid research can also help businesses avoid following fads. If Levi Strauss had a better fix on its lead users, it would have foreseen the potential for a quick demise as teens suddenly wanted baggy jeans and just as suddenly didn't. They were late to each of these realizations because they don't understand yet that the teen market's priorities are for change—new fashions at all costs, just as in haute couture. The solid understanding of priorities and how to learn from early (if not anticipated) changes is critical to continuing success.

■ DEVELOP NEW BUSINESS MODELS WITH SUPERIOR ECONOMICS

The Strategic Anticipation® skills we hope to popularize go beyond just reacting to change in an era of discontinuity. They condition us to identify future opportunities rapidly and to act on change by redesigning the business model whenever necessary. A corollary to the anticipation skill is to pursue redesign of the business model just as quickly as possible, perhaps a year or two or more before your competitors figure out what's happening. Of course, this means risk taking and the willingness to take a few arrows as the pioneers did, but in times of rapid changes the fast implementers get the lion's share of the market, provided they fund the effort with sufficient resources and intensity.

MCI Worldcom is a good example of a company that went all out to capture market share once it identified the trend toward global fiber-optic telecommunications over the Internet. It achieved its goal of becoming a dominant player by aggressively pursuing acquisitions. MCI Worldcom is a provider of local, long-distance, and Internet communications services to business, government, and consumer customers through a network of fiber-optic cables, digital microwave, and satellite stations. In rapid succession it acquired WillTel, UUNET, MFS Communications (for $14 billion in 1998), Brooks Fiber Properties, ANS Communications, CompuServe, and finally MCI (for $37 billion in 1999). This young company is now the number two long-distance provider behind AT&T, with a revenue stream of over $60 billion in less than 10 years. Obviously Bernie Ebbers is pursuing his business model with great speed, commitment, and focus.

An economic revolution is in the works with consumer catalog companies. For many years their marketing approach involved dropping millions of catalogs in the mail to prospects in the hope of getting perhaps a 2 or 3 percent response. With the advent of the Internet and e-commerce applications, these companies are at an inflection point where their costs can go down dramatically and their reach can expand. The Internet significantly reduces the cost of fulfilling orders by reducing or eliminating order clerk and customer service involvement. There is also a significant reduction in marketing expenses. So the economics of the business change dramatically. The cost of sales attributable to producing catalog mailings are significantly reduced, consumers have 24-hour access, and brand name companies like Williams Sonoma, Lands' End, Intimate Brands, Tiffany, L.L. Bean, Victoria's Secret, and so forth stand to benefit substantially.

As new cost models evolve—and before intuition is refined—explicit attention to nonlinearity is critical.

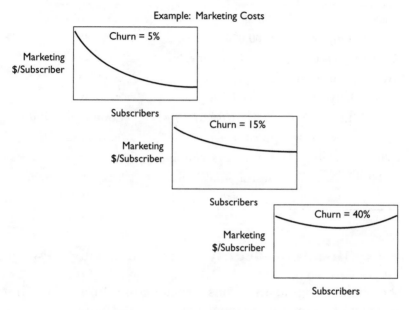

Example: Marketing Costs

Figure 3.1 Supply Analysis: Nonlinearities.

Source: © Mercer Management Consulting.

➤ Use Interactive Modeling to Build New Intuition

With today's software and instant recalculation capabilities, it's much easier to present "what if" versions of models to get an idea of the impact of certain actions or business conditions. For instance, when calculating the marketing cost per subscriber for a newsletter company, as shown in Figure 3.1, the marketing cost per subscriber at a 5 percent churn—*churn* being the failure-to-renew rate—steadily drops, whereas at 15 percent, the decline is a much more shallow curve and then flattens out. Finally, at a 40 percent churn, the marketing costs quickly start back up after a short decline. Illustrating a wide variety of options helps focus attention on what the outcomes might be with nonlinear cost profiles.

Table 3.3 The Bookselling Business

	Super Store	On-line Model
Titles	200,000	2,500,000
Sales per employee	$100,000	$300,000
Occupancy cost	12 percent of sales	4 percent of sales
Inventory turnover	3–4 ×	50–60 ×
Product delivery	Immediate	3–7 days
Accessibility	Walk/drive to store	Computer dial up
Product viewing	Instant	30–60 seconds
Reviews/readers' comments	No readers' comments	Readers' comments
	Testimonials/review excerpts	Third-party reviews/ testimonials

➤ Use Models to Identify Economic Leverage Points

The bookselling business has already gone through a major redesign of its business model. Take a look at Table 3.3. It contrasts the brick-and-mortar bookstore model with the online version.

The model for the bookselling business has undergone further refinement with the advent of specialty on-line college textbook sellers. The idea is to give students easy and instant access to books from all publishers. Think how many of us were out of luck and got behind in classwork due to unavailability of texts in campus and local bookstores.

■ ANTICIPATE COUNTERREVOLUTIONS

Revolution often spawns counterrevolution in the grand scheme of things. In a business setting, the counterrevolution may be in the form of a new business or economic model or a new twist in marketing. Customers change and markets change.

Table 3.4 Strategic Anticipation® Perspective

Traditional Analysis	Economic Anticipation
Core buyer profile	How could the demographics change in 5 years?
Core buyer values	What could change buyer values in 5 to 10 years?
	What will tomorrow's buyer value the most?
Benefits customers expect	What benefits might they value that haven't been explored yet? (Use market research tools to identify them.)
Current players	What economic forces will drive competition and profits tomorrow?
Profit distribution	*Surplus creation.* How can we increase the overall pool of value?
Static structure	*Dynamic evolution.* What does the end game look like?
Industry rating	*Decision making.* How should we pursue future opportunities?

Key to anticipating counterrevolution is knowing about your business and your customers. Table 3.4 outlines some of the categories of knowledge you need.

Among the factors we have identified that thwart sustainable success are:

➤ *Size.* Size tends to be disproportionately related to speed. The will to change is thwarted by the mindset of complacency, and the ability to change is thwarted by the size and complexity of the organism created to perpetuate the paradigm, which brought success.

➤ *Success.* Once you have scaled the peak, there's a tendency to want to enjoy the view. You don't immediately look for a bigger mountain to climb. Also, competitors and even the marketplace can look quite small. I recall an Anheuser-Busch executive once remarking to a consultant in a discussion about the microbrewery business that "we spill more beer per year than the microbreweries make." Thus, they are not taken seriously.

► *Paradigm limitation.* The paradigm that fueled the original success rarely works as effectively in maintaining success. The reasons for this are that customers change, markets change, and competitors learn to adapt. The survivors will likely find strategies and tactics that eventually hurt the leaders.

► Widen the Radar Screen

One of the ways to keep a sharp eye on the horizon is to think outside the cockpit. Develop broader vision. Let's look at a business periodical publisher. The center of their radar screen (Figure 3.2) might focus on *Business Week, Fortune,* and *Forbes* magazine. At the next circle out they might list the business newspapers like *The Wall Street Journal, The New York Times,* and *The Economist.* Then business book publishers might be considered. Further out, they might list the small business publications like *Success, Inc., Business 2.0,* and *Fast Company.* And to add to the mix those seeking immediacy or insider information, there are the newsletter publications, such as *Kiplinger's,* and finally the technology circle would loop in the on-line database companies and desktop publishers and business web infosites. By broadening the target, we get used to picking up on broader trends that might impact the business model before it's too late. And often we are able to identify opportunities based on trends we see early.

► Anticipate the End Game

A logical extension of our strategy here is to project what's coming. Like a chess player, we need to see several moves

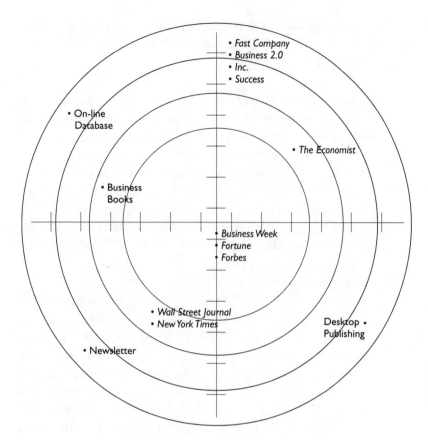

Figure 3.2 Radar Screen: Publishing.

Source: © Mercer Management Consulting.

ahead to the ultimate object of the strategy. The tactics are what get us to the realization of the strategy. An example would be the actions—mergers and alliances—of both AT&T and MCI Worldcom in the telecommunications world and Microsoft in the domination of the software industry. When Bill Gates talked about a PC on every desk, it seemed like a really futuristic scene. Today he's talking about software everywhere, whenever you need it, on a device you can hold in your hand. Funny how that doesn't seem so far away anymore.

On a more granular level, once the leadership demands research for the future, it is important that the process be a good one. These steps work:

1. *Leaders must discuss and describe their perspective, biases, and needs.* What decisions will be made? What do you need to know to make them? How much time do you have before the decision is made? What do conventional wisdom and current beliefs tell you; that is, what are the ongoing hypotheses and expected results? What do you expect; what will you accept?

   It is frequently useful to role-play reactions to various types of findings. Where there may be disbelief or push-back, consider what other information would be helpful to verify the results.

2. *Determine who the business' best (future) customers are.* Until the team knows this, it will not be able to design an effective research tool. If 20 percent of your customers provide 80 percent of your business, why bother to measure the other 80 percent? And though it may be hard for executives to get away from the notion that every customer is king or queen, you should analyze customer segments to determine their lifetime economic contribution.

3. *Explore relevant past research.* As noted, best-practices companies maintain a "knowledge book" that summarizes what is already known about the marketplace. It is amazing how many organizations start with a clean slate each time they talk to their customers. Instead of wasting both time and money, the research team should develop a database of key indicators that includes ongoing competitor analysis, environmental scans, and cost comparisons. The point is to build on institutional memory, not to reinvent the wheel.

4. *Investigate parallel work.* Don't ignore information learned in past organizational failures. As inviting as it may be to sweep disasters under the rug, the infor-

mation learned in a market failure may be even more valuable than that learned in a market success. Be sure to talk to participants about lessons learned and add outside case studies if appropriate.

5. *Summarize what has been learned so far.* Have the research team describe on paper your customer base and the research objectives, hypotheses for the outcomes, and what decisions will be influenced or changed as a result of the research.

6. *Review the research methodology. Qualitative* work can help define issues; it includes focus groups, one-on-one interviews, and other directional but anecdotal studies. *Quantitative* work involves statistically projectable surveys, mall intercepts, and the like. This research should be used to explore the kind and number of customers who feel a certain way. Decisions also have to be made as to:

➤ *Universe definition*   Who are you sampling? The top 20 percent of customers? All of them? Do age, gender, and socioeconomic characteristics matter?

➤ *Sample size*   This should be determined by the statistical basis for the results; for results within plus/minus 5 percent accuracy, a sample size of 400 customers must be used.

➤ *Instrument design*   To the extent possible, use questions that allow for baseline comparisons. Be sure to use open-ended questions to support those answers where decision makers will need further explanation.

➤ *Instrument dependability*   Are the questions understandable, and do they mean what you intended to the intended recipients? Test the instrument and repeat the development process until you are satisfied that the answers you get will give you the information you need. While these can seem to be minor details, if you are not confident of the source of the information, you will not act on it.

7. *Check the research in process.* If both qualitative and quantitative data are being gathered, the qualitative work should be done first and steps 5 and 6 repeated after that research has been completed.

8. *Review the research.* Review findings for each question. Ensure that the hypotheses that initiated the study have been fully validated or rejected.

■ ALIGN YOUR ORGANIZATION TO THE FUTURE

Our final and concluding plank in the Strategic Anticipation® platform is to point everyone in your organization toward the future. Those who have successfully adapted have left some clues. Some sound like bromides, and others are clearly tough to accomplish. But the accomplishment is necessary for the future of the company, the managers, and absolutely the employees and customers. Here are the seven exhortations:

1. Tolerate and encourage competing points of view.
2. Adopt a presumption of no privilege, no entitlements.
3. Use your sensory organs, not just your brain and hands.
4. Never stop learning.
5. Inject new DNA. Get more brain cells in on conversations.
6. Be patient . . . but learn to give up when necessary.
7. Replace "ready, aim, fire" with "fire, aim, fire, aim, fire. . . ."

When the rate of change in the marketplace exceeds the rate of change in the organization, the end is in sight.

—Jack Welch

■ NOTES

1. B. Joseph Pine II and James H. Gilmore, *The Experience Economy* (Boston: HBS Press, 1999).

2. The Economist, 7/31/99, p. 51.

3. "Memories of the Future" (interview with Arie de Geus), *Across the Board* (July/August 1997): 39–43.

4. Ibid.

5. For further information about marketing and product life cycles, see Theodore Levitt's books on marketing and his articles in the *Harvard Business Review*.

6. Thomas J. Peters and Robert H. Waterman, Jr., *In Search of Excellence* (New York: Harper & Row, 1982).

$Chapter$ 4

Researching the
Future Brand

Brand building calls for more than brand image building.
It calls for managing every contact that the customer might
have with the brand.

—Philip Kotler

Let's dig in deeper. Strategic Anticipation® is about much
more than looking over the horizon; it is about applying the
outlooks gained in the process to every aspect of your business. In the remainder of this book, we will apply Strategic
Anticipation® to each of the five critical dimensions of every
business: brands, customers, competitors, channels, and
employees. Then we will examine the most unanticipated
revolution of modern history—the Internet. Finally, we will
crank the microscope down on the research function and
how it can best serve your needs for Strategic Anticipation®.

Brands are what make Strategic Anticipation® worthwhile. They are every business's defense against pernicious
price competition. Economic theory tells us that competition
drives profits toward zero. Brands push in the other direction, enabling businesses to earn exceptional profits. The
intangible value of a brand is very tangible to a firm's financial health. This value must be developed, protected, and

grown in the face of an ever-uncertain future. What better application of Strategic Anticipation® might there be?

Never before have customers had so many brand choices. Ironically, the difference between competitive brands is often intangible. What does it take to break out of the pack with your brand and set it apart from the competition and, most importantly, place it first in the minds of customers? Creative advertising and package design are the most visible manifestations of each brand's attempt to be seen as uniquely wonderful, but these are just the tip of the iceberg. Skillful brand positioning is the base. Properly communicated by effective advertising, as well as the entire marketing program, and fulfilled by the product or service itself, it is the *right* positioning that builds brand loyalty and delivers exceptional profits. The profit premium that a brand earns in excess of its commodity value is the expression of brand value in financial terms. At its simplest, the net present value of the difference between the brand's future profit stream and that of an equivalent commodity's is the prize marketers seek. It is this brand asset value that they are charged to develop and build or, at least, maintain. *Brand stewardship* are far from empty words. Brands are a business's crown jewels, but unlike those in the tower of London, they are put to work, and put at risk, every day.

Brand positioning is communicated through packaging and advertising and promotion, but the most important element is the product or service itself. In positioning the product to consumers, marketers, too, have a choice. In *Competitive Strategy,* published in 1980, Michael Porter identified these choices, positing two generic strategies. The first was differentiation, competing on the basis of value added to consumers (quality, service, and differentiation) so consumers would pay a premium to cover higher costs. The second was cost based, offering products or services at the lowest cost. Quality of product or service isn't unimportant, but the focus is on costs. Porter posited that a firm couldn't successfully do both.[1]

Subsequent work by Porter and others suggests that a cost saving is a weak structure upon which to build brand loyalty.

Perceived relevant differentiation is the key to earning customer loyalty.

What does brand loyalty mean to your organization? Profitability. The link between it and a strong bottom line has been so well established that it hardly needs to be discussed here. In *The Fourth Wave,* from the Coalition for Brand Equity, co-authors Larry Light and Richard Morgan cite 15 different marketing experts who have found a clear correlation between the two.[2]

If perceived relevant differentiation is the key to customer loyalty and enduring profitable growth, how can we get some? Marketing research guidance is essential to the quest. Differentiation among brands can be found in a laboratory or in a marketing plan, but only the differences that are understood and meaningful to your customers matter. If your brand's benefits are not relevant to them, they are not relevant, period. Finally, those relevant differences are not effective until they have been communicated effectively. Understanding each of these requires hearing from your customers, via research, to know where you stand and how you are doing. Those businesses that fail to undertake market research to establish an effective brand position squander their resources. Too often, without market research guidance, the product or service is seen in consumers' minds to lack value, ultimately making all the advertising, promotion, and other marketing expenditures worthless investments.

Conversely, experience after corporate experience demonstrates that well-thought-through marketing research can create a blueprint for development and franchise building of a brand and provide information over the short term to sustain market share. Just as a weak brand image may keep an otherwise competitive product from getting so much as the attention of curious consumers, a strong brand image predicated on sound research can earn market share against vigorous competition. Further, Strategic Anticipation® can prevent discontinuous change from causing lost market share by alerting management in time to sudden shifts in trends and developments. Researching the future can be key to brand management. By understanding what your brand equity is, you can know what your brand can and cannot do. For instance, Coca-Cola was able to introduce a diet version without losing the luster of its name and even brought legitimacy to the category that Pepsi had helped establish. In fact, Diet Coke sold more than Diet Pepsi from its introduction 15 years after Diet Pepsi's launch. Miller and its Miller Lite had the misfortune to lose its leadership when Budweiser lent its brand luster to its light brand. Similar to the situation with Coca-Cola, Budweiser was strong enough to overcome even the strength of a competitor such as Miller.

■ THE NEW COKE CASE

In answer to those executives who question the worth of marketing research, Sergio Zyman, in his book *The End of Marketing As We Know It,* observes that although no one can predict the future accurately at all times, preresearch, or careful hypothesis testing, can help. Contrary to what some executives believe about the objectivity of consumers surveyed, Zyman believes that "consumers are usually pretty honest in answering the questions that you ask them, but they won't answer what you don't ask."[3] Zyman, who played a big role in both the introduction of New Coke in 1985 and the subsequent decision to reintroduce Coca-Cola Classic 77 days later, writes that "marketing isn't about knowing all the answers when you start out. It's about experimenting, measuring the results, analyzing them, and then making adjustments based on what you find out. . . . I know from experience that marketing conducted scientifically produces better results. It gets more people to buy more products more often than marketing that is 'intuitively' approached. The reason that Coca-Cola's volume rose from 10 billion cases to 15 billion cases from 1993 to 1998 is precisely because we applied scientific principles: assume, experiment, review, and revise."[4]

In one instance, Zyman chose to cancel Coca-Cola's advertising in Canada for a whole year and spent the money on packaging instead. Research showed that Coke's generic packaging was doing harm to the brand. A contour package could do more than distinguish Coke from its competitors than a bunch of commercials on TV. The data proved correct. Sales after the introduction of the new contour bottles proved that repackaging was a better investment.

Zyman is a firm believer in using marketing research not only to chart a course and make course corrections but also to review successes to confirm the accuracy of assumptions. Debriefing enables marketers to figure out what is working and why so that a business can replicate the success. It also determines those occasions when initial assumptions were incorrect despite sales meeting or exceeding plans. Zyman gives the example of repackaging detergent into supersizes to meet the laundry demands of large families. Not only did sales meet expectations, they exceeded them. Surprisingly, marketing research determined that sales came not from families but single consumers who preferred the larger size because it meant less frequent shopping trips. They have groceries delivered and they don't mind the oversized packaging sitting in their kitchen. Research provided two strategic consumer insights: First, singles are a market for supersized packages; by targeting more advertising to them, this initial success story can be sustained and even grown. The other insight is that the marketers had yet to find a way to appeal to larger households! In the absence of research, superficial intuition would have led to the wrong conclusion, the wrong marketing actions, and failure!

■ A MARRIAGE OF INSIGHT AND JUDGMENT

You may wonder why we have cited Sergio Zyman, someone who was involved in the infamous New Coke episode, in favor of marketing research. The episode is often cited as a failure of research. But Zyman led Coca-Cola to learn quickly from the firestorm and, through research, not only did he and his team act rapidly, but they also learned enough to help ensure that Coke's future would be even more successful.

The indictment often made about marketing research related to the New Coke incident is that the taste tests were blind—that is, no brand names were revealed to respondents—but of course, those buying cola in stores and restaurants look at brand names and packaging. Clearly what was learned (and arguably should have been known by Coke) is that taste tests without brand identification are interesting but not important. Furthermore, the tests and questions did not really posit the loss of the traditional Coke that drinkers grew up with and cherished. This was a failure of judgment, not research.

Marketing research is not an oracle that tells you what to do; it is the best source of information about what your customers want. The rest is up to you. The consumer insights you draw from the research, the business opportunity you find in them, the marketing activities you plan to address the opportunity, and the successful execution of those plans all depend entirely on the judgment and skill of the brand manager. Despite the often-expressed concern that research may constrain the manager's prerogatives, it is, in fact, her best friend. The effective marriage of research-based insight and creative marketing judgment is a formula for success.

The argument in favor of researching the future posits that a company must have a firm understanding of buyer values to provide a context in which to react, if not anticipate, what might occur. Blind taste tests would never be the basis of any decisions about a flagship brand (in any category) other than possibly a cost-reducing subtle shift in the product formula to be introduced without public fanfare. A significant marketing program would support any major change. The consumers' experience would be the combination of the product change and the impact of the marketing blitz on their perceptions. The research would need to take both effects into account to reasonably represent the likely marketplace outcome. The cynical view is that the management of Coca-Cola really wanted to build category momentum and made the move for that reason and not at all because of taste tests, using them publicly solely to justify the move.

Secondly, had Coca-Cola worked with lead users, especially their core users (e.g., the 20 percent who consume 80 percent of the product), the company would easily have understood what would happen and, perhaps, plan the New Coke and Classic Coke dual-existence strategy in a more efficient manner.

Here's another example of a disconnect between marketing research–based insight and marketing judgment that was used by Peter Drucker to argue that marketing research cannot tell us about product areas for which no product currently exists. The year was 1974. Xerox undertook research to determine, via consumer responses, businesses' need for urgent messages delivered outside their organizations, the amount of time within which these messages had to be delivered, the nature of the messages (number of pages, graphics), the bearer of the cost, and the like. Research estimated sales of facsimile devices based on existence of customer need, rather than on intention to purchase such a hypothetical product, at one million units. So why wasn't Xerox the developer of the fax? The answer is that Xerox believed it had a better product concept—that is, a system in which computers would communicate with one another, with the receiving computer putting the message on paper by means of Xerox imaging technology. Unfortunately, Xerox chose the wrong path to this latent market. The research did, indeed, identify the need for a product that had yet to exist. The problem lay not in the research-based consumer insight but in Xerox's choice of how to execute the opportunity. The marketing research offered a valuable insight, but Xerox *fumbled its future!*

Marketing research can offer management valuable information but, as the Xerox experience demonstrates, its final worth is determined by the judgments made based on the data.

■ THE ROLE OF MARKETING RESEARCH IN SUCCESSFUL BRAND DEVELOPMENT AND ENHANCEMENT

The secret to good marketing research, in general, is that the nature of the marketing problem defines the research used, not vice versa. Further, the results must have relevance in marketing terms, not simply research terms. Good marketing research should provide insights at key decision points; its purpose is not to facilitate day-to-day decisions. Finally, it must be communicated to the right decision makers at the right time in language that is clear and decisive. These general guidelines are as applicable to researching issues related to brand introduction and growth as they are to all the business applications identified in this book. There are both quantitative and qualitative techniques that your marketing researchers can use to enable your business to better position both product or service brands and the corporate brand. Various issues must be addressed in the development process, at the introduction stage, later in the growth stage, during the mature stage, and finally during a brand's decline, should that need to occur.

Research is critical to product development. Who are you developing the product for? What do they expect of a product of this type? What are the consumer's needs that are being fulfilled by existing products? Which ones are the drivers of purchase or usage? Which of these could be meaningfully improved? Are there unmet needs that your product can fulfill? Marketing research must lay this foundation if you are to avoid managing a product in search of a market nowhere to be found. Excessive reliance on unfettered judgment (aka guessing) may find you with a product only *you* would buy!

During the introductory stage, it's critical to identify the single driving customer need that your brand will use to make a beachhead in the competitive landscape. How many other brands are like yours in the consumer's mind? How entrenched are they in the consumer's repertoire? At this stage, the product may be just out of development, and you'll be using advertising and promotion to create demand. Marketing research can determine how best to communicate the brand's benefits and how to promote to gain trial without undermining perceived brand value.

During the growth stage, positioning discipline becomes even more important—which means, so does marketing research. Research-guided advertising has to be used to build a marketing relationship between the consumer and the brand. It should also be alerting you to opportunities for line extensions, targeted marketing opportunities, or reaching up or down the price/value continuum to enter new niches. Most importantly, research can help the brand stay true to its positioning and its basic value proposition. There is always great temptation to seek additional volume in ways that may dilute the brand's positioning and confuse its consumer franchise. When the brand loses its identity, it loses value.

The mature stage will have marketing research focused on ways to sustain consumer loyalty. The details of building customer loyalty are the subject of the next chapter. For now, suffice it to say that the critical performance metrics of brand loyalty lie unseen beneath the surface of brand performance. Research is required simply to be aware of this situation, which is central to a brand's profitable future. Research must identify the insights that can be exploited to increase the brand's share of requirements among those key consumer segments responsible for the majority of its profits. Long after a brand has become solidly entrenched in the category, with a market share that may seem impossible to budge any further, research can point the way to profit growth even with an immovable market share.

During the declining stage, a key role of marketing research should be to identify new products or services as well as sustain returns as long as possible, although research might also alert your business to marketplace trends that you can use to reposition your product. For instance, wax paper was replaced by plastic film to keep food fresh but then found another purpose with the introduction of TV dinners. Theodore Levitt, Professor emeritus of economics at Harvard Business School, has posited that preplanning during product introduction should extend the life span of products. Such thinking "can be a great help in developing an orderly series of competitive moves, in expanding or stretching out the life of a product, in maintaining a clean product line, and in purposely phasing out and dying costly old products," he writes.[5]

➤ Overview of the Research Toolkit

Many marketing research techniques can help brand management succeed, from brand positioning and brand introductions to brand extensions. Conjoint analysis determines the relative preferences respondents assign to each attribute when selecting from among several alternatives. Attitude and usage studies typically involve mail or telephone interviews and are designed to get a broad profile of the characteristics, practices, attitudes, product usage, and beliefs of consumers in a category. More often than not, these studies focus on the benefits or problems associated with a brand. Brand-mapping studies also involve various types of interviews, but their purpose is to measure the degree of satisfaction or dissatisfaction with product attributes as well as those attributes' impact on purchase or usage. Product-positioning maps reflect the perceived relationships among brands in consumers' minds, with shorter distances between brands indicating greater similarity in perception of relevant attributes. Segmentation studies are often built on attitude and usage studies but analytically reveal when and where various types of consumers use the product to address various needs. This enables the researcher to construct consumer segments that have similar characteristics and can be effectively targeted with a single marketing program. Positioning concept tests obtain consumer responses to written descriptions or mock-ups of packages of products under development. Attitude ratings, likes and dislikes, and intention to buy are related to a control product or other norm to learn if the new product might succeed. Simulated market tests involve personal interviews after consumers are made aware of different product concepts based on advertising and given "money" with which to buy those products they want in a simulated store. The goal is to measure purchase intent in a simulated market environment, and it can be used to test various components of a marketing plan. We are beginning to see some of these techniques migrate to the Internet (which we will explore in Chapter 9).

➤ What Is a Brand?

A brand is most simply a promise, an offer that profitably delivers a unique perceived benefit, or set thereof, to target customers better than the competition can. In short, a brand has value and, as such, is an intangible corporate asset. Interbrand's Kylie Trevillion and Raymond Perrier, writing in *Accountants' Digest* (March 1999) observe that brands qualify as assets because (1) they are identified in law as separate pieces of property; (2) they are protected through trade mark registration; (3) they are theoretically transferable through assignment; and (4) they are enduring in that trademark registrations, though granted for finite periods, are renewable by owners time and time again.[6]

Trevillion and Perrier point to the stock market's recognition of brand value, noting that companies that base their businesses on brands had outperformed the stock market over a 15-year period (from 1983 to 1998). A study undertaken by Interbrand, in conjunction with Citibank, compared share prices of a group of 59 companies dependent on their brands with *The Financial Times* (FT) 100 index and found that the branded group did consistently better. Branded group companies included Cadbury, Schweppes, and Unilever that rely on branded products they sell and businesses such as British Airways, in which case the corporate brand is what's important. The basis on which companies were included or omitted from the 59 centered on whether the brands were main drivers of revenue.

Given the impact that brands can have on shareholder activity, it is no wonder that efforts have been undertaken to put a value to brands. A relatively new concept, brand valuation, is undertaken for such purposes as brand management, merger and acquisition planning, fund raising, taxation, and licensing arrangements. Brand valuation is suitable where the brand is clearly identifiable, where the brand ownership is not in question, where the brand can be sold separately from the business, and where the brand represents a premium value over the equivalent commodity product.

Interbrand's approach to brand valuation is one of several techniques offered, but it is the most widely accepted model. It is a six-step process: (1) identification of forecast revenues and earnings over a five-year period, assuming current management budgets and plans, supported by historical data; (2) deduction of return from tangible assets and working capital to determine brand earnings (Trevillion and Perrier compare these earnings to those generated by the business if it did not own any of its fixed assets and instead leased them from another party); (3) determine the impact of continued ownership of the brand, itself a five-step process from which comes a Role of Branding Index; (4) application of a tax rate across all brand tax earnings to determine posttax earnings; (5) assessment of brand risk, which is done by comparing the brand with competitors and to the ideal, risk-free brand, from which is derived a Brand Strength Score; and (6) capitalization of future brand cash flows. "A valuable brand is dependent both on a good financial performance and also a strong marketing position," write Trevillion and Perrier. "Sometimes even if short-term earnings performance is weakened, investment in the brand can produce better long-term results, a stronger brand and, consequently higher brand value."[7]

Interbrand uses seven attributes for its Branding Index: pricing, product quality, availability, customer service, awareness/familiarity, innovation, and breadth of product range. These characteristics would seem applicable to both consumer and business-to-business marketing.

Companies in the business-to-business market, for instance, must offer a value proposition that improves a customer's position in one or more of the following areas: market position, productivity, cost, customer service, reduced time to market, or some other dimension of business that the customer values highly. For instance, Baxter International, a good example, studied its target customers—large hospitals—and learned that they wanted to cut costs, reduce waste, streamline distribution and inventory, and leverage better prices. In response, it rolled out a number of initiatives, including shared-risk partnerships to help its customers set cost targets and to allow them to share in the resulting savings. Baxter provides hospitals with their annual supply needs for a fixed price; an inventory management program, in which the company manages customers' inventory and delivers directly to the hospital floor; and procedure-based packaging, under which Baxter works with hospitals to standardize products used in particular procedures and then packages and delivers these products accordingly.

With these initiatives, Baxter gave its target customers compelling reasons to purchase products and distribution services. It dramatically reduced costs, cut money and resources spent on inventory and distribution, minimized product waste, and made doing business easier. The results for Baxter were higher sales and many new clients as well as increased shareholder value.

Baxter created an array of packages for one targeted segment, but other companies develop winning value propositions with different market segments in mind. IBM, for instance, offers numerous models of its top computer systems and focuses on providing an easy-to-use application engine featuring worry-free installation, postsales support and services, and the like.

Measuring the asset value of a brand is a useful exercise but only if it motivates you to recognize the need to protect and develop that asset. Otherwise, it's like a weather forecast—you may feel good or bad about it, but you always feel helpless to influence the outcome. Market research can do so much more than simply measure the value of your brand, although that is a useful start. More importantly, it can help you assess the impact of alternative marketing programs, or other internal initiatives, as well as environmental and competitive events.

➤ The Issue of Differentiation

As we mentioned earlier in this chapter, differentiation is critical to building brand value. Brands built on price become thought of as commodities, not as solutions to consumers' everyday needs—items they can depend on, to be preferred over the host of alternatives offered to them. When managed in this manner, brands, corporate and product, can provide for very durable and profitable revenue streams.

Brands with high recognition benefit by greater access to distribution. Retailers take on the product line because they can be more confident that the product will move off their shelves. The same is true for e-commerce; good brand reputations off-line translate into credible business on-line. Research by John Phillip Jones, a Syracuse University professor, indicates that established brands can advertise more efficiently than less well known brands.[8]

Even when a product isn't that different from the competitors', branding can personify the differentiated positioning so crucial in helping it stand out. So Andersen Consulting found out. Its decision to advertise before its competitors created such a strong presence that it achieved a marketplace relationship that has endured. But remember that everything about the brand communicates to consumers, either supporting or conflicting with this positioning. For example, the use of package design can help bring a brand's image to life. Packaging gives physical form to the image you've chosen to project. Consider how organizations that offer products such as L'Eggs have used packaging to turn a commodity into a premium product.

Research is essential to identify the benefits that will differentiate your brand for maximum profit. Techniques such as conjoint analysis enable you to sort through the possibilities to construct the best possible benefit bundle. Perceptual mapping enables you to see where your brand fits into the customer's mind, and other mapping techniques show where your product fits into the customer's life. Research enables you to sift and evaluate, searching for the greatest appeal to the greatest flow of profit. Convenience, functionality, durability, prestige, efficiency, speed—which is the glue that will bond your brand to the most profitable consumer segment? Don't guess, there's too much at stake!

➤ Positioning a New Brand with Research

Later we will describe some success stories in which marketing research played a key role. Here, let us share how one research tool might be used if management wanted to know how a new brand should be added to its line. Discrete choice analysis is a favorite technique among marketing researchers, providing models of which product a consumer is most likely to choose given attributes of a set of alternative products from which he or she can select. These attributes typically include such key marketing variables as features, packaging, pricing, and promotions, all elements of brand positioning. Consequently, marketing managers can use choice models to assess the impact of given sets of features, types of packaging, pricing, or promotional strategies on consumer choice behavior.

In discrete choice analysis, respondents provide information on their usage in the categories, including which brand they last bought, which brand they buy most often, how often they buy in the category, and the like. They then perform the discrete choice exercise in which the primary question is, "Which of these products would you be most likely to buy if you were shopping for (category) and saw these on the shelf?" Finally, respondents provide standard demographic information, such as age, income, family size, and gender.

Table 4.1 Choice Set A

Brand	Hilton	Sheraton	Marriott	Other
Cost	$195	$200	$180	
Includes breakfast?	No	No	Yes	
Exercise room?	Yes	No	Yes	
Distance to meeting	10 minutes	5 minutes	15 minutes	

Table 4.2 Choice Set B

Brand	Hilton	Sheraton	Marriott	Other
Cost	$205	$195	$200	
Includes breakfast?	Yes	No	No	
Exercise room?	Yes	No	No	
Distance to meeting	5 minutes	10 minutes	10 minutes	

One specific approach to discrete choice modeling is Strategic Choice Analysis® (SCA) as used at Mercer Management Consulting by Eric Almquist of Mercer, Ken Roberts of Lippincott & Margulies, and others. This instrument measures the (added) value of the brand within the content of virtual purchase decisions. The key to SCA is giving respondents choices (i.e., discrete choice sets) as might occur in the marketplace. For example, a respondent who is a business traveler might be given choices such as those shown in Table 4.1 and Table 4.2 a scenario involving a typical business trip to a specified location.

The analysis is quite powerful, and businesses can actually model the price consumers will pay for a benefit such as an exercise room or "free" breakfast. You can also compute the brand value vis-à-vis competition by looking at the premium price that respondents might pay if all else is equal. This can become the basis of building up from this value to the aggregate value of a brand over time or new consumers. Articles by Almquist and Roberts fully explore this analytic technique.

These marketing research techniques are designed for gaining insights into the present situation or for short-term forecasting of the results of immediate decisions. But to anticipate the impact of discontinuous change on brand value, your firm should be using a more future-focused technique, such as information acceleration, which identifies tomorrow's most likely strategic environments; discrete choice analysis, which models the economics of these environments; lead-user analysis, which learns from consumers who already live in the future; and the Delphi technique, which taps diverse, expert opinion.

➤ Extending a Brand with Research

A strong corporate brand can enable you to move into new, related product categories on the strength of your name. High corporate brand awareness translates into the ability to move into certain unexplored product categories while trading on the brand equity of the corporation as a whole. The key is, as always, in how consumers perceive your brand. If they define you narrowly, you may not be able to move out of your current category without diluting the brand's identity. If they see the brand representing a broad quality, such as innovation, or comfort, or safety, you may have a great deal of opportunity ahead. Market research is necessary to learn of consumers' perceptions and can even test the viability of specific brand extensions. Canon, for instance, was able to move from cameras to copiers, and Sony has gone from the Walkman to recorded music. Disney has made the transition from movies to theme parks to television to licensed goods. Honda, too, has undergone a successful shift—from motorbikes and cars to chainsaws—based on strength of its corporate brand name. An example of how a corporate brand name may not work is when Barnes & Noble took its bookstores online. Rather than make a change, the organization chose to do no more to its name than add the suffix ".com" when it launched a site to compete with Amazon.com, one of the most popular sites on the Web at the time. It forgot that up against tough competitors familiar with a new distribution channel, a long-standing name might not work effectively. Recently, Barnes & Noble announced that it was changing its domain name to www.bn.com. Another case in point is Starter, an athletic apparel firm, which believed it could trade on its name to enter the sports beverage market and beat out rivals Gatorade, Powerade, and All Sports. Its product made little impact in the market.

Obviously, brand extensions are not without risk. In some cases, companies that have tied new releases to established brands have seen short-term profits because they didn't have to buy initial awareness and trust to the extent that they might otherwise. But often, over the longer term, the decision can be a poor one. As Jack Trout and Al Ries have documented repeatedly in their books, a single brand can't stand equally for two conflicting positionings with their own value propositions.[9] Typically, the brand will be defined—in the consumers' mind and eye—with one or the other or, worse, will end up as a blur standing for nothing.

When you have responsibility for the brand, it is impossible to be objective. Market research provides the consumers'-eye view of the marketplace. What does your brand stand for? Can that take you into another flavor? If your brand means chocolate, you may not ever be able to be vanilla. If your brand means rich flavor, you have many options. There's only one way to know how far you can go.

■ WHAT IS BRAND EQUITY?

Its time to ask the fundamental question, what is brand equity and how can I get more of it? *Brand equity* is a set of assets and liabilities linked to a brand, its name, and its symbol that add or subtract from the value provided by the product or service to a firm or that firm's customers. Brand equity can be divided into five issues, insights into each of which can come from marketing research. The five elements are:

1. *The brand's physical characteristics or attributes:* cleans better, lasts longer, has fewer calories. These attributes are relevant to consumers and differentiate the brand from others based on research into consumers' needs and desires.

2. *Brand awareness.* You want consumers to say about your brand, "It's one I know and can trust." Research helps develop tactics, such as advertising, that are memorable and create a media plan that effectively earns this awareness.

3. *Consumers' beliefs about the brand.* Do consumers think the brand will make them successful, sexy, or happy? Such insights, too, can stem from research. Conclusions reached are reflected in the brand's communication vehicles, especially advertising.

4. *Perceived relevant differentiated quality.* Such a response to a product or service offering leads to the brand receiving consumer consideration and being preferred. Research leads to the right positioning, the right communication, to gain this special place in consumer's minds.

5. *Consumer loyalty.* From the right positioning, the brand can ultimately wind up in this special place in consumers' hearts. Preferred above all others, even at a somewhat higher price, because it is believed to be better.

There are various levels of brand loyalty, with each level representing a different marketing research challenge. Larry Light, president and CEO of Arcature Corporation, uses the analogy of a ladder, with each consumer existing on a rung. Those at the bottom rungs are price-sensitive consumers little moved by the brand reputation. On the next level are buyers satisfied with the product or at least not dissatisfied and consequently without a reason to want to change. Above them are satisfied buyers who won't switch because they recognize they would have to pay to do so—from a risk of poor performance or time lost to actual financial losses. Above that level are those who like the brand and even consider it a friend. Finally, at the top level are the committed buyers. These individuals not only use your product or service but also recommend it to others. "These individuals," suggests Light, "are so enthusiastic about the brand that they might actually switch stores or postpone the purchase until they could find it."

The most compelling case for a product is based on two aspects: behavior and attitude. Behavior is what the consumer does (purchase loyalty); attitude is how the consumer feels about the brand (his or her commitment). Behavioral loyalty may be the result of heavy promotion, which is not the commitment that bears profitable fruit for the brand over the long run. Therefore, it is important to examine both attitudes and behaviors to really understand consumers.

In addition, loyalty or brand choice is generally situation specific. Consumers use one soap for the face, another for the bath, and still another for their hands after changing the oil in their cars. They buy three different brands, and are loyal to each, but their behavior suggests switching. They may also seek some variety, loyally eating three different breakfast cereals in rotation, yet their purchase history would suggest switching brands, not brand loyalty. Carefully analyzed purchase panel data can reveal these patterns. Further, they can help the marketer understand which consumer segments are loyal and which are not, which is to say, which are profitable and which are not.

This insight, if effectively acted on, can enable a company to maximize a brand's profitability. The attitudinal side is, if anything, more important. Finding true commitment, not just consistent behavior, is crucial to identifying the sources of brand profitability. Attitudes also help to identify the reasons for loyalty and, with them, the clues for promulgating loyalty among more consumers, converting sales into profits.

There's no question that loyalty is most elusive and yet most essential in product categories that are considered to be commodities. Be it credit cards, long-distance calls, audit services, or airlines, most marketers excuse the churn of their company by complaining they are caught in a commodity marketplace. But, as Theodore Levitt has observed, you can differentiate anything. That is what the winners do in these industries. For instance, Southwest Airlines outperforms its rivals, as do MBNA and Nucor. The key is to follow a process that focuses on what keeps customers. Fresh research is needed to marry attitudinal and demographic information with the behavior data of the company. This allows it to pursue traditional segmentation analyses before determining the actual profitability of the customers in each segment.

The company can then determine which segments to target for loyalty programs (that is, which segments can the business make more loyal *and* more profitable). Through the melding of attitudes (e.g., proclivity for loyalty and satisfaction with the company) and behaviors (e.g., the company can serve profitably), the company can isolate groups that become the magnet for building a profitable future.

Using this insight means avoiding trying to please some of the highest-volume users—the ones who always demand a discount and often are attitudinally uncommitted. Always, this means marketing to the target both through products and services and emotional connections (communications, icons, etc.) that are meaningful. The old AT&T slogan, "Reach out and touch someone," is the classic emotional appeal that prompted incredible loyalty when the monopoly was ended and consumers could choose their carrier.

But remember: Buyer values work must incorporate both rational and emotional values. Simply having the right features and price does not guarantee either sales or loyalty. Conversely, as Marlboro learned a few years ago, even the best emotional linkages are not sufficient if price gets too high.

■ HOW GREAT BRANDS GOT (AND GET) THAT WAY

The importance of positioning stems from the sameness of so many products today. If you think about your own firm's products, chances are that their physical attributes are not very different from those of your competitors. Consequently, awareness, as Stuart J. Agres, senior vice president for Young & Rubicam, Inc., has observed, isn't enough.[10] Agres notes how in the past the model for brand success was AIDA— awareness, interest, desire, action. Awareness didn't just lead to action; it also led to "loyalty" if the product delivered as promised. A brand manager's toolbox for securing trial and then keeping consumers coming back for more was the four *P*s: product, price, promotion, and place. No more, says Agres, who cites these trends as cause for change:

➤ *The alarming rate of product failures.* Twenty-five years ago, the new product failure rate for packaged goods was 65 percent—today it's 95 percent despite substantial promotional support.

➤ *Generics and store brands compete successfully with name brands.* Consumers seem willing to abandon branded goods in favor of generic, private labels and store brands.

➤ *Margins are shrinking for even the great brands.* Consumers aren't willing to pay a premium even for high-quality, reliable brands.

Awareness, as Agres observes, is no longer enough. Brands must stand out when they start out. Today, marketing research has discovered that successful brands are founded on four new pillars: differentiation, which reflects the distinctiveness of the brand; relevance to consumers; esteem or regard consumers have for the brand (Does it live up to expectations?); and consumer knowledge and understanding of the brand.

Young & Rubicam has spent over $20 million to verify this four-pillar formula for corporate success. As Agres says, "The old rules, no matter how passionately embraced, will not give birth to the blue chips of tomorrow."[11] As examples of firms that epitomize this model, Agres points to Boston Chicken, now Boston Market, and Barnes & Noble, the bookstore. In both instances, growth occurred with a strong first pillar and over time strengthened the other measurements.

Once brands get great, they can stay great—like Disney. But brands, even famous, top-of-mind names, can fade. Y&R's study found a reverse pattern to successful start-ups. The first pillar was severely depressed, the second and third were following downhill, and the last pillar was still holding up. The research suggested that the first pillar, differentiation, was the critical one. "To have a chance in today's marketing world," says Agres, "a brand must be perceived as different and unique. While differentiation, in general, is very strong among the successful brands, it is usually the first pillar to dissipate for those going bankrupt."[12]

In 1993, Starbucks was just getting started. It had a healthy start-up pillar pattern, according to the Y&R research. Although the awareness-related pillar—knowledge—was zero for Starbucks in 1993, the differentiator pillar presaged well for the fledgling firm. By 1997, the first pillar was still growing fast, but the other dimensions were also moving up. Starbucks is now developing the potential that Y&R predicted four years before. Not so fortunate is Foxy, according to Agres. "After four years of trying to establish a brand name in lettuce, they've made little progress in differentiating their lettuce from competing brands."[13]

Agres cites another company, Kmart, that is high on knowledge, the last pillar, and low on differentiation, the first pillar. However, Kmart is still seen as relevant, even if not differentiated. Pricing, distribution, and packaging can truly drive relevance. What these *P*s are unable to drive is differentiation and profit margin. Agres adds, "No matter how relevant the brand, differentiation is what gives a brand the foundation it needs, building customer loyalty as well as margin opportunity."[14]

■ MANAGING BRANDS FOR PROFIT WITH EFFECTIVE RESEARCH

Today much is written about brand management. Discussion about positioning often cites the importance of targeting the right consumers, awareness of the competition, the need for marketplace credibility for the offering, and clearly defined benefits to the consumer. But obviously the central focus of all those issues is always consumer needs and wants. Creating a profitable brand demands that you research these in depth, noting emerging trends or evolving interests.

The benefits your brand represent to consumers may trigger emotional feelings that can motivate them to consider your brand as superior to your competitors'. The benefits themselves have to be credible and presented in language that consumers understand. Take the Always brand of sanitary protection from Procter & Gamble that is designed to pull wetness away from the skin. P&G chose to name this feature "Dri-Weave," which is certainly more consumer friendly than "Spaghum," the term initially used by an Australian competitor with a similar product offering superior absorbency. A benefit-based analysis of the competitive environment enables marketers to differentiate your brand for consumers, which means that you should be periodically studying your marketplace to look for any restructuring that may be occurring. This could be due to a new competitive product offerings like Ensure, once solely a nutritional supplement found in hospitals but now being advertised as an everyday food supplement for those with insufficient time to have a good meal. It could be due to consumers redefining a product category, like their increasing preference for healthy snacks like white tortilla chips and popcorn because they are less oily and more wholesome.

Earlier we said that a brand is a promise and that promise must always be kept. It's curious that we speak of "brand loyalty" when we usually mean "the consumer's loyalty to the brand." Yet brand loyalty is not a misnomer because the cherished consumer's loyalty requires that the brand be loyal to her. It's easy to forget this basic tenet of brand management as you struggle to grow a brand. But keep in mind how word of mouth multiplies many times. Don't lose a good brand name through bad customer service. The initiative by Hilton Hotels, to be described later in this chapter, underscores how important performance is to brand equity.

Understand what is behind a brand's identity: It's not only the product itself but also the services associated with use of the product or the wide array of products within the line. Product quality or service must lend credence to the brand. Starbucks' founder Howard Schultz has said about the impact of service on brand, "Starbucks' success proves that a multimillion-dollar advertising program isn't a pre-requisite for building a national brand."[15]

■ THE PROMISE

Another successful use of marketing research concerns Saturn. Research enabled the company to understand the market well enough to develop position a new positioning in an extremely well established and diversified category.

Although much has been said about this success story, little mention is made about the initial risk. Consider the situation when the car was launched in January 1985. The company planned to introduce into a highly competitive and oversupplied market a new U.S. car to an audience that was predisposed to buy cars from other countries, specifically Japan. Honda and Toyota were household names, but Saturn was not. The organization used correspondence analysis to identify the most discriminating attributes and brands. Perceptions of quality explained 50 percent of variance between makes, but value was next most important dimension, responsible for 25 percent of variation in brand perceptions in the market. Although Honda and Toyota didn't score poorly on this attribute, the make most associated with value in consumers' minds at the time was Geo. Other factors that determined differentiation were how much fun the car was to drive and looks, and a make that performed well on these criteria, but not necessarily on quality or value, was Mazda. This was the climate when Saturn was launched.

Awareness of the Saturn brand name climbed to nearly 70 percent by year's end, compared to the pretest study that found only one in three people recognized the name. Studies showed that the ads worked better than others among people who saw the ads but had not experienced the brand. But when the ads were combined with the Saturn experience, the full effect was evident. The conversion from familiarity to purchase consideration was 20 percent higher than the norm and more similar to that achieved by foreign rather than domestic models. Those who conducted research prior to launch and after the advertising campaign point to the value of the research to identify the weaknesses of other car makes and to challenge the status quo. A well researched and conceived positioning enabled Saturn to slip into a crowded marketplace, successfully addressing a new consumer segment with a new promise. All too often, people use research to view the world only as it is and not to think about how it might be.

➤ Renewing the Promise

A well-known brand name isn't enough. There has to be value behind the name, which is the problem that Hilton Hotels faced in the early 1990. With competitive hotel supply expanding up and down the price point ladder and a proliferation of new brands creating ever-narrowing market segments, it had become difficult to differentiate products and services in an environment threatened by potential overcapacity. So Hilton Hotels adopted an aggressive growth strategy, one designed to leverage the Hilton brand while reengineering business practices to gain a leadership position in the hospitality industry. The Hilton initiative was built on ensuring substance behind the brand perception.

Hilton began by examining its position in the marketplace. Extensive research showed Hilton to be in a comfortable but middle position among its competitors. Using a comprehensive conjoint analysis, customer research identified key attributes where Hilton hotels were not meeting customer expectations. Further, research showed that quality was inconsistent, especially between franchise and owned/managed hotels. Despite the efforts under way at many of its hotels to improve performance, Hilton senior officers realized that their efforts were fragmented and disjointed.

The survey results led to a plan focusing on creating value for its constituents that truly has transformed the company. Hilton changed its business design, the system by which the business delivers services to its customers, by redesigning its organizational and support structure with a focus on action-oriented tactics. Finally, Hilton devised the means to measure results and communicate them and the strategy throughout the organization. In this manner, Hilton translates its strategy, through measurement and alignment, into daily operations. A key driver of the system is brand management, leveraging the widely known and respected Hilton brand.

Hilton's strategy itself is built on three elements— research, education/training, and brand standards. Extensive research is conducted to determine what is important to its customers and how it is performing vis-à-vis its competitors. Education and training acknowledges the importance of today's information-based environment by communicating brand standards and also develops and utilizes team member knowledge. This approach explicitly recognizes the price of nonconformance if one doesn't adhere to brand standards by investing in the education and training of all those who deliver the products and services that customers expect. Hilton chose the balanced scorecard, the concept developed in the early 1990s by Robert Kaplan and David Norton, to gauge whether the company's strategy is working. The balanced scorecard quickly translated corporate strategic direction into property level goals and became the critical link in Hilton's value chain.

At a strategic level, use of the balanced scorecard has increased brand equity by reinforcing quality control of the standard Hilton experience. This has been directly transferable to the Hilton Garden Inn, a new franchise product that commands a rate premium over competitors and is meeting with success as evinced by over $1 billion in new hotel construction currently under way.

➤ Your Brand Name As a Promise

Your brand name speaks your promise to the consumer. A respected brand name doesn't make marketing unnecessary, but it can make your programs much more effective. On the other hand, a poorly perceived brand name may make all the advertising, sales promotion, and even public relations work you do worthless. A good brand name (1) projects your positioning, (2) identifies the function of the product or service, and (3) lends itself to creative advertising.

An example of how marketing research successfully led to a name change involves CVS Pharmacy, a major store chain located primarily in New England, and Peoples Drug, a chain located in the Washington, D.C., area. After CVS purchased Peoples Drug, it undertook a major renovation of every one of the 400 stores and then undertook an eight-week promotional effort. Unfortunately, the store renovations and subsequent marketing effort produced only moderate sales results, according to Mark G. Kolligian of CVS, Inc. Besides the lukewarm sales results, major inefficiencies in operating and marketing two similar drug chains with different names prompted management to consider changing Peoples Drug's name to CVS.

The change was risky primarily because, says Kolligian, Peoples Drug was a 90-year-old institution in the D.C. area— almost a household name. Further, marketing worried about consumers' distaste for meaningless acronyms. And CVS had no positive associations in Peoples Drug's regional market. It didn't help, either, that recent name changes in the industry (Osco/Sav-On) and in the local retail market (Hardee's/Roy Rogers) had been disasters.

So marketing research was undertaken before a decision was made. The goal of the research was not only to determine how consumers would react to the name change but also how marketing should effectively position and communicate the chain. The study took the form of a brand imagery study, comparing Peoples Drug's profile to local competition and to CVS in a core New England market. The research involved 500 in-depth interviews in Washington and Boston.

The research rated the two stores on three different levels of attributes: (1) operational characteristics such as pricing, services, and assortment; (2) benefits/values of an ideal drugstore; and (3) brand personality characteristics to help the firm focus on the right areas in terms of imagery building (e.g., an honest, caring, socially responsible company). People's Drugs did well on all three. The chain got a strong rating on most of the key tangible, operational characteristics, according to Kolligian, because of the renovations. Although sales after the refurbishing had not met full expectations, the fraction rating "excellent" or "very good" on store characteristics made the effort worthwhile.

The ratings on benefits/values also were fairly strong. The highest ratings were awarded to those attributes considered most important to consumers—customers' feelings of confidence that prescriptions would be filled carefully and accurately. Peoples also scored high on the shopping experience. Again, this seemed to stem from the renovations.

The brand imagery also appeared to be fairly strong. The chain's imagery was widely seen as "knowledgeable," "successful," "professional," and "modern." There appeared to be opportunities to build excitement in the stores. But there was a problem. Despite Peoples Drug's strong brand equity, Kolligian and his staff found that its key competitor in the market, Giant, a well-run local food/drug store, had an even stronger profile. Peoples Drug had a perceived price advantage over Giant, but Giant was seen as being outstanding in terms of overall service, "shopability" (merchandise being easy to find), and the assortment and quality of private-label merchandise. Giant also had a significant advantage over Peoples Drug in terms of time savings—Giant was seen as providing one-stop shopping. On the other hand, Peoples Drug was seen as a more exciting/fun place to shop, in part due to the recent promotional efforts.

Because the objective was to determine if Peoples Drug's name should be changed to CVS, the performance and imagery data was compared with similar data on CVS in its strongest market, Boston. CVS's equity was extremely strong compared with local competition. "CVS is truly an institution in most of New England. In fact, the name for many consumers in this part of the country was synonymous with the drug category overall," Kolligian recalled.[16] CVS's image in its core market surpassed Peoples Drug's image in its core market on all three levels of attributes. CVS received significantly higher rankings on tangible/operational store characteristics, benefits/values dimensions, and personality/imagery. In the case of the last, CVS received significantly higher associations with positive imagery items such as "successful," "popular," "caring," "understanding," "modern," "helpful," and "friendly," among others. CVS also received a significantly lower association with "disorganized," "messy," and "confusing," which appeared to be a result of some of Peoples Drug's negative baggage prior to the refurbishing.

All the brand imagery advantages enjoyed by CVS, according to Kolligian, translated into shopping behavior. CVS's customer base was far more loyal to CVS than Peoples Drug's customer base was to it. Indeed, as a percentage of all customers, CVS's core customer base (those committed to the store behaviorally *and* attitudinally) was found to be twice the size of Peoples Drug's core customer base. This finding was critical, suggesting that despite the modest gains already realized by Peoples Drug, a significant upside still existed—not just in imagery but in real sales and shopping behavior.

Most important, the study found that CVS and Peoples Drug had similar imagery profiles. Although one was stronger than the other was, they were fundamentally similar. Consequently, it made sense to move forward with the name change.

The research also asked consumers a number of direct questions about the proposed change to identify the most successful communication approach. One approach being considered focused on the past and the continuation of services and benefits already perceived as strengths. The other approach focused on continued change for the better. Based on consumer response, the latter was seen as having more impact. Combined with previous imagery data, this finding led to a massive name change communication program with the slogan "Same thing, only better."

The survey responses proved themselves. The campaign was a major success. The renamed Peoples Drug stores have a share advantage over Giant, and perceived disadvantages versus Giant have been eliminated.

Note that this research fulfilled the three key points mentioned earlier in this chapter. The nature of the problem defined the research procedure to be used; the results were clear in management terms, not just research terms; and the focus reflected key decisions, not day-to-day operations. In describing his efforts in *The Journal of Advertising Research,* published by the Advertising Research Foundation, Kolligian further pointed to the importance of how research needs are positioned to retailers to be of value. Given retailers' action orientation, he writes, "You can't tell a retailer that they have a perceived weakness on pricing that needs to be fixed."[17] You have to specify actions to be taken.

■ RELATIONSHIP MARKETING

If there is one major shift in marketing initiatives, it is away from driving sales to winning customers for life, with high customer service emphasis, high customer commitment, and high customer contact. We will detail the challenges and benefits of earning customer loyalty in the next chapter. For now, just note that relationship marketing is the heart of maintaining and developing brand value. Relationship marketing is predicated on the notion that a customer represents not merely the next sales opportunity but rather a lifetime revenue stream.

One organization that has long seemed to practice relationship marketing with utmost skill is Procter & Gamble. It

is known for its ability to turn products such as Tide, Head &
Shoulders, Crest, and Pampers into market leaders. In each
case, it accurately defined the brand through market segmentation research, named and packaged it in an appealing
fashion, pumped ad money and promotions into the media
and trade to draw buyers and users, and leveraged its distribution channels. It is so skilled at branding that it has even
used the formula for brands acquired from others, such as
Richardson-Vicks (which it acquired). For instance, Pepto-
Bismol was retargeted for uses such as traveler's diarrhea,
and Oil of Olay was retargeted to young women and more
recently developed into a full line of cosmetics. How can
they do this successfully almost every time? This kind of reliability does not come from a flash of insights—it comes from
fact-based discipline. The research department at Procter &
Gamble was recently renamed "Consumer and Market
Knowledge"—they go to great pains (and expense) to *know*
the consumer—and it pays.

Another excellent example of good brand targeting is
Geritol. Until recently, the product line languished because
of its image as a geriatric product; most people at 50 years of
age don't think of themselves as old. Consequently, Geritol's
management rebranded it as Geritol Extend, repositioning it
as a multivitamin that was perfect for active, over-50 consumers. Backed by promotions including wing dance com-
petitions and walking rallies for seniors, Geritol Extend went
from negative sales trends to annual sales gains of 19 percent. This didn't just happen. Research identified the central
consumer insight and then ensured that everything communicated to consumers (including the wing dancing) reflected
the right positioning.

Many other examples demonstrate the power of marketing research to enhance brand equity and with it brand
profitability. At United Airlines, a segmentation study of
consumers was conducted to learn their attitudes, behaviors, and preferences as it related to the airline in order to
build a brand value proposition that would work around the
world. Scott Praven, director of brands and product development for United, found that the company had years' worth

of information on its best customers and customer performance ratings but that little was being done with the information. He shared that information with President John Edwardson, who in turn took the information to the firm's board of directors; the board gave Praven the go-ahead to conduct research to increase its share of high-yield passengers, among other goals. Praven recalled, "We carried a lot of people but at a lower yield than some of our competitors. And we had no clear image. One of my boss's favorite quotes was, 'There's no reason to fly and no reason not to fly [United]'. That wasn't very pleasing for an airline like ours, with a 70-year history."[18]

United conducted a segmentation study of customers, surveying around two thousand U.S. flyers to learn their attitudes, behaviors, and preferences related to the airline and where it stood in terms of brand imagery. The company also conducted qualitative research among flyers in eight countries to learn their feelings and attitudes—the things that you sometimes can't find in a quantitative study.

The studies showed that the way United saw its business and the way its customers saw the world of travel were very different. United saw itself as a provider of transportation, whereas its customers, according to Praven, "made it clear we were looking at things much too narrowly. They look at the total experience, how they are treated and at the certainty of that experience . . . the travel experience begins the minute they think about travel and continues until they get where they are going."[19] The conclusion caused United to do touch-point analysis to find suitable behaviors within each stage of the customer experience. It also did focus groups. The result was awareness that flyers wanted a simple and seamless process.

Since implementation of the research findings, United has experienced improved "yield performance." In the three-year period between 1993 and 1996, its yield improved 4.6 percent, while industry yield as a whole dropped 0.9 percent, equating to a $657 million advantage for United.

At Minute Maid positioning groups, reason-why groups, hot-button research, and positioning-optimizing tests were used to reposition the brand and develop a new advertising effort to turn around brand equity and increase market share. The studies showed that consumers weren't satisfied with a product that tasted like fresh squeezed. They wanted a juice that recreated the experience of eating an orange, a brand philosophy Minute Maid adopted as its own. During 1997, research helped develop and evaluate advertising copy behind the brand, with positive results. Equity signs showed strength, and volume rose significantly, as did market share.

Once you get such volume, how do you retain it? Our next chapter looks at customer retention.

■ DIAGNOSTIC

Do you know . . .

➤ The lifetime value of your most valuable customers?

➤ How your most valuable consumers see your brand positively or negatively relative to alternative brands?

➤ Which of these differences are important enough to drive their purchase and usage behaviors?

➤ Which drive their loyalty?

➤ Are you adequately communicating your relevant differentiating benefits through your advertising and other forms of marketing communications?

➤ Are your price, promotions, and packaging consistent with this positioning?

➤ Is it distributed where consumers can find it?

➤ Does it come in the right forms and flavors?

➤ Can you expand your current customer base with a new brand extension?

➤ Can your brand enter new product categories?

➤ What is the financial value of your brand?

■ NOTES

1. Michael Porter, *Competitive Strategy*, (New York: Free Press, 1980).

2. Larry Light and Richard Morgan, *The Fourth Wave: Brand Loyalty Marketing* (New York: American Association of Advertising Agencies, 1994).

3. Sergio Zyman, *The End of Marketing As We Know It* (New York: Harper Business, 1999), 55.

4. Ibid., 49.

5. Theodore Levitt, "Exploit The Product Life Cycle," *Harvard Business Review* 43, no. 6 (November–December, 1965): 115.

6. Kylie Trevillion and Raymond Perrier, "Brand valuation—A Practical Guide," in *Accountant's Digest* (London: Interbrand, March 1999): 405.

7. Ibid., 37.

8. John Philip Jones, *When Ads Work: New Proof that Advertising Triggers Sales* (New York: Lexington Books, 1995).

9. Jack Trout and Al Ries, *Positioning: The Battle for Your Mind* (New York: Warner Books, 1993).

10. Stuart Agres, "How Great Brands Got to Be That Way," in Brands in The Fast Forward Future (New York: Advertising Research Foundation, 1997).

11. Ibid., 27.

12. Ibid., 28.

13. Ibid., 29.

14. Ibid., 29.

15. Rebecca Saunders, Business the Amazon.com Way (Oxford, U.K.: Capstone, 1999), 97.

16. Mark Kolligian, "What's in a Name? The Conversion of Peoples Drug to CVS," *The Journal of Advertising Research* 38, no. 6 (November–December 1998): 47.

17. Ibid., 48.

18. Scott Praven, quoted in Research Conference Report (Skokie, IL: RFL Communications, February 1998), 1.

19. Op. Cit.

Chapter 5

Researching the Future Customer Loyalty

> As long as you depend on the statistical aggregates we now call information, you'll know a great deal about your product, a good deal about your services and not a blessed thing about your customers.
>
> —Peter Drucker

Business growth can stem from mergers and acquisitions, price increases, new products or services, geographic expansion, new customers, or additional purchases by existing customers. Of the three, the last represents the most stable platform for long-term growth. Companies have to do much to develop a customercentric culture. Yet few collect the information required to quantify the asset value of their customer base. Worse, a recent Mercer Management Consulting survey of large U.S. companies found that few CEOs or boards spend even a small fraction of their time looking at data on their own customers—even if their research departments do conduct the research—despite the amount of lip service given to "customer focus."

Management has explanations for this situation, including such arguments that there is no way to get the true facts, that market research is vague and imprecise, or that senior managers generally don't have time for this stuff but must instead focus on the balance sheet and the bottom line. If you agree, you need to heed the advice of Tom Peters and treat the customers as an appreciating asset.

■ OPPORTUNITY

There is impressive evidence that retaining valuable customers is directly related to value growth (i.e., the bottom line). It is even clearer that losing valued customers—or valued employees, as we'll describe later—costs incremental dollars that would not be spent without each such loss (if only in having to recruit and orient new customers or employees).

Replacing customers lost to competitors is five to six times more costly, maybe more, than retaining existing customers, and customer retention is a driver of net growth. Mercer projects that retention of 5 percent of a company's customer base can increase profitability by as much as 125 percent.

Some more numbers: According to the Technical Assistance Research Programs Institute (TARP), customer loyalty drops by about 20 percent if a customer encounters a problem. The affect on the bottom line is that for every five customers who experience a problem, at least one will leave or purchase another brand the next time he goes to the marketplace. If your average customer is worth $1,000, then you can estimate that for every five customers with problems, you lose one customer and $1,000 in revenue.

TARP refers to this reduction in loyalty as *market damage*. If you need financial figures to justify the cost of remedying the problem, you can quantify the level of market damage. You can also test solutions by doing your calculations in reverse, quantifying the value of loyalty building initiatives to justify their costs.

And, in some industries, interestingly, old customers pay higher prices than new ones. This is sometimes due to trial discounts for brand new customers, as in the retail and magazine fields. More often, however, the price difference is self-selected. A bank promotes special CD rates from time to time but finds that long-term customers rarely take advantage of them. A retailer offers a coupon to all customers but finds that long-term customers don't often use them. Loss leaders make up a small portion of an old customer's shopping cart.

■ LOYALTY CAN BE BAD

It might sound like heresy, but the fact is that customer loyalty is not always good. If, for instance, you are losing money in serving a particular set of customers, the last thing you want to do is to invest in forging long-term relationships with them. And if your customers' loyalty is to old products and services, you may be lulled into a false sense of security that leaves you vulnerable to new competitive threats. A blind devotion to the concept of loyalty can be dangerous.

On the other hand, ignoring loyalty is even more dangerous. Companies that give little or no attention to building loyalty among their customers (and, unfortunately, most still fall into this category) are doomed to eventual decline. Either they will succumb to terminal customer churn or, more likely, they will lose their best customers to a competitor with a more compelling value proposition. We see such fates played out again and again in the business world, as once prosperous companies take their market positions and customers for granted. Remember that many of the original 1955 Fortune 500 companies—once the most powerful enterprises in the business world—no longer exist. They had loyal customers at one time, but they lost them.

A case in point about the value of customer loyalty: Honda spends far less in advertising than other Japanese car makers in the United States, yet it is the largest foreign supplier of cars because of its repurchase loyalty rate—68 percent. Analysis of dollar savings in advertising costs further demonstrate the value of loyal customers. Honda spends only $150 per car on advertising compared with its Japanese competitors Toyota, at $300, and Nissan, at $400.

A wide body of research now shows that customers' satisfaction as a single measure is misleading if not dangerous. You can give caviar and champagne to coach airplane customers and satisfy them (for awhile), but that won't ultimately improve profitability and shareholder value.

■ THE PRINCIPLES OF CUSTOMER LOYALTY

Mercer Management Consulting's work in helping companies build loyalty among their most profitable customer groups identified four principles of loyalty (Figure 5.1) that are applicable to virtually every company, though each flies in the face of conventional thinking about the topic.

➤ Principle 1 — Focus on Specific Types of Customers

Attention should be on the most profitable segments of customers. Avoid those who are at the bottom of the loyalty ladder, price sensitive, or otherwise likely to easily change products. Furthermore, accept that you can't (afford to) please all the people all the time. The key is to determine which ones you can profitably afford to please.

There are numerous successful examples of the worth of this from the past: American Airlines was the first airline to institute a frequent flier program. Budweiser got involved with ESPN because Anheuser-Busch knew that its core customers—those who used its products in great volume— were into sports. *Sports Illustrated*'s development of *Sports*

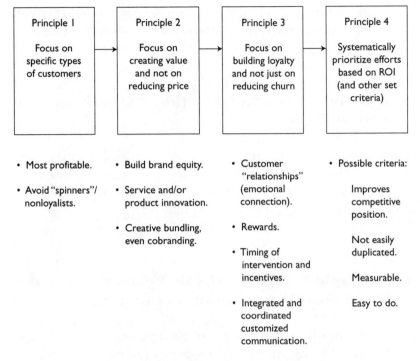

Principle 1	Principle 2	Principle 3	Principle 4
Focus on specific types of customers	Focus on creating value and not on reducing price	Focus on building loyalty and not just on reducing churn	Systematically prioritize efforts based on ROI (and other set criteria)

- Most profitable.

- Avoid "spinners"/ nonloyalists.

- Build brand equity.

- Service and/or product innovation.

- Creative bundling, even cobranding.

- Customer "relationships" (emotional connection).

- Rewards.

- Timing of intervention and incentives.

- Integrated and coordinated customized communication.

- Possible criteria:

  Improves competitive position.

  Not easily duplicated.

  Measurable.

  Easy to do.

Figure 5.1 Principles of Loyalty.

Robert Duboff and Lori Underhill Sherer, "Customized Customer Loyalty," *Marketing Management* 6, no. 2 (Summer 1997): 20.

Illustrated for Kids was a tactical coup because *SI* readers tended to waver in their loyalty as their children grow older.

➤ Principle 2—Focus on Creating Value and Not on Reducing Price

As it is said, if you discount long enough or deep enough, your customers will learn the real value you put on your product. Two alternatives to discounting are building brand equity and providing service or product innovations. The key is to understand what your segment(s) value and provide it, because you can't bribe someone to be loyal for long.

➤ Principle 3 — Focus on Building Loyalty and Not Just on Reducing Churn

The goal should be to cultivate a positive attitude and engender an emotional connection (think "customer relationship"). Such loyalty can be developed by integrated and coordinated customized communications.

➤ Principle 4 — Systematically Prioritize Efforts Based on ROI (and Other Set Criteria)

Let's consider these principles in greater depth.

The first principle is controversial because it forces a company to admit that some customers are more desirable than others. But building loyalty among *all* customers is more often than not detrimental to the long-term health of a business. After all, customers exhibit dramatic differences in their buying behavior and their cost-to-serve, leading to equally dramatic variations in the profitability they generate for a company. Building loyalty among nonprofitable customers can thus undermine a company's bottom line. Moreover, trying to please the least profitable customers (who tend to be the most demanding) can impede your firm's ability to serve its most profitable customers. Designing business systems to meet the needs of all the diverse customer types, for instance, keeps businesses from tailoring their products and services to the needs of the most attractive customers. Those banks that try to provide top-notch electronic, ATM, telephone, and branch services, for example, can't compete effectively with more focused competitors that master only one of these distribution channels. The marketing advantage will always lie with the specialist.

Certainly this is evident in the credit card business in which innovative specialists such as MBNA and Direct One have grabbed the most lucrative customers from traditional banks. Similarly, old-line department stores have found it extremely difficult to counter attacks from more narrowly focused specialty stores. Furthermore, the banking industry has shown that maintaining a high level of expensive lobby-based services may satisfy the few people who value this traditional experience but can drain resources that could be better spent to capture and please other types of customers.

Although the criteria for choosing customers to target may vary, a company should focus on satisfying those who will be more profitable to the firm *and* those who will be willing to be loyal. The mistake most stock brokerage houses have made is to target those individuals who are the most wealthy and most active. They are all going after the same market, a market that is savvy enough to be loyal to none. Studies have pinpointed these "high rollers," "players," or "big ticket traders" as a segment that can provide high revenues. However, the people in this segment are quite aware of their value and quite sophisticated in their ability to select investment opportunities. Further, they enjoy the game—part of which is finding the best deal on every transaction. Loyalty carries little weight in their choice of broker. Most maintain multiple accounts and develop patterns that are hard to change.

What about principle 2, focusing on creating value and not on reducing price? Though this may be counterintuitive to some executives who see discounting for one's best customers as a part of doing business, the fact is that cheap prices alone will not provide a stable foundation upon which to build loyalty.

The problem is that discounting, in isolation, has negative ramifications: It suggests that prices have been set higher than value—and the offerer knows it. It also suggests that the only reason for loyalty is, in essence, the bribe the consumer will get. All of this diminishes the perceived quality of the brand and sets up a relationship wherein loyalty is bought and sold—as we see today in the telephone long-distance market. In the current world of long distance, only a person who cares little about money would choose to be loyal to any one provider. By switching regularly between competing carriers, even a frequent caller can show a positive cash flow by accepting the highest offer each month for switching or staying. No other industry has yet paid up to $100 cash to keep or entice a customer with no barrier to exit when the next offer comes a day or two later.

This similar scenario was evident among the (then) Big Six to Eight accounting firms. The issue was whether or not they should continue "buying business" in the audit practice. Clients wanted cheaper audits, and the theory was that low-balling an account would get the firm into a relationship that would ultimately be profitable. Analysis showed that this strategy rarely paid off. Most of these clients continued to apply price pressure. Further, client satisfaction studies for the same firm demonstrated that the most satisfied clients were actually paying higher hourly fees on average than less satisfied clients.

Michael Porter's formula still seems valid. There are two choices: either be the low-cost provider or differentiate in a manner for which customers will pay a premium. If you can do the former (a very hard battle), you can offer everyday low prices. Far better is to provide other forms of value, perhaps in addition to pricing tactics. Innovations, particularly those offered only or first to valued customers, are the best strategy if your target is young consumers or business people. Bundling and cobranding can also enhance loyalty. Another route to building value-based loyalty is to use databases to acknowledge key events in the customer's life (e.g., a child's birthday) or to track and accommodate personal preferences, which is what Amazon.com does for its customers. Other routes include providing special previews of new offerings and creating customized packages of services that meet specific needs.

In some instances, loyalty can be enhanced at little or no cost. Many marketers, for example, are seeking access to the high-end business market—a market that is held captive on planes and in hotels. These marketers could partner with hotels and airlines, allowing them to reward their best customers by giving them access to (perhaps even possession of) these new products. That's a loyalty win-win-win.

The importance of building a positive value perception underlies the third principle: focus on building loyalty and not just on reducing churn. One can reduce churn fairly simply. Focusing wholly on churn typically leads to a series of costly, last-ditch efforts to stop customers as they are about to walk out the door, efforts that typically amount to too little, too late. The better approach is to understand the underlying drivers of loyalty and use that understanding to preempt churn by reinforcing loyalty at critical junctures throughout the customer's life cycle. Discounts, presents, and timely interventions work, but only until a competitor tries again.

If they want to stop churn, most companies try bribing. The problem is what this ultimately does. As the long-distance industry has learned, attempts to stop churn can boomerang. Initially, it is true, customers didn't leave—but then a month or two later, when a better offer came along, they were gone. In fact, over a two- to three-year period, churn went up for all three major U.S. players—and so did the costs of retaining customers. Customers started to believe long distance was a commodity because the providers acted that way, using price as the only marketing sales lever. The best way to build loyalty is to understand why people will stay loyal, to learn what will win both their hearts and minds. After all, brand loyalty, as we said in Chapter 4, stems from both attitude and behavior. This requires an emotional connection with customers through communications and a reward or thank-you after behavior rather than an incentive at the front end to induce it.

To determine that connection, data must be acquired that analyzes the path of loyalty. First, the marketing team must learn the danger spots: what events (e.g., the first bill, a change in residence) form the critical trigger that can cause churn or those that can engender more loyalty. This latter point is often neglected. For instance, the sign-up is rarely a cause for churn but is almost always an opportunity to enhance loyalty by engendering positive feelings and setting proper expectations (similar to the check-in process in hotels).

A related inquiry is to map out a customer life cycle, identifying where points of churn typically arise and determine (through fishbone, root cause, and other analytical techniques) the reasons.

Rather than consider reactions and last-minute save efforts, the process should encourage thinking about how to solve any underlying problems. For instance, if consumers leave after their first bill, that means the company didn't set expectations properly or it attracted the wrong customers in the first place. A more candid sign-up process that sells the benefits for the cost is a better solution than a massive telemarketing effort to reconvert someone after price shock.

The next step is to brainstorm for practical ways to engender loyalty. Of course, this presumes a true understanding of the targeted customers in terms of both their needs and their value systems. Once this point is reached (that is, once a set of solid ideas can be converted into marketing programs), then the company can progress to test alternatives, measure outcomes, and capture learnings. Of course, marketing research plays a critical role throughout this process. Never to be forgotten, loyalty programs, like quality programs, aren't free. Each such program must be rigorously tested to ensure that it is working and paying off. The fourth principle is the logical conclusion of our initial point. Loyalty is not a good idea if it means keeping unprofitable customers longer. It is a necessity if it means—as it should—developing and retaining a profitable group of customers. These points raise managerial questions for a service company as shown in Figure 5.2.

Although each enterprise is unique, the process of developing a loyalty program can be generalized (see Figure 5.3). The first step is diagnostic and contains two equally important interrelated elements:

1. Identify the key drivers/causes of both customer retention and customer defection.
2. Identify customer segments that can be profitably served.

Figure 5.2 Managerial Questions.

Rob Duboff and Carla Heaton, "Employee Loyalty: A Key Link to Value Growth," *Strategy & Leadership* (January/February 1998): 8–13.

Each of these diagnostics must be based on research—and, in the case of the drivers of defections, it must be blind research in which the sponsor is not identified. Relying on what customers told the sales force is not enough. Too frequently, companies believe what they want to believe about why customers don't return and have only the vaguest ideas abut what truly motivates their most loyal customers.

The segmentation effort must encompass customer attitudes, behaviors, and demographics, and it should be tied to actual customer history if such databases exist. Only by looking at both rational and emotional factors can segments be constructed that both describe and (at least partially) explain

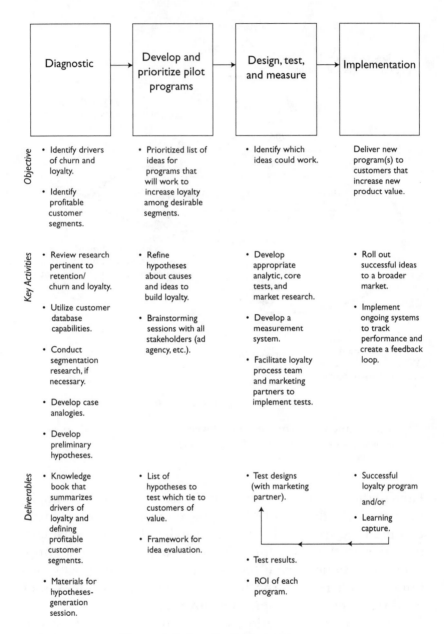

Figure 5.3 Loyalty Program Process.

Rob Duboff and Carla Heaton, "Employee Loyalty: A Key Link to Value Growth," *Strategy & Leadership* (January/February 1998): 8–13.

behavior. The segments must then be carefully analyzed from an economic perspective to determine reliable estimates of their profitability over time.

Key outputs for this step are a document that summarizes what has been learned historically and from any fresh research as well as a set of hypotheses about potential loyalty programs. Once segments and motivations have been determined, the team must hypothesize how to combine the learning—that is, to develop hypotheses about what program(s) will improve the loyalty of which profitable segments.

In the second step, these ideas are triaged. Those deemed most promising are fully defined and then refined. At this stage, it is important to ensure that all the ideas are practical (that is, that they can be implemented) and that the potential impact is relatively large, with incremental revenue exceeding program costs.

The next step is to test the potential programs. This demands careful design with explicit criteria and measurements, both of revenues and costs.

The final step is to implement the program(s) while continuing to rigorously measure the impact. Feedback mechanisms must be built in, with flexibility to amend or enhance the program as it continues. It is also critical that marketing and communications to customers are part of what is tested and monitored over time.

■ BEYOND THE HYPE

Now that loyalty has become a management issue, many businesses will launch new programs. If yours is one such business, you should be aware of the pitfalls that can thwart success. The principal barrier is an inability to recognize that different customer segments have different values and thus must be served differentially. As noted, these differences usually manifest themselves as different wants and needs both on the left brain (e.g., product features) and the right brain (e.g., emotional connection) sides. The key is to communicate appropriately to each valuable segment. Given today's sophisticated marketing tools (e.g., database modeling, interactivity, etc.), this is now technically feasible, which makes loyalty programs potentially far more powerful than before the days of database manipulation and the possibility of customized communications. Even after a targeted approach is taken, executives must avoid these pitfalls:

> ➤ Not focusing on the future—serving only today's needs instead of anticipating what key customer segments will want in the future.

> ➤ Not doing the hard and necessary work of pinpointing which segments are likely to be able to be served profitably in that future.

> ➤ Failing to connect acquisition efforts with loyalty programs. A key sign of danger is if those involved in acquisition are organizationally distinct from the loyalty team. For example, many magazine companies have a sales force (acquisition) team with incentive to add customers distinct from those charged with writing the magazine and those getting renewals. Often all three of these units are targeting different people or—just as bad—acquisitions and renewals are battling with each other.

> ➤ Failure to measure properly and comprehensively. A company shouldn't look at customers' tenure, short-term revenues, or even their profitability. In fact, each program should assess the proper weighing of at least four dimensions of loyalty:

>> —Length (tenure of the relationship).

>> —Depth (amount of spending each year).

>> —Breadth (number of accounts, services used).

>> —Width (other household members or referrals).

Too often, a program focuses on only one dimension. An effective program should, at least, decide which of these to increase and progress accordingly. You can reward customers for longevity (e.g., a recognition or present after passing certain milestones) or for usage each year (as the airlines do) or for the number of relationships. This is an underexploited area. Many businesses want to cross-sell, but they don't directly reward the customer for continual breadth (beyond typically a one-time incentive).

As always, there are psychological barriers as well. Common excuses include the following.

➤ *"We don't have a good database to study and then track loyalty."* This is a good excuse for lazy management, but it's not a rational argument. Even traditional market research provides many means for the assessment of customer loyalty levels—syndicated consumer panels, survey techniques to capture claimed previous purchases and intended next purchases, and purchaser intercepts are just a few. Although you may not be able to track the impact of programs individual by individual (as you can with a good database), you can assess the impact of a program in the aggregate through a panel or a predesignated control group.

The best counter to this argument is that companies invest millions on advertising and other marketing programs without a database to track individual impact.

➤ *"We focus on customer satisfaction. If we can increase satisfaction, loyalty will follow."* This belief, although widespread and logical, isn't necessarily true. Satisfaction is usually necessary but not sufficient for loyalty.[1] This has been proven over and over again by looking at client data. Match satisfaction scores by customer from a year ago with behavior during the past 12 months. Typically, there will be correlations (i.e., more satisfied people will be more likely to remain customers), but the relationship is far from perfect. Even satisfied customers leave. Furthermore, often the most satisfied customers are not the most profitable. Thus companies must de-average their satisfaction scores to focus on the most valuable customers.

Finally, "satisfaction" measures vary dramatically. Many are very left-brain oriented, focusing only on product or service attributes that may be fine (i.e., "very satisfactory") but still does not meet needs or competitively superior offers. At a minimum, satisfaction measures should be a combination of questions that the company has found statistically (e.g., with regression or time/series analyses) to contribute to profitable loyalty behavior. There should be probing on trust and perceptions that the company cares as well as comparisons with competition.

➤ *"All our customers are equal. We want them all to be loyal."* This philosophy is quite positive and in many companies forms an important driver of an internal culture that produces quality service (USAA is a prime example). However, it is simply foolish as a marketing practice for everyone. Few businesses can afford to invest in developing aggressive efforts to satisfy all customers in the future. The businesses' limited resources must be allocated where they will do the most good. New initiatives must be designed to meet the needs of those who will return the company's investment over time. If there is sufficient funding for every marketing program you can come up with, it's time for a major shareholder dividend!

Making loyalty more than a fad requires doing it right from the start—with in-depth analysis followed by alignment and dedication. Like any initiative that requires major change to be effective, this requires, above all else, the continuing commitment of top management, which takes us to a key step you must take to build a customercentric culture within which loyalty programs can prosper: Develop a measure of customer assets.

A related, equally critical lesson to learn is that not all segments can be motivated to the same level of loyalty. You can design a Maslow's hierarchy (Figure 5.4) for each segment to understand how much behavior and loyalty you can engender. Some segments for some businesses can approach the top—they can become emotionally tied to your business and actually become an advocate, almost a salesperson. Other segments can become more loyal or spend more (even

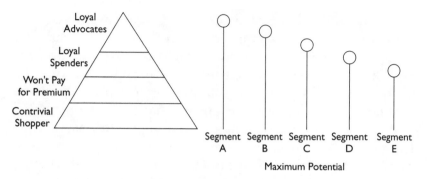

Figure 5.4 The Loyalty Hierarchy.

better) but will not become—or want to become—"emotionally" bound or, by nature, won't ever proselytize for you. Although you may not learn this as you start the process, good trial and measurement work will guide you over time. This is why you continually need to test the ROI and look at all four potential dimensions.

➤ Toward Managing Customer Assets

Our belief is that the only purpose of a business should be to build sufficient customer assets to meet the long-term financial goals of management. All else should be seen as a means to that end. You should be focusing, above all else, on deepening relationships with existing customers or by adding appropriate new customers to the asset base.

Given the importance of businesses' assets, then, it would seem natural that among marketing data on customers—such as measures of customer satisfaction, customer needs, customer preferences, and even brand equity—organizations would be collecting the information required to quantify the asset value of their customers. But apparently few collect such information. Despite all the lip service in mission statements about being customer oriented or customer driven, most firms don't know the value of their customer assets.

In its simplest terms, a customer's value as an asset is a function of the costs required to attract and serve that customer and the revenues derived from that customer over the years he or she remains a customer. Why is this information so important? Without it, companies cannot effectively evaluate their marketing or ensure that they are attracting and retaining the most valuable customers. Just as accurate financial information is essential for responsible management, so, too, are measures of customer assets, but whereas measures of financial assets are descriptive, measures of customer assets can be prescriptive: They not only tell management what's happening but can also indicate how a firm would evolve given its current direction.

Let's assume that you head up a large service firm. Traditionally, the firm has analyzed its business solely in financial terms, monitoring the financial losses and gains in key accounts. On the other hand, it did no marketing research or customer-profitability analyses. Assume further that the company begins to suffer a steady increase in number of defections by key customers. If the company had been conducting marketing research, it would have found that it had numerous problems in customer service and that competitors were doing a better job at satisfying consumers. Further, there was a direct correlation between the satisfaction of a customer and the level of profitability generated by that customer for the firm. That is, the more satisfied the customer, the higher the profit margin.

To ensure actions are taken to improve service on the dimensions proven to drive satisfaction, you would need to raise the organization's awareness of the importance of customer satisfaction. To do this, a single, research-based measure of the customer asset—say, the percentage of major customers who said they were very satisfied with the company's service—would have to be introduced, measured regularly, and used as a yardstick to measure the enterprise's efforts. An action plan could be developed to improve service in ways that marketing research shows will provide a return on the investment.

The result would be a corporate culture that is truly customer driven. In terms of results, as the game plan is achieved, defections will have stabilized and profits will have rebounded. This measure (or a series of such measures) could be used as a beacon—a sign of reality as important as the stock price.

The measure for your company need not be the percentage of major customers who say they're very satisfied with your firm's product or service. The measures of customer assets that companies track are dependent on their strategic objectives, just as measurement of financial assets also reflects strategic interests. So a company might track the ratio of profitable customers to all customers (higher is better) or the ratio of profitable new customers to all new customers (higher is essential). Or the company might focus on the average tenure of all customers or the average tenure of all profitable customers. Then again, a business might concentrate on the share of all purchases made by most profitable customers in a given category. A company could use one of these measures or a combination of these or others.

Choosing the most appropriate measures for a business requires a four-step process of marketing research and analysis:

1. Segment the customer base according to current and projected profitability.

2. Learn the relationship between the customers' feelings and satisfaction levels and their buying levels and profitability.

3. Run simulation models to project how the growth of each segment (more business per customer, longer tenure per customer, or additional customers) would impact the business.

4. Hold top management meetings to reach consensus on how best to measure customer assets and, in turn, how to grow them most effectively.

As secondary benefits of this process, a company should gain a deeper understanding of branding issues as well as strategic insight into whether the business needs to expand or alter its core competencies to grow profitably. But the immediate return is that once the measures are established and a marketing strategy in place, marketing and sales will be able to focus on profitable growth and assess their progress accurately. Products and services that are found to be purchased primarily by low-value segments can be eliminated. Promotions can be designed not only to attract more sales but also to attract or deepen existing relationships with the highest-value customers. Likewise, the objectives for and assessments of new products can be clarified. The information will also serve to guide other management actions. Mergers/acquisitions and licensing decisions can be viewed on how much impact they might have on the customer asset. Let's say an acquisition is under consideration. Assuming the core competencies are to remain unchanged, a test of pursuit of this course might be: Does it lead to growth of customer asset, either by bringing in new customers within high-value segments or by strengthening the relationship with existing high-value customers?

In the area of marketing, research will become more precise and of more strategic worth. By focusing on customer segments defined by value, sophisticated buyer modeling will be able to determine the attitudinal and behavioral attributes that distinguish high-value customers—the basis for brand loyalty—from the rest of the customer base, thus enabling all marketing programs to be focused on the drivers of the purchase decisions of the high-value segment. Ongoing research can also be directed at profitable segments instead of on random samples of customers or prospects, which inevitably depict the "average customer" rather than customers the company really must monitor. Ultimately, marketing research will be able to track return on assets and return on income for customers just as accounting does on the financial side. Moreover, it will be able to help the enterprise anticipate changes in the environment that will affect the attitudes and behavior of key customers.

■ CUSTOMER RELATIONSHIP MANAGEMENT

From the concept of customers as assets, we clearly move to considering our valued customers as a portfolio of customer assets that must be actively managed, with resources allocated accordingly. You need to recognize your company's responsibility to manage the customer's total experience, which means all moments of truth between your customers and company's employees, and further increase the portfolio by acquiring new profitable customers as well as developing and maintaining the profitability of existing customers. Mercer Management Consulting's research into the 100 U.S. companies that have sustained the highest rate of profitable growth shows that most achieved their gains by extending their existing core capabilities into new markets or deepening their penetration of existing markets through new products or new sales channels. In effect, these firms have been nurturing their "customer franchise," or portfolio of customers with whom these firms enjoy a privileged relationship and to whom they dedicate their efforts for creating and delivering value.

A typical portfolio includes customers with a wide range of asset values, both positive and negative. If all customers were arrayed based on their profitability, total franchise value would increase sharply with the most profitable customers, reach a maximum, plateau (with break-even customers), and finally begin to decline (with unprofitable customers). The diagram shown in Figure 5.5 of this portfolio value curve is important to understand as the first step in effective customer franchise management.

For many companies, particularly those fortunate enough to serve a relatively small number of high-volume customers with long-term contracts, determining franchise value can be a straightforward process. But not all businesses are so fortunate. In most instances, determination of franchise value requires complex, probabilistic estimates of customer purchase rates and relationship duration.

Because not all customers are good candidates for inclusion in a franchise, the challenge for companies is to

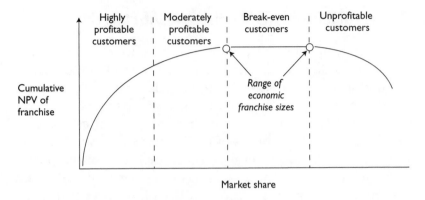

Figure 5.5 Portfolio Value Curve.

acquire, develop, and retain only those relationships that, in time, have the greatest potential for creating value for the company. Meeting this challenge demands, above all else, a concrete understanding not just of customers' needs but also of their long-term potential for generating profits for the company. The latter is the true definition of *value*.

Customer valuation is a technique that enables customers to be segmented on the basis of their profitability to the supplier. It provides a systematic way for a business to identify attractive customers for acquisition, development, and retention. Because most businesses serve customers who make numerous purchases during the course of their lifetime, effective valuation requires that customers be viewed as long-term assets. As Figure 5.6 shows, the sources of customer value include not only the original sales volume but also the potential for increased sales, increased margins, cross-sales of related products, and even indirect revenues from referrals.

The net present value of a long-term customer asset can be calculated by multiplying the dollar value of the customer's yearly purchases by the margin earned on the sales and then by the projected duration of the relationship (in years). The product is then adjusted by any appropriate discount rate, and the acquisition cost is subtracted.

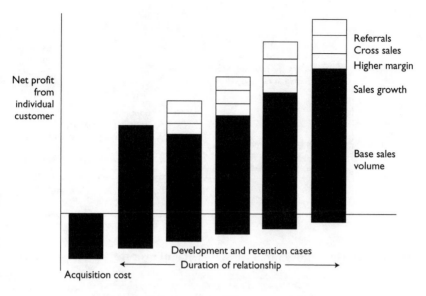

Figure 5.6 Sources of Customer Value.

The customer is profitable only if his or her asset value is greater than zero. Beyond that point, the value of a customer relationship is determined primary by three factors: volume per period, margin per unit, and duration of relationship. In principle, value of a customer asset may be increased by raising any of these variables while holding the others constant. In reality, though, volume, margin, and duration may conflict. For example, increasing volume may entail price and margin reductions that, depending on price elasticity and discount rate, may increase, decrease, or leave value unchanged. Therefore, the optimal value proposition is unlikely to entail simply the maximization of any single variable. Rather, it demands a careful balance among all three as Figure 5.7 shows over the life cycle.

Research is a key component. "Organizing that achieve breakthrough customer service know that a commitment to customer satisfaction must be backed up by a complete understanding of their customers."[2] Earl Naumann and Kathleen Giel, in their book *Customer Satisfaction Measurement*

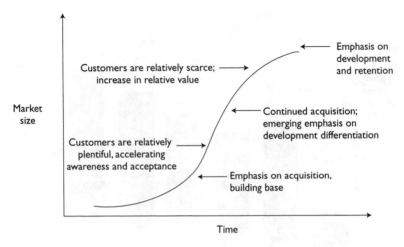

Figure 5.7 Customer Franchise Management over the Market Life Cycle.

and Management, point to the importance of having a customer satisfaction management (CSM) program embedded in the firm's corporate culture. "If the CSM program is just a 'program,' another tacked-on activity, it will be of little value. Even though it probably won't be a total waste of time, its full potential will never be realized. But when a CSM program is fully backed by the organization, the results can be impressive." If there is a definition for a CSM program with which we would agree, it is these authors' when they write, "A CSM program is a formal mechanism for soliciting ideas for improvement and innovation from customers."[3]

Certainly, given the importance of your most valued customers, you must monitor their level of satisfaction. If you can't keep them contented, then your focus won't work, and they will leave you for one of your competitors. You must know not only their current needs and interests but also what their future needs and behaviors likely will be. Whether the approach is ongoing Delphi panels or feedback from user groups, whether it involves a customer "board of directors" or tracking of trends, companies must stay in touch with emerging developments.

As should be evident by now, these future profitable customer segments should be the focus of most of the research the business pursues and, in particular, of lead-user inquiries. (Conversely, any defections from this group should be studied quickly.) Furthermore, as stated earlier, satisfaction initiations can be justified only to the extent that they can be shown to drive loyalty and are focused on these profitable segments.

■ CUSTOMER SERVICE

Any discussion of customer loyalty must include discussion of customer service. Despite all the talk about customer-centric cultures, says Vincent P. Barabba, author of *Meeting of the Minds: Creating the Market-Based Enterprise,* lack of understanding and failure to deliver what customers want and need continues to promote poor quality of service. Yes, companies send out surveys to gauge customer satisfaction, but customer service is more than a functional area. Rather, "it is an operating philosophy that, to be fully effective, must extend through all phases of a business—weighing every action from the standpoint of how it affects the goodwill of the institution, recognizing that its quickest way to profits—and the permanent assurance of such profit—is to serve the customer in ways in which the customer wants to be served."[4]

Authors Paul Cole and Bob Wayland, in their excellent, still timely book, *Customer Connections,* provide evidence of the importance of commitment to loyalty principles. Their work used a survey of 200 executives from Fortune 1000 firms and, upon analysis of underlying economics, showed that those in the higher-growth companies were far more involved in understanding their key customers (Table 5.1).

In another study, Deloitte & Touche studied 860 companies in the top 25 percent in sales in 36 countries and found that customercentric firms (25 percent of those studied)

Table 5.1   Segmentation of Growth

	Higher Growth	Lower Growth
Percentage with an "extremely clear view" of most valuable customers	38	22
Percentage of revenue from top 10 percent of customers	46	32

Robert L. Wayland and Paul M. Cole, *Customer Connections* (Boston: HBS Press, 1997).

outperformed the rest as 50 percent of them exceeded goals (versus only 22 percent of the rest).[5]

Jeffrey Gitomer, author of *Customer Satisfaction Is Worthless, Customer Loyalty Is Priceless,* takes us full cycle back to the issue of loyalty with which we began this chapter, pointing to its importance in customer retention. Mackay points out that "satisfaction is the lowest form of loyalty. Satisfied customers will shop anywhere—loyal customers will fight before they switch and will get others to do business with you by referral. Satisfied customers are apathetic. Loyal customers will be your advocate."[6] When you assess the quality of customer service, we posit you must reflect loyalty based issues. Don't ask yes or no questions but rather why and how questions that will determine what needs to change and document and interpret the results. You've determined your customer assets; now benchmark all your daily customer interactions and develop best practices in your interactions with them. Identify the most effective or efficient or considerate way and then see that everyone of your employees does it that way through training.

We have been talking about loyalty throughout this chapter—how to gain it and how to measure it. How to *retain* it can be guaranteed by never forgetting the customer after the sale. The company with loyal customers is one that solicits their reaction after the sale and periodically thereafter. Personalized attention, interest, and care translate into customer loyalty.

➤ Standards

These are the standards (from *Enterprise One to One* by Don Peppers and Martha Rogers) for superior customer service:

1. The customer tells the enterprise what he wants by means of interaction and feedback.
2. The enterprise meets these specifications by customizing its product or service to the needs of that particular customer and then remembers these specifications.
3. With more interaction and feedback, the customer will have spent time and energy teaching the enterprise more and more about his own individual needs.
4. Now, to get an equivalent level of service from any other firm—even one offering the same exact level of customization and feedback—this customer will first have to reteach the competitor what he has already taught the original firm!

The authors add the following questions as follows:

➤ Does it take only one call or e-mail from a customer to handle any issue?

➤ Is each purchase that a customer makes more efficient than the one before it?

➤ Customer Loyalty Diagnostic

➤ Do you know your key profitable segments? Can you identify their attitudes, demographics and behaviors? Have you computed their lifetime value?

➤ Who is the customer? Who decides to make a purchase? Who chooses the brand or company?

➤ Who actually uses it? Who influences, suggests names, and so on? What is the role of points in the distribution chain?

➤ What are the buyers' values—that is, the needs that prompt a purchase and the benefits conveyed? How do they vary by key segment?

➤ What is the purchase cycle (the ratio of trial to repeat)? When are customers are most likely to defect?

➤ What are the break points? What prompts initial purchase in the category? What can prompt switching?

➤ How do target segments (even individuals if possible) prefer to be communicated with?

   —By what name?

   —By what media?

➤ What are your competitive strengths and weaknesses? Which are unique? Which are sustainable/unfixable?

➤ Whom do you *really* compete with?

➤ Do you know what it is costing you to gain a customer?

➤ Do you know what it is costing you to retain one?

➤ In both instances, what is the return on investment?

➤ Do you only target—or aggressively market—those who fit the profile of a profitable customer?

➤ Have you customized programs to ensure the loyalty of the most profitable segments of customers?

➤ Is customer loyalty an element of your operating philosophy or corporate mission?

➤ Do you know as much about your customer as best practice-type companies?

   —History with your firm/initiation of relationship.

   —History of other household members.

   —Incidents in the relationship.

   —Household details and preferences.

   —Key dates (birthdays, anniversaries, etc.).

➤ Are your communications to key customers:

   —Customized by segments?

   —Sent to them alone or to their spouse, if requested, with the correct salutation.

➤ Do you know the key elements of customer service? How do you prepare for and handle moments of truth that can either engender or destroy loyalty?

■ NOTES

1. Two of the finest articles on this point are Thomas O. Jones and Carl Sasser, Jr., "Why Satisfied Customers Defect," *Harvard Business Review* (November–December 1995), and Kaki R. Brose, "It's Customer Loyalty, Stupid," *National Productivity Review* (Summer 1995).

2. Stanley A. Brown, *Breakthrough Customer Service* (Toronto: John Wiley & Sons Canada, Ltd., 1997).

3. Earl Naumann and Kathleen Giel, *Customer Satisfaction Measurement and Management: Using the Voice of the Customer* (New York: Van Nostrand Reinhold, 1995).

4. Vincent P. Barabba, *Meeting of the Minds* (Boston: HBS Press, 1994).

5. Cited in *Financial Times*, July 9, 1999.

6. Jeffrey Gitomer, *Customer Satisfaction Is Worthless, Customer Loyalty Is Priceless* (Bard Press, 1998).

7. Don Peppers and Martha Rogers, *Enterprise One to One* (New York: Random House, 1997).

Chapter 6

Researching the Future Competition

> Business is war.
> —Japanese proverb

The business landscape is littered with examples of leading businesses that lost their competitive edge by failing to keep tabs on their competitors. Sometimes they weren't even sure who was really competing with them for the hearts and minds of customers. Most upscale department stores failed to pay adequate attention as Wal-Mart grew slowly from a small chain of Arkansas stores to a U.S. powerhouse retailer. Apple ignored the growing influence of Microsoft's Windows technology in the business world, preferring to focus on the consumer market to develop a loyal customer base among students. Merrill Lynch put on-line brokers in a different category than theirs, but their customers didn't.

The evidence is clear. The business world follows the same evolutionary rule as the rest of our planet: survival of the fittest. And size doesn't always make a difference. Companies, like the dinosaurs, face extinction.

Why do giants shrink? Too often, the reasons are internal more than external, even when a company is large enough not to be constrained by an inability to invest.

The following are factors we've uncovered that can lead to extinction:

➤ Winners become the hunted and can lose the ability to hunt.

➤ Size tends to be disproportionately related to speed. Therefore, the will to change is thwarted by the mind-set of complacency. And the ability to change is thwarted by the size and complexity of the organism created to perpetuate the paradigm that brought success.

➤ Competitors find it easy to hit a visible target—particularly if it moves slowly or is a straight line.

➤ Psychologically, the risk of losing what you've won often looms larger than the opportunity for incremental gain.

The ability to strategically anticipate the future certainly requires constantly monitoring and evaluating your competitors. And a majority of businesses do, in fact, kept a watchful eye on the competitors they see. Some even dedicate an entire staff for competitive analysis. But why then do many businesses still disappear, becoming only footnotes in the annals of U.S. enterprise?

Too often, competitive analysis is limited in scope, focusing solely on the competitors of today and their current performance. Other key elements in the marketplace remain overlooked, often those that literally are right under your nose. The ability to sustain competitive advantage requires you to broaden your view of the business landscape. To effectively monitor the competition, your business needs to understand how your own customers—and your own channels—perceive the purpose of your products and services. You need to "become" your consumers and channel partners, in addition to walking in the shoes of your competitors and could-be competitors. Market research techniques can help you achieve a better understanding of customers, their unmet needs, and the abilities of new or existing competitors to possibly fill those needs ahead of your business (or raise performance bars in same way as Amazon.com has done so far for e-commerce).

Let's consider, for example, a sports arena and how its management might view its competition. It could be any one of the following:

➤ Other sports arenas.

➤ All sports arenas in the area.

➤ All entertainment venues and options in the area.

➤ All leisure venues and activities.

Often the most accurate competitive analysis can be found by determining exactly what your customers consider as the real alternatives. And when not taken to account, what can appear to be only an ancillary challenge can quickly turn into a full frontal attack. As noted earlier, eBay's auction Web site—considered by some as nothing more than a downscale flea market—did not at first appear to threaten Sotheby's or Christie's elite-style auction business. Therefore, any business that is involved in the industry in which you compete—or that is targeting the same core customers—must be on your radar screen. Those that are growing or attracting positive reviews from your customer set must be monitored.

To effectively anticipate the future, your business's radar screen should be wider, and the perspective broader, than it generally is today. First, an enterprise needs to maintain a healthy share of wallet and share of mind (e.g., sense of loyalty) of its customers and, to this point, a business must keep abreast with who else going after its core customers. Often this evolves in continuing to understand best practices— what great businesses are doing to progress because ultimately what they are doing will have an impact.

As a way to co-opt potential competition and to understand possible game changers, benchmarking can be valuable. Looking at companies that excel at a facet of your business delivery means you can use a different business than yours—package delivery, for example—which can have a major impact on customer expectations on speed of response, for example. This can provide a model for how to improve or even point to potential partnering opportunities—such as sending out orders to valued customers via overnight delivery rather than relying on a slower delivery process.

But the hype of benchmarking can become a detriment for many businesses, particularly small companies. As Edith Wiarda and Daniel D. Luria of the Performance Benchmarking Service at the Industrial Technology Institute in Ann Arbor, Michigan, advise in "The Best Practice Company and Other Benchmarking Myths: Five Lessons from Real Data," companies need to be cautious in seeking benchmarking partners while being aware of five key issues:

1. You're probably not as good as you think you are. But when armed with hard data, you can shock your organization out of complacency.

2. Standard benchmarking how-tos are often poorly suited to smaller companies. If you manage a small business or one that doesn't receive much managerial or technical support from your corporate parent, then you'll have to craft a benchmarking approach that will work for you.

3. Searching for an "all-around best practice" partner is a waste of time. No one company is good at everything.

4. Use value-added per employee for a quick meaningful assessment of your overall performance. Focus your improvement efforts by considering what stands in the way of large gains on this measure. *Value added* is defined as sales less the cost of any purchased parts, materials, and services. It measures the market value of the work done in a business.

5. Be prepared to mount a resourceful, committed search for best practice partners. Many excellent firms never get written up in the trade press. So look beyond the usual literature searches.[1]

The following are some guidelines you can use:

➤ *Don't rely on intuition.* Although intuition is powerful, it has limitations because it is based on our past experience. Today's competitive marketplace is constantly breaking patterns we've learned from our past.

➤ *Never rely solely on experts.* There's a major difference between expertise and being considered an expert. Expertise can be considered as a body of knowledge, and we have seen that past knowledge is one of the least reliable ways of judging the competitive marketplace. Experts, however, have been certified by their profession as holding the correct body of knowledge. This investment in prestige is one of the root causes of organizational tunnel vision.

➤ *Don't allow past investments to influence your views.* Businesses typically continue to focus on that which enhances prior investments. But loss of competitive advantage often occurs because those investments no longer produce returns for a particular group or individual.

So whom can you listen to? It's critical that you listen to your customers and channel partners as honestly as possible. The most important thing you can do is to explicitly understand your areas of strategic vulnerability. Don't just focus on your critical success factors—those things which are most important to your success—but also focus on your critical failure factors as well.

Strategic anticipation® can apply to any size organization. That's why it is critical to delineate strategic vulnerability: No one business can anticipate on all fronts, but everyone can focus on vulnerability and watch for threats to key success drivers. Organizations need to have a finite number of critical things to watch. Therefore, as you begin to think of your strategic vulnerabilities, remember to be specific. Clearly, customers are critical to your success, but what kind of customers? Children, married women, diabetics, and men over 60 all fall under the category of customers, but they are quite different in their surprise potential. Knowing your lead users (or future profitable segments) allows you to focus on them.

When money becomes a strategic vulnerability, be as specific as you can. Do you need access to funds at reasonable interest rates? A steady flow of capital?

If you can detect a major development that could negatively affect your strategic vulnerability early on, you will likely avoid crisis. If you can anticipate something that would *positively* influence your strategic vulnerability, however, you can create a competitive advantage that may remain for years.

Of course, knowing what to look for is only half the battle in developing an action plan. Understanding how and where to look is also vital.

■ LEARN FROM THE FUTURE

Ignorance kills. There is a large body of work advocating the value of becoming a learning organization. But learning is not just about history or about the present. Every business must know how to learn from the future. This will perhaps be the most important twenty-first century skill—that of Strategic Anticipation®.

■ FOUR SKILLS FOR ANTICIPATION

Although life-and-death decisions probably are not part of your daily business routine, for some professions, the ability to anticipate literally means the difference between life and death. We can learn a lot from these professions as part of our understanding of how to anticipate the future.

Which professions *demand* that their practitioners anticipate as a regular part of their job? Wayne Burkan, in his book *Wide Angle Vision,* cites jet fighter pilots, snipers (a legal division within the U.S. Marine Corps), and the Secret Service. These groups have five things in common:

➤ They have been trained in how to search using "splatter vision."

➤ They have learned how to develop mental models.

➤ They have developed specific methods of reading the signs.

➤ They have specific early warning systems.

➤ For them, anticipation is a matter of survival.[2]

➤ Splatter Vision

In business, *splatter vision* means never becoming so focused that you expect your challenge to come from a specific direction. Burkan cites the Maginot Line—named for France's war minister, André Maginot—which was an elaborate, permanent fortification, a 200-mile line of defense designed to prevent an assault by the Germans during World War II. The French, as it turned out, were so solely focused on a frontal assault along their northeastern border that they never expected the Germans to outflank the line and invade France in 1940 (just as Xerox focused on copiers or DEC on minicomputers).

By focusing on an expected future outcome, businesses create their own Maginot Line. Surprise turns into crisis not because business managers don't look to the future but because they look to a *single* future or tightly define the battlefield (i.e., trains in the train business, buggy whips in the buggy whip industry). Change usually hits us where we least expect it.

When asked to list areas of strategic vulnerability, many businesses focus on the most obvious, usually targeting only a few core competencies. They may have very thorough plans in place to cover those few critical areas and think that they are protected from surprise.

➤ Mental Model Development

For most businesses, a mental model usually is off-the-shelf material. A sales forecast, for instance, is a mental model of the quantity, rate, and mix of products or services your business expects to sell. Your strategic plan contains assumptions regarding the future business environment. These are all part of your mental model.

We all have mental models. If the model is implicit—as they are for most businesses—then it filters our vision and stops us from recognizing the future's signals. When the model is explicit, however, businesses can use it to detect those signals and anticipate the future. Even when your assumptions are explicit, there's no guarantee you will actually use your mental model. Take the U.S. automotive industry, for example. As foreign competition exceeded 30 percent, the companies failed to act on this critical signal. Contemporary press reports described automobile executives acknowledged that although oil prices were going to skyrocket, they were not adjusting their business plans.

To be effective, follow these guidelines when developing your mental model.

Be As Explicit As Possible

What business are you in? What are your assumptions regarding your customers and competitors? What about suppliers and regulators? Remember not to limit your assumptions to only those that reflect changes. If you are assuming there will be no significant new changes, then state that assumption as well in your mental model. (You may even get a chuckle someday when you review this assumption, which undoubtedly will be proven wrong.)

Ironically, most organizations that explicitly state their assumptions only record those that go beyond their sphere of influence. It's true, inflation rates or raw material prices definitely can have a financial impact on your plan, but there is nothing your business can do to change those variables. Competitive thrusts usually have a more fundamental and systemic impact on your organization, but because their influence is less visible, they are often omitted from your filter.

Be As Detailed As Possible

As you build your model, make sure that every area of your business explicitly states its assumptions. For example, accounting may assume that there will be no new competitor price cuts (or regulations regarding transfer pricing or the price at which one division sells to another). Sales may be assuming that Microsoft's Windows 98 will grow 5 percent in corporate acceptance. A challenge to one assumption is indicative of a possible change to your future. Insist on detail. That way, your model becomes more than just a useful tool for you organization. It also will help you to develop anticipation skills throughout your organization.

Be Consistent Throughout

Several applications exist here. For some businesses, such consistency means that every group must apply the same assumptions in both type and amount—for example, every business unit uses the same inflation numbers. Although this is more convenient for the corporate staff, it does diminish the autonomy of the organization as a whole. Consistency should mean that everyone uses the same assumptions, but each group can decide the amount. In this case, the corporate staff acts as a clearinghouse by communicating its specific view of the future and reporting on discrepancies between divisions. Each group ultimately has the power to decide which numbers it wants to use.

Monitor Carefully

Usually this task is shared by both corporate and component groups. It's important that everyone understand early on when variations become evident. Keep in mind that the sensitivity of your monitoring should vary, depending on whether you are tracking the mainstream or margin. Therefore, it's preferable to track rate of change. For example, it is crucial to understand that sales are up more than 6 percent as well as that the rate of growth is increasing. The rate of change holds the most valuable information.

Before you monitor variations to your mental model, be sure to assess what deviations in your lead indicators might mean. Revenue per customer is a critical one; drops here are often linked to the heretofore unrecognized competitor. More broadly, if your business is a university, then ask yourself what it means when the number of credits per student begins to drop. If you are a manufacturer, what does a decrease in the lead time of orders indicate? You should explore the significance of deviations before they happen for two reasons:

➤ You can look at the changes more objectively when you don't have daily performance pressures. This will give you time to explore the meaning rather than to try and explain it away once it happens.

➤ You have time to consider alternatives, which is, after all, the benefit of anticipation. The more lead time you can give yourself, the more reasoned your actions will be.

Explain in Real Terms

During the 1980s the agricultural division of a chemical company was facing declining sales. During the monthly performance review, the group's sales manager blamed the disappointing performance on the eruption of Mount St.

Helens. Indeed, the devastating eruption caused a major set-back for agriculture in the Northwest that affected pesticides sales. But during the next several months, sales continued to spiral downward, and each review began with the statement: "Our performance continues to be hit by Mount St. Helens." After the first few months, the president of the division questioned how a sales decline in the Southeast could be attributed to the eruption in the Northwest. Each time he was given an intricate explanation of the cause and effect factors at play. Finally the president forbid anyone to mention Mount St. Helens. Suddenly a landslide of competitor factors, heretofore undisclosed, came rushing to the forefront of the review. The other problems would have surfaced sooner had the company employed anticipation techniques to review explanations of variations.

➤ Early Warning Systems

Scanning for business risks can be a rather monotonous task because many of the factors you track will barely move, especially over the short term. This can lead to "being blinded by the crowd," a phrase used by Secret Service agents as they scan a crowd while protecting the president. The solution? Use computers to handle repetitive tasks. Create systems that regularly audit your leading indicators and scan the environment for you. When a variation occurs, the computer will tell you what has changed.

■ TOOLS YOU CAN USE

Beyond benchmarking and monitoring competitors, an effective system of Strategic Anticipation® strives to understand the strategic options of these competitors so as to project several alternative paths potentially available to them.

These competitive scenarios can be combined with the enterprise's own scenarios and plans as part of the assessment about what could happen in the future and how to position the enterprise today to best prepare for tomorrow.

Research skills are key here in a number of respects. First, the competitive radar screen should be developed by disciplined review of public documents, including continual review of competitors' Web sites, as well as by constant interviews with customers and channel partners. Once a company is on the screen, a competitive intelligence function, which logically should be part of a research project, can take over to scrutinize activities, analyze results, and develop insights. There are various tools to accomplish these goals.

Purchasing power and buying habits information uncovers the financial strength and economic attributes shared by your target market. You can use this information to answer the following questions:

➤ What is our average sales per customer segment?

➤ What is the average dollar amount spent on purchases or products or services similar to ours? (Trends are key here.)

➤ Where do they live and/or work?

➤ What is the competition at each juncture?

Marketplace competition research gathers information about other companies within your area of business and answers these questions:

➤ Who are our primary competitors in the market?

➤ How do they compete with us?

➤ In what ways do they compete with us?

➤ What are their strengths and weaknesses?

➤ Are there profitable opportunities based on their weaknesses?

➤ What is their market niche?

➤ What makes our business unique?

➤ How do our competitors position themselves?

➤ How do they communicate their services to the market?

➤ Who are their customers?

➤ How are they perceived by the market?

➤ Who are the industry leaders?

➤ What is their sales volume?

➤ Where are they located?

➤ Are they profitable?

Environmental factors information uncovers economical and political circumstances that can influence your productivity and operations. Questions to be answered include:

➤ What are the current and future population trends?

➤ What are the current and future socioeconomic trends?

➤ What effects do economic and political policies have on our target market or our industry?

➤ What are the growth expectations for our market?

➤ What outside factors influence the industry's performance?

➤ What are the trends for this market and for the economy?

➤ Is the industry growing, at a plateau, or declining?

■ COMPETITOR FOCUS

Having a person or team familiar with each competitor (there need not be only one competitor per person) will allow management to be able to garner real-time perspective as specific issues emerge. A key here is to develop scenarios reflecting likely strategies these competitors might pursue.

The extent to which competitive analysis can elicit what competitors perceive to be likely futures will greatly enhance the enterprise's own views on scenarios and competitive strategy as events unfold.

In addition to these strategic perspectives, good competitive analysis also produces value at a more tactical level. First, through surveys or customer satisfaction measurements, research can pinpoint specific competitive advantages and disadvantages in performance and in marketing. Here, a best practice is not only to compare with direct competitors but also with whatever company respondents feel is best overall in a category (for example, handling telephone inquiries; having a great Web page, etc.). Asking respondents to identify the best company provides input for the radar screen and for benchmarking.

A related possible second activity is to employ "mystery shoppers," customers who are blind to your enterprise (and to your competitors) who actually shop and buy to access performance in a focused apples-to-apples manner. (This is appropriate only for businesses in which there are no cost or confidentiality issues in having researchers actually open accounts and deal with competitors.)

A third possibility is to interview channel partners or other third parties about various competitors' performance vis-à-vis the enterprises.

■ DIAGNOSTIC

In addition to the questions just posed about purchasing power, marketplace competition, and environmental factors, consider the following:

➤ Do you know who are the two or three key competitors for the hearts and minds of your core customers at each stage of marketing? Which company—even if not a major player—is growing fastest in customer preference on each of these variables?

—Awareness.

—Image.

—Channels (availability).

—Point of purchase (presence).

—Service.

➤ Do you know how you rank relative to these competitors?

➤ Do you have someone (or a team) accountable for tracking each key competitor?

➤ Do you have a point of view on each competitor's strategy? Is this updated at least twice a year?

COMPETITIVE ECONOMICS

Traditional competitive analysis focuses on the future economics of the industry:

➤ Can we claim a sufficient share of the market demand?

➤ Will ruinous competition destroy the surplus?

➤ Can we rise above the fray?

➤ How will costs grow as revenues grow?

Traditional industry economics focuses on important questions about the industry:

➤ Who are the players we face today?

➤ Who has the power to claim the industry's profits?

➤ What is the structure of our industry?

➤ How "good" is our industry?

Strategic Anticipation® requires focusing on a new set of questions:

Traditional Industry Analysis	Economic Acceleration
Current Players	Driving forces: What economic forces will drive competition and profits tomorrow?
Profit Distribution	Surplus creation: How can we increase the overall pool of value?
Static Structure	Dynamic evolution: What does the end game look like?
Industry Rating	Decision making: How should we pursue future opportunities?

■ NOTES

1. Edith Wiarda and Daniel Luria, "The Best Practice Company and Other Benchmarking Myths," *Quality Progress* 31, no. 2, (February 1998); 91–94.

2. Wayne Burkan, *Wide Angle Vision* (New York: John Wiley & Sons, 1996).

Researching the Future Channels

All great change in business has come from outside the firm, not inside.

— Peter Drucker

The actual process of going to market breeds ambivalence among marketers. They consider it a challenge, a barrier, even a nuisance. They see it as a question of logistics, negotiation, or even unseemly bribery. But going to market is a critical link in the business process, one we believe can be optimized through Strategic Anticipation®.

Distribution channels have seen their power rise, fall, and rise again. The turbulence experienced during the past several years undoubtedly will continue well into the next half-decade as the Internet penetrates further. The rate at which channel patterns play out will accelerate, stimulating the emergence of completely new opportunities. The impact of the future, consumers needs and desires, and economics may be tough to forecast, but we can anticipate the most important scenarios.

Market research turns the chaos into a strategic advantage in three ways:

1. *Anticipate the destabilizing future shifts that may occur in the distribution process.* Consider what's already occurred: the evolution from local retailing to dominant national chains in almost every category from shoes to banking; the transformation of manufacturers to retailers in closed, integrated marketing systems; increased elimination of retailers by direct-to-consumer sales; the rise of mass merchandising and super stores; automated electronic replenishment that links retailers to a closed set of suppliers through an electronic umbilical cord; and, of course, e-commerce. Successfully anticipating and preparing for any of these phenomena made a valuable difference to those who made the effort. Strategic Anticipation®—assessing consumer response to possible futures and their concomitant economics through market research—made it possible.

What seismic changes lie ahead? B. Joseph Pine II and James H. Gilmore present a provocative perspective in *The Experience Economy,* subtitled *Work is Theater and Every Business a Stage* (Cambridge, MA: Harvard Business School Press 1999). In so many categories, shopping has been transformed into an experience and occasionally even entertainment akin to a visit to a theme park. Although they have changed in recent years, a visit to the original Banana Republic stores had an exotic flavor. A few minutes inside a Disney store conjures everyone's inner child. The Hard Rock Café and all of its imitators provide much more than a good burger—you are assured of being cool just because you're there! Where does this go next? Imagine what can be achieved on the Web, where every e-commerce site has the capability of transforming itself into your own personal fantasyland. How will we survive and, better still, exploit these discontinuous transitions? Strategic Anticipation® holds at least one answer.

2. *Understand the role of distribution in winning the consumer's attention, preference, and (ultimately) loyalty.* Gaining additional distribution often is considered the fastest route to incremental sales volume, but it may not be in the brand's best long-term interest. Consider some current positionings;

some are clearly mass, whereas others aspire to or already exude class. Coke is ubiquitous, while Hermes prefers exclusivity. E*Trade launched itself as the new, smarter way to trade on-line, forcing Merrill Lynch to reluctantly join the on-line trading channel. Supermarkets sell L'Oreal cosmetics; department stores sell Lancôme cosmetics (same company and, sometimes, the same products!). The goal is to ensure that channel strategy remains consistent with brand positioning. Salon hair care products adamantly fight to *not* be distributed anywhere but salons, but other hair care brands fight tooth-and-nail to gain any additional distribution. In-depth research that achieves exploitable insights into the bond between brands and customers is readily extended into this setting. You must understand the customer as a product user, but it's equally important to understand the customer as a shopper. The former is widely recognized; the latter is rarely considered. Market research offers as much leverage for distribution issues as it does for advertising and promotion. This spill-back effect of distribution on the brand and customer issues, which we have already covered, should not be overlooked. Strategic Anticipation® can enable you to identify future marketing advantages from this arena that your competitors may not see coming. The greatest discontinuity ever may be ahead of us courtesy of the Internet. Some brands may be compatible with an on-line image, others might work best with an off-line image, but can any enjoy the best of both worlds? Imagine the cognitive dissonance of encountering an Amazon.com bookstore—unthinkable! Experience has shown that a Barnes & Noble e-commerce site may have been equally unthinkable, hence bn.com. A call from your E*Trade broker would be downright disorienting, but Schwab seems to have been able to exist in both worlds. Making the right call on e-commerce may be the single most important decision every business must make *now*. Strategic Anticipation® and all that it can offer is absolutely essential.

3. *Drive marketing down to the local level.* Consumers in a specific market have unique characteristics that may impact

their choice of products and brands. And these local differences don't end at the market level. Even within one market,
neighborhoods differ (consider New York City!). As a result,
more stores are differentiating themselves—Food Emporium
versus C-Town. Regular shoppers in a given store may constitute a somewhat unique group, with unique product and
brand preferences. Just a decade ago it was impractical to
exploit this. The data requirements were astronomical, the
processing power was unavailable, the analytical expertise
was too expensive, and the organizational barriers were
insurmountable. Today each of these barriers has been or is
being overcome. Market research disciplines formerly
applied primarily at the national level and rarely at the
regional level are now commonly practiced at the local level.
Is the next step to put these to work individually for every
major store? This is the current trend in distribution, but the
influences of technology, economics, and the major players
are due to make some leaps. Where they land may be good
news or bad news for your business. One thing is sure—
Strategic Anticipation® will enable you to play it to your greatest advantage.

Let's consider each of these opportunities.

■ SHIFTING CHANNEL PATTERNS

The greatest opportunities may come from the successful
Strategic Anticipation® of significant and often discontinuous
shifts in the patterns of distribution. Consider the following
five trends that may redefine the future.

➤ Multiplication

Customers generally were comfortable purchasing products
through one or two standard channels. But customers today

want to buy in different ways. They look for more buying options because they have become far more varied in their needs and preferences. Technological change is a major trigger for multiplication. Sophisticated voice-mail systems and home-shopping cable channels replaced hundreds of sales representatives. Rapid evolution of the Internet has created another distribution channel. In addition, deteriorating economics due to channel dysfunctionality also encourage multiplication. Channels not properly matched to how customers want to buy result in inefficiencies, increased costs, and low profitability. Channels more closely aligned to how customers prove asset efficient and highly profitable.

Example: Book buyers in the past went solely to bookstores. Today, they have multiple channels available, including a wide range of retail outlets (supermarkets, airports, etc.) as well as book clubs, phone, mail, and the Internet. Similar situations exist throughout the retail industry.

If you want to make this transition work for you: What are your options? As astute observers of your industry, it should be easy for you and your colleagues to draw up a list of new, emerging, and anticipated outlets that might be suitable for your product or service. Nevertheless, you may want to consult two additional sources: your channel partners and your customers. A Delphi study among retailers and distributors might reveal some surprises. There may be more coming down the road than you anticipate! You will see their business from your perspective, not theirs, and the view from their side of the desk may be quite different! Your customers may also have some good ideas. Focus groups, using some projective techniques to free their thinking, may generate novel concepts.

Research can help you decide which of these new channels might be appropriate for your brand and your customers or specific customer segments. Discrete choice analysis, strategic choice analysis, or similar techniques for determining the impact of specific elements of the total brand attribute bundle on consumer preference would be a logical place to start. Treat access to the product as a brand attribute. Which forms of access add or detract? This is likely to vary by consumer segment and even by occasion or need state. Some elements of your product line may be better suited to certain channels than others. This step, coupled with an economic analysis, can help you to identify some promising new options as well as avoid some potentially damaging missteps.

If you have distribution in some of these channels, what do your lead users think? A lead-user study will help you understand what they are doing. Are these sales incremental or cannibalistic? Are they more or less profitable for you? Are they helping you claim a greater share of customer requirements and hence loyalty? Has this changed customers' perception of your brand? Positively or negatively? Without lead users, an information acceleration technique might be applicable. Bring your customers into a world with new means of accessing your product or service. How would they change their purchase or usage behavior or attitude toward your brand? What does this mean for your business model?

➤ Concentration

For many industries, channels traditionally were characterized by vast numbers of small-scale outlets that provided local access with personalized service. Value shifts when a newcomer brings economies of scale to such a fragmented, high-cost market, and consolidation occurs. And customers are willing to accept consolidation because they can buy more for less and receive better service.

Example: French company Carrefour successfully created hypermarket stores that went against the grain of traditional small shopkeepers, which historically defined French retail culture. The rise of Wal-Mart in the United States transformed customer expectations and supplier relationships alike. The power shift has been palpable.

Another approach in the concentration pattern involves acquisition of small players (e.g., mom-and-pop businesses, etc.) to create one large, market-leader position. The physical format is different, but the benefits of economies of scale and improved customer service remain the same.

Example: Service Corporation International consolidated the funeral home industry in the United States by buying many small funeral homes but continued to provide localized service—a critical aspect for the industry. Operational efficiencies and value growth were achieved, however, through resource sharing, cost minimization, and elimination of large price variations.

National retail chains have been replacing local stores ever since McDonalds went coast to coast and bulldozed the local hamburger joint. First it was the Gap on every block, followed by Banana Republic and now Old Navy. There's no longer an independent sports wear retailer in sight! More importantly, these integrated retailer/manufacturers are closed to other makers. As a result, other manufactures, most notably Levi-Strauss, have been pushed into retailing.

If you want to make this transition work for you: Answer these five questions:

1. Has channel concentration occurred, or is it likely to occur in your industry?
2. How do (will) your customers relate to the newer outlets?
3. Should you compete or partner with them?
4. What brand strengths do you have to work with?
5. What solution is compatible with your brand positioning and your business model?

Answering the first question may not be as simple as it seems. As with the multiplication issue, you may want to consult the experts through a Delphi study. The information obtained can serve as the basis of a scenario-planning exercise to identify the possible futures you may have to contend with. What might they look like, and what would be the business implications for you?

The second question is key because the underlying business issue is this: Will the channel concentration result in a power shift that leaves you out in the cold? You may experience a total loss of distribution or a severe paring of your line. You may find negotiations tougher and new concessions demanded. But these are issues only if your customers are attracted to the newly concentrated channels. Here's where brand equity and customer loyalty can really pay off. Will your customers switch retail outlets if you are not available? This is a highly researchable question that has been explored in surveys quite frequently. Such a survey could also help sort out the partnership issues. For example, a perceptual map of you, your competitors, and your key channel partners would literally paint a picture of the best possible relationships. It would also indicate those less likely to succeed. Once you understand your relative brand strengths, you can develop an informed strategy. The central idea of Strategic Anticipation® is to not wait for this to happen to you but to anticipate it and develop a strategy so that you can head this off while you still have some negotiating leverage.

➤ Compression

Multistop distribution systems (wholesaler, distributor, and retailer) are classic features of the business landscape, but there's a price to pay: long cycles, high cost, and low responsiveness to market changes. Consumers in search of lower prices and greater convenience apply pressure to these systems. The result: compression of traditional distribution channels in favor of more efficient and closer relationships between customers and suppliers. Streamlined delivery turns customer dissatisfaction into satisfaction.

Example: The National Association of Convenience Stores (NACS) has been experimenting with and promoting the use of EDI (electronic data interchange) for automatic stock replenishment. Point-of-sale (POS) data informs the reordering system of the volume of retail off-take. Using a highly disciplined shelving plan and minimal inventories, the reordering system automatically calls for new product. The NACS estimates this process could generate incremental profits of $758 million by reducing inventory and eliminating out-of-stock conditions.

Example: The Grocery Manufacturers of America (GMA) conducted a similar study of store-to-door delivered products. EDI-based automatic product replenishment resulted in a 2.9 percent sales increase.

If you want to make this transition work for you: Ask yourself what compression means for your business model. Compression is a profit strategy for certain types of retailers based on sales velocity and markups. Scanner or other point-of-sale data sources will enable you to assess the velocity of your items compared to your competitors. Brand-switching data from purchase panels will enable you to evaluate various item-trimming strategies. Making some assumptions about comparative markups, can you develop a scenario in which your line in a given category would be more attractive to the retailer? Taking into account the greater share of shelf, what would the business outcome be for you? Can you construct a hypothetical win-win? Use Strategic Anticipation® to be preemptive!

➤ Reintermediation

Compression—in its most extreme form—leads to complete disintermediation, which completely eliminates low-value distributors and creates a direct link between the supplier and company. The Internet accelerates this pattern.

In a growing number of cases, a pattern of reintermediation follows. This allows ousted distributors or new players to return to the picture in a different capacity because direct relationships are often limited to transaction processing. They provide the value-added services and face-to-face experience that customers come to miss. This requires retailers to completely rethink their role.

Example: Rosenbluth International, a travel agency, eliminated the use of various airline reservation systems it felt were biased to each respective airline and created its own system. Called Dacoda, the system allows corporate clients to link directly into the system and create their own travel arrangements.

If you want to make this transition work for you: You must identify unmet needs around the product's purchase, service, or use that you can fulfill as value added to the purchase process. This could begin with qualitative research to stimulate some hypotheses. Alternatively, in situations in which it may prove difficult for customers to think of truly new ideas, ethnographic techniques may be more productive. These tools of cultural anthropology involve observing customers in the act. This could be live, announced or unannounced (as in a store), or video recorded. In the process of objectively watching customers do what they do, the little disconnects may become apparent; once identified, these may be probed for further depth. The insights derived from the research need to coalesce into an opportunity. What are you going to do about it, and can you make any money in the process? Finally, the desire for action is developed into a product or service concept.

Once you've reached the concept stage, you have a testable hypothesis. If the concept is fairly far afield from common contemporary experience, you need to engage in information acceleration to equip the respondent to provide an informed answer. This is a delicate process because you need to provide an adequate basis for an opinion without leading the consumer to the answer you are hoping for. Concept tests can be elaborated to incorporate product features and marketing programs and should include price, although alternatives can be examined. Be cautious when it comes to very new concepts. Respondents have difficulty accurately reflecting their willingness to pay for a product or service for which they have no frame of reference.

➤ E-Commerce

This phenomenon will be dealt with extensively in Chapter 9. For now, suffice it to say, this may be the biggest change to hit retailing since Sears met Roebuck. The potential for virtual retailing to undercut its brick-and-mortar older sibling is enormous, as is the potential for manufacturers to sell directly to consumers, disintermediating retail entirely. The outcome, however, may not be so black and white. More than likely, customers will segment by category and need or occasion. The same person may buy books only on-line but purchase clothing only in the traditional way. Or certain kinds of books, say, nonfiction, may be purchased on-line, whereas novels read for pleasure may require a *browseable* store. Then what are the economics of such a segmented market? Millennial opportunities are appearing for manufacturers, distributors, and retailers alike. Keep an ear to the ground and an eye to the horizon and invest in researching the future!

Although traditional test-market techniques may be too costly and time consuming in so many situations, the Web may be the exception. E-commerce applications can be developed far less expensively than constructing a physical store, although a full-featured application, required for a fair test, may not be that inexpensive. Target-group customers can be invited to a secure site for an evaluation. This test can capture their overall experience rating and future intention to purchase as well as numerous diagnostics that may lead to an improved concept. Of special importance is the need to assess the navigability of the site. Often, what seems a clever idea to those fully immersed in the development of a Web site is totally opaque to the casual visitor, thus preventing them from becoming a customer. Is the purpose of your site instantly identifiable? Can the visitor immediately determine if you offer products or services of interest? How many clicks does it take to get to the product or service they want? Do you provide enough information to close the sale? What barriers do you place between your customer and a purchase, and how can you eliminate them? How can you ensure total satisfaction and, more importantly, return business? Most important of all, how can you transform your visitor first into a customer and then into a loyal customer? Mastering this conversion process requires a consistent program of research-based learning, but these questions can be answered making your foray into e-commerce successful. One of the most useful tools the Web provides to marketers is the *cookie,* which allows you to tag visitors, enabling you to recognize them upon their return. From a marketing perspective, the ability to execute one-to-one relationship marketing schemes is instantly realized. From a research perspective, you are able to track customer behavior to determine how successful you are being in converting visitors to customers and customers to loyalists. The flip side is that cookies are viewed with some concern by many as a potential invasion of privacy. In fact, they are no more an invasion of privacy than those frequent-shopper cards we willingly submit at every visit to the supermarket. Nevertheless, they need to be handled with care, which means informing your visitors that you're setting a cookie and allowing them to opt out if they so desire. Going a step further, if you ask your customers to register with you, providing some information about their preferences and characteristics, you will be able to segment them for a sharper understanding of how to market to them. Registration also has its perceived dark side. You must develop a privacy policy—what you will and won't do with the information they are giving you. This is especially acute if you are requesting any personally identifiable information such as a name, address, or phone number. Privacy policies should be available via a link on your homepage. It is truly a brave new world! The power of the Web for fully integrated efficient product or service distribution, relationship marketing, and market research is unprecedented—no, it is undreamed of! This vehicle is so powerful that great care must be taken to not abuse that power. We believe that the greatest e-businesses have not been thought of yet; this is the most amazing field of play yet for Strategic Anticipation®!

Understanding the likely response of consumers is key to deciphering all of these near and distant future opportunities.

What do your customers want from their shopping experience? Selection, convenience, price, fun, romance, service, speed, cachet, identification . . . the list of possible attributes goes on and on. Use qualitative research to compile the list and identify attributes you may not have thought of, especially when taking a disciplined look at the role of the shopping experience for the first time. In addition to standard focus groups, other techniques prove useful in the retail setting. Exit interviews catch the shopper fresh from the shopping experience. These can range from open, in-depth (but brief) probes to structured, quantitative evaluations. Passively observing shoppers in the act can be enlightening, particularly when combined with a brief interview. Videotaping shoppers where your products are shelved is highly unintrusive, and the insights gained can be remarkably potent.

The quantitative research recommended in Chapters 4 and 5 to provide the insights that can maximize your relationship with your customers should be extended to include distribution channels as another brand attribute. Although you may not have direct control over this attribute—as you do with packaging, for example—you can seize the opportunities presented by shifting channel patterns as they occur. For example, the Internet affords unprecedented opportunity to disintermediate traditional channels.

Studying lead users (those early adopters of new channels) can be highly informative. As with any lead-user research, you must understand how these early adopters may differ from the rest of the market that will follow. Nevertheless, lead users can help evaluate the numerous initiatives to come from the retail entrepreneurs, especially the "dot coms." Truly moving ahead of the pack may require understanding where the retail industry is going. A Delphi study among relevant retailing executives could point the way—or at least the *ways*. Such an exercise would not likely result in consensus, but we would expect a small number of alternative scenarios that could be explored in greater depth. Each is likely to involve different economics, depending on the level of retail intermediation.

➤ Purchase Marketing: The Shopping Experience As a Brand Attribute

Purchase marketing focuses the merchandising, marketing, and buying functions of suppliers and retailers on what the consumers actually want. Consumers benefit from purchase marketing in two ways:

➤ It provides the products that consumers want or need, in areas of the store where they can find them, and displayed in ways that make choice easy.

➤ It introduces consumers to products that they don't know they want or need, in areas of the store where they will come across them, and those products are displayed in ways that prompt purchasing.

Purchase marketing can help you develop a strategy for your brand in an individual retail account by allowing you to determine the best approach for the supplier to influence that account. Understanding the relative importance of the purchase environment in relation to the prepurchase environment for the category becomes crucial.

The prepurchase environment includes the marketing activities that influence consumers' brand choice before they enter the store, including such things as product and packaging design, above-the-line advertising, and direct promotions to the consumer. A usage and attitude study is a market research tool you can use for developing plans to influence the prepurchase environment. Consider the in-store activities that influence the shopper: availability on shelf, shelf position and space allocation, communications, and in-store promotions. Once you understand how important these tools are and what each tool can accomplish for each brand in the specific retail account, you then can use them to develop a purchase-marketing strategy that is in harmony with the brand's positioning and overall marketing strategy.

Four features basically characterize consumer purchasing behavior:

- ➤ Single-brand loyalty.
- ➤ Price focus.
- ➤ Promotion focus.
- ➤ Active versus passive shopping.

These four components describe the core of the purchase decision and occur to different degrees depending on the level of interest in the category, brand choice in store, and the amount of price/promotions activity.

Research conducted by Tandem Consulting in Canada in conjunction with Research International offered some surprising results:

➤ Only six basic segments describe the consumer's purchase behavior, although two of the segments have up to four variations.

➤ The different behavioral types described by the segments are very different from each other, which is not always the case in segmentation analysis.

➤ Not all categories exhibit all six of the purchase behavior segments.

➤ Some purchase behavior segments in particular geographic areas can be very different from one category to the next.

➤ Specific brand (or retailer's own brand) users will often have different proportions of the individual segments than the category as a whole.

The research companies used this segmentation technique in different geographic markets, with some interesting findings that have increased our understanding of the dynamics of purchase marketing.[1] In Canada, for example, the retail scene is very fragmented, with few truly national multiples. Not all brands have national distribution across retail chains, and prices and promotions often differ considerably. Price promotions are common, coupons are used extensively, and shoppers know to search for their particular

brands through an offer or a deal. Active shopping consti-
tutes a regular feature in many categories, and hunting for a
price deal or promotion is commonplace. Consumers start to
watch retailers' advertising, wait for key brands or prices to
be featured, switch stores to take advantage of the offer, and
stock up.

Stimulating hunting behavior poses serious risks to both
manufacturers and retailers because it can seriously undermine brand loyalty. If a brand loyalist becomes conditioned
by the availability of offers to buy only in bulk when the
brand is heavily reduced, the brand's profitability will
diminish even with the incremental volume.

EASTMAN KODAK

Although shoppers historically stated via direct-questioning
methods that they had no difficulty shopping for photographic
film, observation of consumers at the point of purchase indicated otherwise. Cognitive modeling approaches—employing
such techniques as paraphrasing, concurrent and retrospective think-alouds, and vignettes to reveal key components of a
decision process (comprehension, retrieval, judgment, and
output)—were applied to hopefully capture the consumers'
thought process in real time.

Kodak already was looking into video observation as a market research technique that could help to reexamine and
improve elements of the marketing mix, so the company used
it to study the film display. A video camera set up in various
retail locations produced some surprising footage. The time
consumers spent at the display was much longer than the time
spent in similar product categories. In addition, a variety of
nonverbal behaviors surfaced, indicating that some consumers
were confused and frustrated during the purchase process.

Exit interviews were conducted with the participants of the
video observation. Surprisingly, no one indicated any great
difficulty shopping for film. This was true even for respondents who spent an inordinate amount of time at the display
and whose behavior at the display clearly showed some level of
confusion and frustration.

(Continued)

(*Continued*)

Kodak knew it had to develop a method other than direct questioning to uncover exactly what was happening at the display. The most straightforward approach was to interview consumers at the point of display and have them tell the researchers what they were thinking as they shopped. This methodology raised several questions:

➤ Will consumers make up their thought processes because they want to look good or feel obliged to produce results for the interviewer?

➤ Even if researchers were able to accurately capture their thoughts, would they be able to organize them in a coherent manner?

➤ Will the results be so unstructured as to generate many different and conflicting interpretations?

The entire interview process lasted about 30 minutes and consisted of the following:

GREETING

When respondents were greeted as they entered the store, interviewers were careful not to set an expectation of a question/answer environment. Rapport had to be quickly established with respondents, and local interviewers were helpful in creating the necessary small talk.

WARM-UP

Respondents were shown several displays in the store using think-aloud techniques before being interviewed on film purchasing. Warm-up started with product categories that were relatively simple and straightforward and then moved on to more complex and involved purchases that required more decision making. The warm-ups lasted between 5 and 10 minutes. The film area was casually introduced to avoid having respondents guess that film was the focus of the interview.

NONDIRECTIVE PROBING

The following nondirective probing techniques kept respondents participating with think-aloud techniques:

- ➤ What you are thinking?
- ➤ What are your thoughts?
- ➤ What are you seeing?

DESCRIBING THE DISPLAY

This part was rotated to address concerns that asking respondents to initially describe the display would bias their normal search process and contaminate the think-aloud. Sometimes display description would be the first step; other times it followed the concurrent and retrospective think-alouds. Kodak researchers ultimately discovered that rotation was not necessary. Most respondents would start describing the display when they started the concurrent think-aloud even when not instructed to do so. It seemed to be the natural first step in their information search.

No matter where it was positioned, respondents usually described a display that did not match the actual display. Researchers realized that respondents were describing the way their mind expected the display to be laid out, an important clue to the expectations respondents had when they entered the store.

CONCURRENT THINK-ALOUD

The nature of the concurrent think-aloud for film was often longer and more disjointed than for the warm-up products. Given the purchase difficulty observed on the video observation, this made sense for the film product category.

RETROSPECTIVE THINK-ALOUD

Summarizing the entire decision process retrospectively was both difficult and intimidating for many respondents. This

(Continued)

(Continued)

technique worked best when specific instances were probed during the concurrent think-aloud. Cues to probe these instances included pauses in speech, nonverbal actions such as twirling the film box in their hands, certain spoken phrases, or mere instances of looking up to the left. The retrospective was useful for filling in the gaps and understanding the decision rules.

REEXAMINING CONTEXT

After the retrospective think-aloud, a more traditional interview took place in a separate room where video vignettes were shown. The respondent was casually probed based on some of the buying context issues previously identified. For example, the respondent may have been asked how her decision-making process would have differed if a specific family member was also present or if she had purchased multiple items in the store that day. These questions provided important insights into variations on the decision-making process that the consumer just described. These questions also brought out inconsistencies among some respondents whose participation in the think-aloud was suspect.

VIDEO VIGNETTES

The video vignettes were compilations of various behaviors that were noted during the video observation project. The behaviors were acted out by the same persons in every scene so that respondents could concentrate on the behaviors and not on the characteristics of the individual consumer. Some of the most valuable research insights emerged at this stage.

The video vignettes acted like a projection technique that respondents used to explain their own behavior at the film counter. For example, a vignette of a woman looking around the store was explained by one respondent as someone looking for her children. This respondent went on to explain how the presence of her children changed the way she shopped at the display. Another respondent said the woman was looking for a clerk to help her and then elaborated on the role that store personnel play in her selection process.

DEBRIEFING

At this point, respondents were asked whether the techniques accurately captured their buying process. Most of the respondents said (rather sheepishly) that the process pretty much portrayed how they shop for film. Some respondents commented that the think-aloud techniques seemed a little strange at first but became fun once they got used to them.

Respondents who participated in other types of market research in the past expressed a preference for the present techniques as being more fun and interesting than discussion groups or surveys.

ANALYSIS

The results were initially analyzed with regard to the respondent's goals, the shopping context, and the meaning of their language for interpreting information and making judgments. A large number of recommendations and insights were generated from the results, and further display tests were based on the research findings.

UNITED KINGDOM

In markets such as the United Kingdom a number of centrally managed and controlled retail chains have full national representation. Key brands usually are distributed nationally, with pricing and promotional activity quite similar between stores. As a result, active shopping rarely occurs, and when it does, it tends to relate only to specific categories or new product markets. However, highly competitive price or promotions activity supported by media advertising, give rise to the scenarios for hunting behavior. One case in point is the cola market.

Research International reassessed a category studied two years earlier.[2] Their goal: to understand purchase behavior and use it to develop a category promotion strategy for the brand

(Continued)

(*Continued*)

across the grocery sector, with a focus on specific retail accounts. When the research firm first looked at this market in 1996, it found very little active shopping across stores in this category because a small number of major chains dominate grocery retailing in the United Kingdom Central management and control allows leading brands in many categories to receive full distribution. Prices and promotional activities usually are carried out at a similar level in all the major chains, so people are less inclined to switch stores based on promotions or attractive pricing. But they will switch stores when it is convenient. In these circumstances, active shopping relates more to specific categories (unusual/different lines for instance) or new product markets.

Research International discovered a relatively high level of promotionally active behavior in the cola category as manufacturers relied heavily on it to encourage consumers to switch between the major brands and their own labels.

Initially, Research International advised its client to continue with a promotions program but link it more directly with the above-the-line advertising message as a way to continue brand building on TV with brand building in store. Indifferent shoppers comprised an important part of the market, and researchers believed the client could encourage more purchasing within this group by boosting awareness in store. On-pack promotions were used given difficulties in achieving greater shelf space.

Price-related promotions were avoided because the brand retailed at a slight premium and competitors were offering price and multibuy discounts to gain more share. The client agreed, using value-added promotions—mostly collectibles that were linked to advertising—to convert indifferent shoppers to devoted loyalists. Because prior research found that indifferent shoppers were interested in collectibles, that strategy used this fact as a means to reinforce the brand at point of purchase and attract potential customers to stores.

During this period, the main competitor introduced a new product into the market using a rolling launch and price-cutting promotions to encourage trial use and build share. The third brand in the market joined the price-cutting strategy.

Two years later, Research International uncovered some surprising findings: The number of people who were promotionally active in this category jumped from 49 to 66 percent; indifferent shoppers declined as they became promotionally sensitized and actively looked for promotions in the category; and loyalty suffered, plummeting 33 percent!

The previous market leader and the client brand's main competitor were totally undermined during that two-year period, while the client's brand strengthened its numbers of devoted loyalists. The promotion strategy appeared to truly pay off!

The challenge for the brand now is to determine the best way to move forward with the promotion strategy for the category. By using the data to model different what-if scenarios, researchers will attempt to anticipate the possible effect on purchase behavior for the different purchase behavior segments.

■ CATEGORY MANAGEMENT—MARKETING AT THE LOCAL LEVEL

Category management addresses these issues by allowing you to fine-tune your product, brand, and variety assortment to the known preferences of the market/neighborhood/chain/store. Similar research drives decisions regarding pricing and promotion choices. Category management, in turn, results in a win-win situation for both manufacturers and retailers because the research enables them to drive inefficiency out of the system and share the benefits. The process, however, is currently hitting some obstacles, which we will discuss later in this chapter.

In addition to category management—which tends to be based on point-of-sale research services such as scanner data—other retail research is gaining popularity. Cultural anthropology—studying how shoppers shop and how they would like to shop—is one such area. Market researchers are relying on everything from hidden cameras in store aisles to computer-based simulated shopping experiences to delve further into the reasons why people buy—and keep buying—products.

All such research leads to a single destination. *Solution selling* is the concept of organizing the store around the consumer's needs, not on what is convenient to the store. Key to all of this is to see the consumer as shopper, purchaser, and user. The brand's distribution strategy needs to address all of these needs. Research can reveal them.

Kevin Clancy and Robert Shulman, authors of the 1991 book *The Marketing Revolution,* anticipated the current marketing revolution and the need for "marketers to do new things in new ways. They will compel marketing departments to abandon myth and ignorance and consider hundreds . . . of alternatives to every marketing decision to find the optimal one. And they will hold marketing executives accountable for a measurable return on the marketing investment."[3]

Category management definitely represents a new thing for market research, a total mind-set change. Retailers and manufacturers historically have been diametrically opposed in their business objectives. Although manufacturers constantly sought maximum distribution, retailers consistently focused on minimizing inventory. Manufacturers always looked to gain the greatest consumer impact and trade dollars, while retailers continually searched for ways to increase slim margins. And both wanted to build their own brand.

But five factors have precipitated this trend toward category management that requires a major shift in the traditional manufacturer/retailer relationship:

1. The U.S. market has become a much more fragmented environment since the 1950s and 1960s, when conformity was "in" and the consumer population was more homogeneous.

2. The media, propelled by demographic and lifestyle diversification, has become fragmented as well, which makes delivery of marketing communications much more difficult and expensive.

3. Manufacturers are finally realizing that the Point of Purchase Advertising Institute (POPAI) actually has a

point: A majority of consumer choices are made in the store, which places greater importance on shelf assortment and shelf layout.[4]

4. U.S. retailers opened their eyes to the fact that they no longer are simply distribution channels but need to be marketers in their own right.

5. Thinning retail margins have created a need to reduce costs and optimize space.

Category management, however, can help both sides achieve greater success by bridging the traditional gaps through a partnering effort that requires cooperation in order to achieve efficient consumer response (ECR) through the following principles:

➤ Categories are managed as strategic business units, not as a collection of unrelated, individual brands.

➤ Both manufacturers and retailers become consumer-centric by organizing their buying, merchandising, and marketing against fulfilling consumer needs and wants.

➤ Marketing strategy is executed at the retail account level to the point where each store can be considered as its own little market and organized to support consumers in that particular market.

When handled correctly, category management achieves efficient consumer response through four key strategies: efficient replenishment, efficient promotion, efficient assortment, and efficient new product introduction. There are five guiding principles you must follow:

1. Work constantly to provide better value to the consumer with less cost throughout the total supply chain.

2. Involve business leaders who are determined to replace the win-lose trading relationships with mutually profitable business alliances.

3. Use accurate and timely information in a computer-based system to support effective marketing, production, and logistic decisions.

4. Ensure that the right product is available to the consumer at the right time by implementing value-added processes as the product flows from the end of production/packing to the consumer's shopping cart.

5. Use a standard measurement-and-reward system that evaluates the impact of business decisions on the whole system.

When properly applied, category management results in data-based supply-chain efficiency that yields lower retailer costs, fewer out-of-stock items, and greater consumer satisfaction. A win-win for both retailers and manufacturers arises when preferences are highly localized, the heaviest shoppers are satisfied, and both sides are able to sell what sells! Coordinated marketing and merchandising are key.

More companies today spend large amounts of time and money to be *the* player in the category management arena by becoming a retailer's "category captain." Retailers appoint companies to provide management expertise for certain categories or sectors in their stores, and the category captains receive a measure of preference in the store in return for managing this business. They maintain their position by enhancing the retailer's business, even if at the expense of their own.

■ PRODUCT ASSORTMENT

Retailers need to give consumers the products they want at the same time they strive to maximize profits from the available selections. These two goals may seem contradictory and often vary by store or store group. Retailers and manufacturers, therefore, must determine what makes for a good product assortment. To do this, they often rely on a common—and, unfortunately, unreliable—method to determine which items to add or to discontinue. *Brand-ranking reports* (which also are known by many other names) are listings of sales for a fixed period of time, usually quarterly, in which each stock-keeping unit (SKU) is rank-ordered by its sales, revenue, profits, or occasionally, the date purchased. Retailers that want to add an item to a fully stocked category often scan the list and eliminate the weakest performers. Manufacturers that are considering a new flavor often review a list of rank-ordered flavors in the marketplace and add the first new flavor that is not in its portfolio. This method is beautiful in its simplicity because little thought is required to make a decision. But the results often turn ugly because it's too easy to make the wrong decision.

The ranking approach often fails for two reasons:

1. Analysis usually is done at the retail chain level or, even worse, at the market level. A particular product may be very strong in the one chain where it is available, but in mixing that data with that of other chains in the market, the product becomes a small factor. It assumes that all products are equally available to be ranked, but that often is true only when the report is run at the individual store level.

2. Ranking reports assume equal product desirability across all consumers, which often leads to the conclusion that the worst-selling products are the least desirable and should be pulled off the shelves. But we know that not all consumers desire all products the same way. Take, for example, the split between premium and budget frozen entrees, one of the few instances when household income becomes an excellent discriminator of purchase probability. Low-income families buy budget; upper-income households go premium. A ranking report, however, combines the two groups of consumers and the two groups of products, leading to possible errors that would be avoided by analysis at the individual store level when a homogeneous trading area cannot be assumed.

To correct these problems, you need to understand the consumer's structuring of your product category and then match that structure to a particular store. That way, you can provide a more optimal shelf set to the consumers in that particular store. Understanding the category—and most importantly; understanding it from the consumer's point of view—will help to ensure success of further category management efforts.

■ LINKING LOYALTY MARKETING WITH CATEGORY MANAGEMENT

The ability to link category management with loyalty marketing is driven both by its potential benefits and by current needs. The potential benefits are improved store performance and higher levels of customer satisfaction that emerge when the two are managed together. The current need is the ability to avoid conflict that can emerge from trying to pursue loyalty marketing and category management at the same time.

Loyalty marketing, the topic of Chapter 5 and extensively treated there, usually targets specific segments of customers to deliver greater value to them than to those consumers who are relatively less important in the total picture. Category management, simply put, divides your business into categories and then manages each category as a business unit with a strict focus on its consumers. But you need to tie together loyalty marketing and category management because if you don't, opportunities will be lost, and in some cases, contention and conflict may arise.

Integrating loyalty marketing and category management ultimately can maximize overall store performance and at the same time reduce costs. To achieve this goal, we recommend you focus on the heaviest shoppers to achieve optimum levels of satisfaction among heavy shoppers through all aspects of store operations—merchandising and promotions.

Retailers often develop frequent-shopper programs to protect what they assume is an existing high degree of shopper loyalty with an aim to preserve existing loyalty and build on it wherever possible. But exclusive loyalty does not exist in today's marketplace. Marketers of consumer products acknowledge that most shoppers spread out their purchases among a group of what they consider to be acceptable brands. Grocery shoppers—particularly frequent shoppers—spend their money among a set of acceptable outlets. The outlet they use is driven by top-of-mind categories for that trip, by the promotion of the week, or by location.

Generally speaking, the top 30 percent of customers generate 70 percent of sales, and this is the group to target. But don't expect undivided loyalty. The problem with loyalty marketing is that a chain's most desirable and valuable customers regularly shop the competitors. Research based on a combination of multi-outlet household panel data and loyalty marketing data shows that:

➤ The average chain captures only 50 percent of its heavy shoppers' spending.

➤ Heavy shoppers typically spend about $4,100 per year, but their primary chain captures only about $2,150 of that total. This leaves a $2,000 potential for this segment of customers alone.

Loyalty programs open up two separate but related opportunities for going after this $2,000 potential:

1. Targeted communications.
2. New information for category plan improvement.

Not surprisingly, targeted communications receive the most attention because household-customized mailings have proven powerful in supporting and strengthening customer relationships. The problem is that most marketers conduct mailings without any strategic integration into category planning. Those who do understand that stores ultimately create shopper loyalty. Discount cards reinforce loyalty, but stores initially build that loyalty. Therefore, using loyalty data to improve store merchandising, promotions, and operations offers a tremendous opportunity.

Winning the battle for share of heavy shoppers lies in your ability to merchandise stores and promote products in ways that increase their heavy-shopper pulling power. Category management becomes a key component of loyalty marketing at retail. The challenge is to integrate loyalty data into that process, with the objective of optimizing category plans against the heavy shopper.

Consider this example: A category manager runs his or her category profitably and effectively using only a single report. Along comes a loyalty program manager who replaces that one report with three distinct reports for heavy-, medium-, and light-shopper segments. Together these reports provide no more useful data than the original one. But simply calculating traditional category management measures by shopper segment only increases the category manager's workload. But let's look at another approach. The data is minded for new merchandising and cross-promotional ideas, which often points to secondary locations or cutting-edge cross-promotions. It can even lead to more tightly focused displays, such as a cold sufferers kiosk, but such efforts at best generate only one-timers and not sustained category growth.

We believe it is important to work through the existing category management process with the aim of enhancing and improving it. Success lies in the ability to assess how well merchandising and promotions are aligned with the chain's heavy shoppers' needs.

Finding measures that add value through clear direction for action over and above existing measures becomes crucial to success. Consider these two illustrations of how you can tie the two systems together.

➤ Define Category Roles

How do categories actually function in relation to the consumer? Loyalty data certainly offers important information for evaluating the roles that particular categories play in

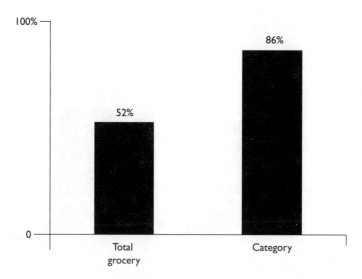

Figure 7.1 Share of Heavy-Shopper Money (Category A).

Source: Glenn Hausfater, "Linking Loyalty Marketing and Category Management," in *Marketing Research Taken to the Next Level* (New York Advertising Research Foundation, 1988), 140.

retail stores. Consider, for example, a *destination* category that can drive a consumer's decision to choose a store and make that particular outlet the primary source of category needs. Research conducted by Partners in Loyalty Management, Inc., shows that a destination category offers strong appeal to heavy shoppers.[5] The problem has been the ability to evaluate whether specific categories function in the roles that they have been slotted for. Until now.

From Figure 7.1 you can see that this Chain A garners only 52 percent of total grocery spending from its heavy shoppers, which reflects the 50 percent upside that we described earlier. However, the chart also indicates that the chain captures more than 80 percent of its total spending on Category A. This spending pattern strongly validates that Category A plays a destination role for heavy shoppers in that chain.

Now take a look a Figure 7.2, which analyzes Category B, a dry grocery item. This is one that quite a few retailers typically use as a destination category. The numbers tell a

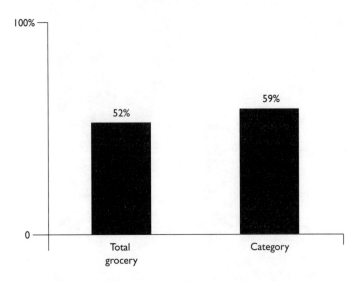

Figure 7.2 Share of Heavy-Shopper Money (Category B).

Source: Glenn Hausfater, "Linking Loyalty Marketing and Category Management," in *Marketing Research Taken to the Next Level* (New York Advertising Research Foundation, 1988), 140.

different story. This chain gets roughly the same share of its heavy shoppers spending on Category B as it does of its total grocery spending. This pattern is more consistent with a *routine* role than it is with a *destination* role.

This type of category role–validation analysis is the first step to linking loyalty marketing to category management by melding loyalty-marketing data from the retailer with syndicated household panel data from third parties. This gives manufacturers of consumer package goods a chance to partner with retailers around loyalty marketing.

➤ Review the Category

This represents another area in which loyalty marketing data can amplify the power of category management. A

Table 7.1 Source of Transactions

Fair Shore	54%
Heavy Shopper Shore	42%
Total	2,620,400

Source: Glenn Hausfater, "Linking Loyalty Marketing and Category Management," in *Marketing Research Taken to the Next Level* (New York Advertising Research Foundation, 1988), 140.

heavy shopper–focused review begins with this question: "How am I doing?" Table 7.1 indicates the chain was lagging the market in category growth mainly because the chain is losing heavy shoppers overall. If heavy shoppers account for a lower-than-expected share of category transactions, this would not in itself destroy category profitability. But it's a strong indicator that a category plan isn't appealing to heavy shoppers, causing overall store performance to suffer. When loyalty data is added to the category review, insights emerge when you look at deal utilization rates by heavy shoppers. Loyalty marketing focuses rewards—both traditional and electronic promotions—on heavy shoppers. If they dislike your promotions, you're in trouble even when your category is profitable.

■ POINT-OF-PURCHASE ADVERTISING

Consumers have grown increasingly self-reliant when they shop. Talented sales staff are harder to find, and those available often lack proper training. Therefore, point-of-purchase (POP) communications have grown more important in the purchase decision process because they offer reliable information consumers can access at the moment they need it.

Despite the huge amount of money being spent on POP—about $13 billion annually—it's probably the most underresearched component of the marketing communications mix. Most decisions related to POP are totally subjective. And traditional forms of recall and persuasion research don't work well because POP is a low-involvement, short-term-memory communications medium that shoppers tend to use and immediately forget. Consumer interaction often takes a fraction of a second, yet it can be very complex. The challenge is to identify research techniques that can measure the impact of the POP medium.

The following are four types of consumer needs, each with its own corresponding POP consumer purpose:

1. When consumers need to find something, POP can provide directions.
2. When consumers need to learn about a product, POP can provide product information.
3. When consumers need to obtain a value, POP can communicate a promotion or bargain.
4. When consumers simply want a pleasant shopping experience, POP can provide ambiance/decor, brand reinforcement, or "framing" of the shopping/usage experience.

The first three POPs are easily measured, and the fourth is somewhat more difficult but not impossible. This one is particularly important for many retailers during major holidays such as Christmas, when a festively decorated store theoretically gets people in the Christmas spirit, thereby getting them to spend their money more freely.

Twelve different methodologies can be used to measure the impact of POP. Some are laboratory techniques, while others take place in the actual retailer environment. Some provide very definitive answers; others are quite open to interpretation. Some should be used very early in the development process to help define a fundamental strategy for POP, while others are designed to analyze results after a campaign.

➤ Environment Rooms

Consumers either rate or actually test the brand's products and in a room filled solely with alternative POP displays. The result: indirect measurements on how different POPs affect brand perceptions or enhance the user's experience in the case of product testing.

➤ Customer Store Mapping

Consumers draw a map of their most-used store on a blank sheet of paper. What is drawn and not drawn reveals what is important to them.

➤ Customer "Need State" Intercepts

Consumers are intercepted for interviews in various areas of the retail environment to gain a better understanding of their needs at that exact moment in time. When used in combination with how much discretionary time consumers spend in each zone, you can define a POP strategy for each zone that is appropriate for their needs and uses the right amount of time to communicate its message.

➤ Eye-Tracking

This device tracks where consumers are looking, for how long, and in what order—and can be combined with recall measures to measure the impact of POP.

➤ Hidden Camera

Video cameras are used in a retail environment to observe traffic-flow patterns and understand where consumers are looking and for how long.

➤ Video "Snakes"

Video cameras hidden in hats are used to look at what consumers see in the brand's actual retail environment. This also can be used to compare the brand with its competition as well as to assess the "real" consumer experience.

➤ "Visor-Cam" Eye-Tracking

This is a combination of video snake and eye-tracking in which a device on the visor of a hat tracks not only what customers see but precisely what consumers are looking at. This can be used in an actual store, as compared with traditional eye-tracking, which relies on simulated shopping.

➤ Merchandising Impact Measurement Study

Stores are matched, and the POP in the experimental group is modified from the norm. The impact on sales is then tracked (or some other measure is used, such as inquiries, test drives, etc.). This can be effective in studying specific POP designs or different mixes of POP (type and quantity). Ultimately, it can isolate the impact on sales of individual POP elements in an attempt to make find the optimal combination or kit.

➤ Promotional Appeal and Readability

This form of copy testing for POP uses a tachistiscope to quantify readability, but it also can measure the ability of POP to catch the eye in peripheral vision as well as its appeal and relevance.

➤ Customer Guided Tours

An interviewer accompanies a consumer as he shops and asks the individual why he does the things he does. This is sometimes combined with postshopping interviews or focus groups.

➤ Executional Audit Correlation

Mystery shoppers are used to rate stores on proper POP execution. Ratings are then correlated to sales performance to measure the importance of proper POP execution.

■ DIAGNOSTIC

Do you know:

➤ The role of distribution channels on your customer's preference for your brand?

➤ The potential value of locally optimized product selection, pricing and promotion? Is there a positive ROI?

➤ The relative effectiveness of your point-of-purchase advertising alternatives?

➤ The ROI of your POP advertising?

Do you have:

➤ Alternative scenarios for the potential channels shifts ahead, including e-commerce and disintermediation?

➤ Contingency plans based upon the opportunity to better serve your customers through these new or evolved channels?

THE EIGHT STEPS TO CATEGORY MANAGEMENT

1. Define the category.
2. Identify the category role.
3. Determine the category assortment.
4. Create a category scorecard.
5. Develop a category strategy.
6. Detail the tactics to drive the strategy.
7. Execute!
8. Review and refine the plan.

■ NOTES

1. Maureen Johnson, "From Understanding Consumer Behavior to Testing Category Strategies," in *Marketing Research Taken to the Next Level* (New York: Advertising Research Foundation, 1998), 89–90.

2. Ibid., 90–91.

3. Kevin J. Clency and Robert S. Shulman. *The Marketing Revolution: A Radical Manifesto for Dominating the Marketplace* (New York: Harper Business, 1991).

4. Laurie Fredman. "POPAI Prescribes Shift to 'Hard Sell'." *AdAge,* Oct. 8, 1984, p. 104.

5. Glenn Hausfater, "Linking Loyalty Marketing and Category Management," in *Marketing Research Taken to the Next Level* (New York: Advertising Research Foundation, 1998), 140.

Chapter

Researching the Future Employee Loyalty

> Ultimately, whatever the form of economic activity, it is people that count most.
>
> —Lord Sieff, Marks & Spencer

So far, this book has covered the traditional marketing terrain (customers, competitors, and channels) albeit through a future-focused lens. However, this chapter—which concerns an area rarely associated with marketing—may be the most important.

The history of business in the twentieth century has had a variety of focal points: mass production, distribution/ logistics, and supply chains; cost economies and downsizing; marketing, branding, growth, and customer loyalty; and so on. Business advice has become a booming industry in itself, given these shifts.

Yet relatively little attention has been given to what will, we believe, be the driver of business thinking early in the twenty-first century: the employee. (A gratifying recent exception to this lack of attention appears in the January/February 2000 issue of *Harvard Business Review*. Peter Cappelli, in his article, "A Market-Driven Approach to Retaining Talent," urges companies to devise highly targeted programs to keep key talent in place.)

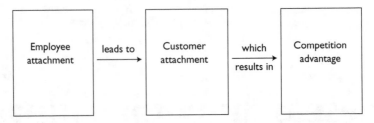

Figure 8.1 Connecting Employees and Customers.

Source: Dan Ulrich, Richard Halbrook, Dave Meder, Mark Stuchlik, and Steve Thorpe, "Employee and Customer Attachment: Synergies for Competitive Advantage," *Human Resource Planning* 19, no. 2: 89–103.

There are a number of reasons for this belief:

➤ Demographic changes will make it harder and harder for businesses to find enough good people in the right age cohorts with the right training.

➤ Attitudinal changes (if not continued downsizing) should continue to make it more difficult for businesses to engender loyalty from their employees.

➤ Growth of service-based businesses (versus product-centric) emphasizes the value of people. The Internet's impact will reinforce this thrust because the Internet requires continuous innovation (i.e., people), continuous learning/improvement (i.e., people), and superb service to a company product/technology quality. (As John Jordan, one of Ernst & Young's experts in e-commerce says, "On the Internet you can have all three—speed, quality and low price.")

➤ Recognition that—particularly in high-end service businesses—the retention of key employees is linked to and may even drive valued customer retention.

These are how a series of books and articles address the linkage of customers with employees. One such article presents the paradigm shown in Figure 8.1 and provides several solid case studies. A growing body of work goes even farther than that to link employee retention to ultimate business goals of shareholder value.

Despite this and other articles, the weight of management literature about customer satisfaction and development of loyalty of profitable customers is unmatched on the employee loyalty side. However, don't expect this imbalance to continue for long.

■ THE BIGGER PICTURE

Since the early 1980s, *Fortune* has published an annual listing of the "most admired corporations"—those businesses with the best reputations for quality of management, products, and services; long-term investments; use of corporate assets; innovation; community spirit; and ability to attract, develop, and keep talented people. The latter is especially relevant here, but together the criteria make for profitable businesses. A review of the list in the 1996 report shows a correlation between exceptional places to work (which assumes low turnover) and bottom-line performance. These best places to work showed up at or near the top of their industry's performance ranking. Further, an earlier report in the same magazine found a positive correlation between the best employers to work for and market value added (MVA) or stock growth over company lifetime and economic value added (EVA), a company's after-tax net operating profit minus cost of capital. The study by Stern Stewart & Company found 8 of the top 10 companies in terms of MVA also appeared among the 100 best employers to work for. More interesting, those with less-than-stellar reputations as employers wound up near the bottom of the MVA/EVA rankings. The 1998 *Fortune* study found five-year annual returns of 27.5 percent versus 17.3 percent for others in the Russell 3,000 listing.

This isn't a phenomenon evident only in larger companies. "Delivering on the Promise," by Friedman, Hatch & Walker, studied the five-year survival rate of IPOs and found higher rates among companies that cited employees as a key competitive edge and could point to high self-assessments on relations with employees.[2] An Ernst & Young study on IPOs showed similarly that the most successful IPOs raised the bar on retaining their employees after they became public.[3]

Studies consistently show a relationship between employee satisfaction and the corporate bottom line. In the October 13, 1997, issue of *Fortune,* in reporting on the reorganization of Sears, author Sherman Stratford notes that Sears has found that although financial figures can report the existence of a problem, employee attitudinal studies can predict future performance problems.[4] (A *Harvard Business Review* article contained similar details.)[5]

A more comprehensive study of over three thousand companies correlates employee loyalty with shareholder value. This work, conducted by Mark Huselid, found that those businesses with programs on employee motivation had higher stock price to book value ratios than other companies. Some programs showed a $41,000 increase in market value per employee. Those businesses that went a little extra mile for their employees experienced even more return; one standard deviation increase, for instance, equaled a 7 percent decrease in turnover.[6]

Hewitt Associates pursued similar objectives as Huselid and looked at 437 public companies divided into one group (of 232) with no formal performance management and one group (of 205) that did. The differences were "remarkable" in outcome (e.g., the latter group outperformed the former on total return, return on equity [ROE], return on assets [ROA], sales per employee, etc.). The conclusion: "Put simply, they were able to do more with the same number of employees."[7]

This study went even further to show that performance managing companies did better after implementation of those policies and found "a strong association with wealth creation by companies after implementing performance management versus companies in their industries that did not."[8]

Comprehensive review work by Jeffrey Pfeffer led to him concluding that "in three-fourths of the cases, significant increases in economic performance were observed" as a result of organization change.[9]

Ernst & Young has discovered that investors do care—which should predict even greater attention to employees in the future. The ability to attract and retain the very best people is one of eight measures that really matter to investors when valuing companies.[10]

Employee loyalty is important, and the spotlight on it is growing. At the same time, engineering retention—much less loyalty—is harder and harder.

First, recent statistics from the U.S. Department of Labor show a flat unemployment rate and a decline in new entrants into the workforce. For example, in June 1999, the Bureau of Labor Statistics reported unemployment at 4.3 percent, essentially unchanged since November 1998. Further, new entrants to the labor force actually declined. So we have a very tight labor marketplace, with demand on the increase and supply flat.

Second, as companies shift from being productcentric to a service orientation, there is more demand for customer-serving employees. June 1999 labor statistics showed growth widespread in the service-producing sector. Employment grew by 151,000 jobs in June, well above the average monthly gain for the previous 12 months.

Likewise, as the workplace grows more and more technologically driven, the difficulty in locating and retaining information technology (IT) employees will become more severe. In June, 15,000 jobs were added in computer services.

The people most critical to competitive advantage in the future (e.g., those with technological literacy and multicultural fluency, with the willingness to be empowered and to work in increasingly delayered organizations) will be difficult to find and even harder to retain, given the shift in employees' attitude in general toward commitment to their employer. Employees have learned from the sports arena and entertainment field that they can make more money if they sell their services to the highest bidder. If the dot-com IPOs continue to flourish, the temptation to join start-ups will be ever more attractive.

At the same time, limited commitment to any single company may also be a residue of bitterness based on treatment in the past from firms going through the trauma of downsizing or reorganization. As one current book notes: "A survey of 12,000 managers worldwide found a sharp decline in loyalty and commitment to employers from early 1980 to the mid-90's. Interestingly, the respondents were more satisfied with their work than with their employer. While about two-thirds of employees in another national survey were satisfied with their jobs, 60% reported that they were less committed to their organization than they had been 10 years earlier."[11]

■ "IT'S JUST A MATTER OF SOUND BUSINESS"

These downsizing companies told the laid-off and the survivors alike, "It's just a matter of sound business." Given the job market, talented employees now can be more assertive and more mobile and can say in turn to their employers, "You're right—it's just good business sense to take my talents elsewhere." A survey of working Americans conducted by Wirthlin Worldwide concluded that "corporate downsizing, whether due to a merger or some other form of restructuring, appears to have a dramatic negative effect on employee perceptions of both their jobs and the companies they work for."[12]

According to the study "Americans on the Job: Rebuilding the Employer/Employee Relationship," the impact of downsizing would definitely seem to be eroding employee morale. The American Management Association regularly surveys businesses in this topic, and the 1994 study, for example, showed that by managers' own evaluations, 86 percent reported a decline in morale (and only barely half reported on increase in profits from the action).[13] Many subsequent studies have reinforced these findings.

➤ Steps in the Right Direction

Companies have begun to put an end to the ongoing jettisoning of employees, either from poor fit within the job or organization or dissatisfaction with their organization and marketability elsewhere. Avis Rent-a-Car has developed a composite profile for its top salespeople. Says Ted Heller, a vice president at Avis, "The make-or-break quality is the ability to listen closely enough. While salespeople have been glibly described as having golden tongues, I honestly feel that the very best salespeople have golden ears. What we need to know is whether an applicant is empathic enough to be able to truly listen and understand where our prospects are coming from." Truett Cathy, founder of Chick-Fil-A, observes that he doesn't approve a potential store manager unless he wants him "to be with us until one of us dies or retires." Brokerage firm A.G. Edwards screens job candidates for those who share the firm's philosophy that the broker's role is "to act as an agent for the customer." Further, A.G. Edwards does not allow market pressures to force it to recruit beyond what it can possibly assimilate. The firm hires at a relatively steady pace and maintains a fairly stable workforce during market ups and downs compared with its competitors that hire far more individuals in boom times than they can assimilate and then do no hiring or cut back during bust times. The firm does no national recruiting advertising, preferring referrals.

Another example: Eighty percent of State Farm's insurance agents stay four years or more, compared with the industry average of 20 or 40 percent of new agents. Frederick F. Reichheld, author of *The Loyalty Effect,* notes that "new agents are hired with the same care that one might use in choosing a spouse." This is evident in the result—the average State Farm agent remains from 15 to 20 years with the firm. The business is expected to go further, requiring agent candidates to serve 2 to 3 years in employee positions before being eligible as agents, thus making the process more like that used for selecting partners in a law firm than hiring salespeople. New agents will know the business fully, and the company will know its agents better as well.[14]

But too many organizations still believe, as Peter Drucker observed in the *Harvard Business Review,* that "people still need us more than we need them." Drucker continued: "In fact, organizations have to market membership as much as they market products and services—and perhaps more." Drucker's use of the work *market* may have been a matter of wordsmithing, but there is no doubt in the minds of the authors of this book that part of the answer resides in marketing to attract and retain valuable employees—including use of marketing research to determine how to attract, satisfy, recognize, and retain employees.[15]

As we noted in Chapter 4, management consultants took the lead in demonstrating the competitive advantage stemming from customer satisfaction and loyalty, with researchers following along to only execute the basics. On the employee front, researchers could provide leadership for management if they grasp the opportunity. For management not to use research tools to help find and keep the talent they need for now and the future would be a costly mistake.

➤ The Losses from High Turnover

As always, the easiest way to get attention is to highlight the bottom line. In this instance, there are costs to consider if marketing research isn't undertaken to identify the drivers for employee satisfaction and thereby more effective and efficient employee recruitment, loyalty, and retention.

First, the amount of spending on recruiting talent is large for virtually all businesses—and not only in terms of out-of-pocket costs but also counting the time spent by current employees, often including senior-line executives, which can be considerable, given difficulties in locating and interning suitable candidates. Often the net is quite wide, with literally tens of people being interviewed per position. For some companies, the cost includes expenses for additional perks and bonuses to lure high-talent employees. Actual costs can be analyzed on a per hire basis as well as shown—typically—as a growing aggregate expense (e.g., training, office equipment, mentoring, etc.). Each year that an employee remains entails other such costs that could be wasted if the person leaves.

The next part of the analysis is to quantify the costs of unwanted attrition. When a valued employee leaves, in addition to the loss of past investment, there are direct exit costs (e.g., exit interviews, farewell party, etc.) and often disruption costs—which are higher if a job is not performed at all for awhile. Then there are the replacement costs (the additional per person hire and acclimation costs and the annual costs of that person to become as proficient as the employee who left). This figure can be high, at least 150 percent of the salary of an outgoing employee if you include the loss of knowledge, contacts, and leads of the defector; the new employee's depressed productivity while learning; and the time co-workers spend guiding him or her. What could also be estimated are the costs of having a less proficient employee than the one who left. Finally, there can be ripple-effect costs in terms of potentially lower morale or even additional loss of valued employees (often people who reported to an earlier departee).

The costs don't end there, either. The true wealth of companies is their intellectual capital, and each departing employee takes a portion of the firm's collective knowledge and experience when he or she moves on. Enlightened companies have been busily identifying ways of capturing that knowledge—in some instances, recreating past triumphs by having the original participants develop histories of the events, and in other instances, creating computer databases that store best practices across divisions—but none of these systems compares with a long-term corporate veteran who has insights from personal experience and is readily available for questioning. Intellectual capital and good will account for up to 90 percent of a business's profitability potential, according to Carla S. O'Dell and C. Jackson Grayson, Jr., president and former chairman, respectively, of the American Productivity and Quality Center. In their book *If Only We Knew What We Know,* they cite these examples of employee knowledge put to use:

➤ Skandia leveraged internal know-how to dramatically reduce startup for new ventures to seven months compared with the seven-*year* industry average.

➤ A Chevron team saved at least $20 million a year by adopting practices already being used in their best-managed fields.

➤ At Dow Chemical, early efforts to manage intellectual capital brought an immediate return in the form of $440 million in savings. Study of existing patents determined which technology streams were strongest and which were weakest, thereby setting the stage for more effective negotiations with venture partners.

➤ Texas Instruments president and CEO, Tom Engibous, with a group of plant managers and teams, identified best practices among its 13 fabrication plants that, utilized throughout the organization, avoided the expenditure of $500 million investment yet provided needed capacity to customers.[16]

High turnover can also mean transfer of employee knowledge to competitors, thereby giving them a market advantage. But there is an even greater problem due to employee dissatisfaction, one that can seriously affect corporate profitability.

■ THE CUSTOMER CONNECTION

Further economic linkage comes by the connection—mentioned earlier—that valued employees' loyalty enhances valued customer loyalty.

Studies have found a strong correlation between employee attitudes about their jobs and their behaviors with customers that can influence, in turn, the likelihood of customer retention and, more pervasive yet, customer comments about a product or service to others, two factors that influence corporate bottom-line performance. Customers who feel they were poorly treated by someone within an organization will tell numerous people—relatives, friends, and neighbors—about the experience. Each of these individuals, in turn, will tell others what the unhappy or dissatisfied customer told them. Consequently, by some estimates, just one unpleasant contact between a dissatisfied member of your business and one of your customers can be reported to over one hundred prospective customers, influencing their feelings about your company and the people in it. This phenomenon was summed up by the firm William M. Mercer, Inc., following a survey of senior human resources (HR) executives in large enterprises. It reported that "more than half of study participants see poor customer service as a consequence of attraction and retention problems. This translates into costs . . . as well as losing customers altogether."[17]

Although the linkage between these two factors is logical, little attention has been given to this relationship. But Mercer Management Consulting is now developing data across industries that builds the case that there are interactions between the two, at least in several industries for the most important customer segments (typically high end). The clearest interaction is not in poor employee performance but in the loss of a valued employee. For example, most dramatically, in the gaming industry, when a host casino for high rollers changes casinos, many of the high rollers move, too. In Mercer Management Consulting's work with a global bank, a similar impact was noted if key customer service people left. The reality is that customer loyalty is often dependent on a specific relationship or relationships with contact employees. The Deloitte & Touche study cited earlier concludes: "Our research shows that employee loyalty is the cornerstone for building customer loyalty in the global manufacturing sector." Thus, the cost of losing such an employee has to include the weakening, if not loss, of key customers as well.[18]

This effect occurs even at lower-value customer segments. In telecommunications retention efforts, using the same employee to follow up contacts from a call center has a positive multiplier on customer retention and even on cross-selling efforts. Similarly, analysis of bank branches has shown that when the employees believe that the branch has an imperative to provide quality service, the customers of that branch, responding independently, report receiving higher levels of service.

A recent book by one of the leading authorities on service quality, Leonard Berry, set forth the summary of our point of view: "High employee turnover drives a stake in the heart of a company's relationship marketing efforts . . . service work is emotional labor."[19]

But the problem isn't solely one of employee job satisfaction and turnover's impact on customer relationship. As with other issues, the key is managerial attention and focus, and there is still too little recognition of the need to work on employee loyalty.

Companies can't and shouldn't take employee loyalty for granted, if only because of the costs. And consequently, even great companies lose people who accept offers to go elsewhere. We believe that marketing research can help here by answering major questions beyond how happy employees are (and even in this realm, HR often bypasses its own market research departments). Research can tell management what kinds of benefits packages will attract the most desirable prospective employees and how it should adapt corporate culture to retain top-flight talent. Research indicates that these workers migrate for other reasons than richer monetary rewards.

Admittedly, marketing research won't enable companies to renew the old social contracts, but it will give them insights to enable them to identify, communicate with, and retain committed employees so long as it is mutually profitable.

What can you do to prevent high turnover of critical employees within your organization and ameliorate performance problems attributable to poor recruitment or employee dissatisfaction? Marketing research, as observed, not only can identify the existence of a problem but can also guide senior management in its development of a solution. Just as marketing research's role extends to providing future direction so, too, can it help management select HR solutions and fine-tune their implementation. If marketing research calculations and analyses serve to get senior management's attention—even if they provide no guidance for the future other than helping to put the issue on the corporate agenda—it is still a contribution, but the tools researchers employ can provide a great deal more. For instance, earlier we mentioned a study conducted by Wirthlin Worldwide that showed dismal performance ratings for management. On the other hand, that same study showed a means to recapture employee goodwill: 83 percent of those surveyed said telecommuting was a good thing for employers, 95 percent of those whose companies offered telecommuting options were positive about their employers, and 98 percent of those who telecommuted themselves gave high marks for working offsite. Thus, the study suggested not only an existing attitudinal problem but also a means of recouping employee support.[20]

You can take general steps to measure employee attitudes, and most large companies do—some but not all. Given the critical linkage of employees to customer loyalty, special steps need to be taken to ensure that the business has the right type of employees who are motivated to help the company help its best customers over the long term.

In essence, research can perform all of the tasks regarding employees that it does with customers. In fact, if you wanted to summarize our advice into one point here: Take all the tools, focus on the customer, and then apply them to employees. First, research can provide the solid base of information needed today. Employees can be segmented according to behaviors, attitudes, and demographics just as customers are. (This type of segmentation should provide much insight about appropriate internal communications strategies and tactics as it has for customers. Today there is typically only mass/broadcast internal communication as opposed to the customization required.) The lifetime value of employees (individually or by segment or even by entry class) should also be computed to highlight the economics involved.

Ongoing employee research, like that about customers, should be focused on learning the drivers of loyalty/retention of the most valuable employees. Won-loss analyses should supplement this work both in recruiting and for exits/lateral entries (i.e., key hires and those that the business can't attract or loses should be interviewed).

With this knowledge in hand, researching the future is just as appropriate for employees as for customers. Information acceleration can help the business understand how valued employees might prefer to be treated in a world of the future (e.g., videoconferencing with cameras built in to PCs/TVs at home, telecommuting, etc.). Conjoint techniques should provide guidance on benefits packaging.

The key techniques of lead user and Delphi are particularly appropriate. In fact, some companies use a form of lead-user research now by forming a committee of relatively young managers to advise (or at least meet regularly with) the CEO. This is a great practice that should be expanded to more rigorously study how these future leaders think and feel about the issues. These lead users should also be exposed to ideas that other companies are trying and could well be a group to build the HR scenarios the business might use to think about the future.

A talent-focused Delphi panel could include some of the lead-user employees as well as senior HR and marketing executives. (This is a good way to force teaming between the people in these disciplines.)

A broader approach could more directly connect thinking for the future, involving both customers and employees and how they intertwine and interact. (Key line employees and customers could both serve on the panel—another best practice.)

■ THE ROLES OF HUMAN RESOURCES AND MARKETING RESEARCH

Of course, marketing research on employee recruitment, satisfaction, and loyalty demands a new mind-set about the roles of not only marketing research but also (and interestingly) human resources. Marketing research is traditionally seen as a tool for looking outward and conducting external scans and is ignored for the role it could play in internal issues. The HR department is stereotyped, too. It's too often seen as being made up of technicians whose role is to manage payroll and benefits, with the sideline chore of setting policies and procedures to avoid legal minefields. As David Ulrich and others have written, HR professionals can and should do much more. Together, HR and marketing research could develop a "talent for the future" agenda and then work on internal communications, retention programs, and training. Such a team effort should be fact based to the greatest extent possible. The key ingredients are to learn about what makes a valuable employee, focusing on the most important attributes for effective recruitment and on the factors that can create and maintain loyalty among these valuable employees and then develop accurate measures of employee performance as well as effective techniques for communicating with these talented workers and retaining those who remain valuable contributors. At the same time, there must be an ongoing effort to understand potential or emerging trends that will impact talent over both the short and long terms.

Although the work should ultimately extend to virtually all types of employees, it is wise to start with those who are now most influential to the company's success. Most often this philosophy will lead to a focus on two areas—leaders-to-be (i.e., high-potential executives) and successful customer contact people (sales or service).

Once the type of positions are selected, a two-prong analysis is needed to determine the profile of the desired employee. On one level, this entails the traditional research tasks of high-level interviewing. In companies with sophisticated HR and multiple levels of measurement and reviews, there will be a wealth of quantitative data once the analysis isolates the model (e.g., the current and past employees at the level in question who are the role models for the future). In the absence of good historical data, the analytic team must conduct a current-state evaluation to determine which traits are most important. The backgrounds of these models (including how they were hired and their path within the company) can then be assessed to lead to a profile of how to hire, acclimate, and manage what types of people.

At the same time, the team has to look to the future. Parallel to how the business itself is assessed, the team must develop scenarios that could impact on the employee environment in terms of whether the profile might have to change to be sensitive to developments that could occur. To the extent that the valuable customer profile is viewed as likely to change, this team must look at the implications, if any, for differing requirements of employees to serve these new types of customers well. The lead-user concept can also be used in the employee environment by identifying valued employees who seem to be in the vanguard of change, representative in some way of a different type of employee. By focusing on this group (and perhaps actively and openly engaging them in the profiling effort), a perspective can be assimilated that often offers real insight.

In general, potential changes in employees' profiles are not as dramatic as those anticipated in business design and even customer mix. Typically, the qualities that lead to successful employees (including leaders) today are pretty close to what will be needed tomorrow. Training and specific skills (e.g., computer literacy) change faster than the underlying qualities that a company should seek and reward.

Change is likely to be needed sooner in the processes by which companies recruit, acclimate, and try to retain valued employees. Analysis along the lines detailed previously allows the team to use research and statistical tools to delineate which hiring techniques have the richest yield for retaining valued employees. There can be similar learnings about initiation, career development, and so on.

A second likely area of change is the expansion of business use of the Internet. Every business has to assess the impact and try to understand this issue's implications regarding employees of the future.

In addition to straight statistics, the prescription for the future should rely on exit interviews of valued employees, benchmarking, best practice reviews of companies that have relevant lessons for the company being analyzed, and structured brainstorming.

The desired result is not a rigid prescription but rather one or two or even three new designs for hiring, career development, training, and so on, all aimed at hiring for the long term. Just as companies should test ideas to improve customer retention, so, too, should they assess improvements designed for the employee side. (The best practice is to do these simultaneously because there is the inevitable and important connection between many types of employees and customers.) Ideas that don't work should be amended and dropped; those that seem to work should be kept and improved. Although the test period is relatively long (i.e., improving long-term employee retention takes decades to definitely prove out), the ongoing monitoring provides the opportunity to continually learn. To the extent that the team follows the precepts of good research and good analysis, hypotheses will be fully documented to provide optimal learning and adjustment over the years. This is especially important with regard to the growing role for the Internet.

The most impactful measures to monitor will be actual retention of valued employees and, if relevant, retention of valuable customers by these employees as well as indicators or predictors of this (e.g., employee satisfaction and other items shown to predict retention in the earlier analyses).

It is also worth noting again that one key lever to valuable employee retention is internal communication. Most companies communicate by rote. Millions are spent on careful crafting of messages to customers and targets through advertising and other expensive marketing tactics. Employee communication is often the province of a few junior public relations (PR) or HR types. Contrast the salaries of the most senior people in marketing with full-time external communication responsibilities to those whose entire job is internal communication. If employee retention is growing in importance and impact, hiring more expert communicators will give companies a head start here.

As an extension of this argument, businesses carefully segment the market and test the impact of each major campaign. With employees, businesses basically push out information and almost never measure the impact. With the advent of Intranets and telecommuting, the opportunity for better communication is both necessary and more difficult. Hiring top-notch communicators for internal purposes is clearly needed.

Any effort to focus on communication to decrease employee turnover and increase employee loyalty must begin with some foundation—that is, management focus. Other lessons have been learned in what are still the early stages of trying to improve employee loyalty. Here are a few:

> Offer varied and interesting assignments. Above-average employees want more than mundane assignments; they want challenge, or they will become restless.

> Provide opportunities for increased employability. Top employees want to get better at the jobs they do. They want to learn and master new skills, for they recognize the worth of continuous skill improvement as a means of earning more money.

> Demonstrate appreciation with more than just money. Top performers are fully aware of their contribution to the organization. They expect their managers to acknowledge this. If they feel undervalued or unappreciated, they won't stick around for long. As with customers, retention requires attention to both the left brain (rational features such as compensation) and the right brain (feeling good about it).

> Set high but achievable standards. Peak performers need to excel. They have a low tolerance for mediocrity and become impatient with low expectations and sloppy work.

> Ensure that top talent performs beside superior co-workers. Winners like to associate with other winners. If a workforce is generally mediocre, it's unlikely to improve, for better workers don't stick around much.

> Provide outstanding supervision. Strong supervisors attract strong workers. Weak supervisors drive them

away. Top-flight employees appreciate the value of effective leaders and want to work for them. Prized employees respond positively to good supervision.

➤ Promote from within. It's a powerful motivator.

➤ Listen. Really hear and act on worthwhile suggestions. Allow workers to participate in making decisions that directly affect them and their work.

➤ Engender and deserve trust.

➤ Be open, honest, and upfront. Keep employees informed. Let them know what's going on and what's coming up.

➤ Demonstrate absolute integrity and unflinching fairness. Maintain your credibility. In essence, don't just say that your employees are your company's most important asset. Treat them as if they really are, which means telling them how they are doing. Be their mentors. Your employees are as important to your bottom line as your customers. Treat them the way you treat your customers.

This means not only communicating with employees but customizing communications to various segments of the rank and file. The critical segments of your workforce should not only be kept in the loop but must also get targeted communication, as would selected customers, to ensure they are familiar with strategic developments that impact their work. Yes, like all your employees, your top talent wants to know about developments that impact their work. Yes, like all your employees, your top talent wants to know about developments in the organization as a whole—new products, services, territories, delivery systems, philosophies, structures, and corporate events—but these key people also want communications that clearly define the role they will play in these developments. Their information needs can be defined from marketing research as can the means by which the communications should be delivered (and the effectiveness of communication so that changes can be made if needed).

The attention that has been focused on customers will now have to be focused also on employees. All the games and tactics from one arena will need to be moved to this arena as well. And, for once, research could be a leader rather than an afterthought.

A final point on communication: The advent of Intranets affords an enabling technology to dramatically improve segmented internal communications.

■ IDEAS FOR RECRUITMENT AND RETENTION

There are companies that, based on research or not, are starting innovative programs to retain those they value most.

Many employers are offering nontraditional benefits to attract new recruits during the tightest labor market in U.S. history. To improve their recruitment and retention efforts, companies are offering training and career development opportunities—offering increased employability as a value for staying on—as well as other alternative benefits as incentives. For years, consulting firms have attracted college graduates by offering loans if they want to go to business school. Now, to combat the appeal of Internet start-ups, these firms are promising equity opportunities with clients and/or seed money to fund the young consultants' own ideas.

Still another approach: Companies conduct vulnerability assessments of their top-flight personnel that look at the risks the key employees are exposed to on a daily basis. This measure ensures that the firm isn't surprised by the sudden departure of one of its most valued workers. It also provides management with data it needs to make hard decisions in what has come to be called the "talent war."

Further, there are management trends such as:

➤ *Creation of autonomous work units.* These independent suborganizations will create greater opportunities for bonding and teamwork, which tend to hold people together. Workers stay with smaller business teams because they feel more a part of what's happening and they see that their work makes a significant difference.

➤ *Relocation of facilities.* Companies are setting up telecommuting programs for those who want to work at home, but they are also moving their facilities to more convenient locations in the suburbs and exurbs to enhance the quality of life for employees. These new locations also will be smaller, enabling employees to enjoy these compact work units and enhanced relationships among colleagues, which are intended to build a long-term commitment.

➤ *Outsourcing.* Companies will outsource, but the intention is to build long-term loyalty relationships between on-site employees and outsourced contracts. Strategic alliances will be built with a familial tightness, allowing people to leave the core to join outsourced contracts and vice versa. In fact, some experts predict dual-employment relationships.

➤ *Electronic commuting.* The number of people working from home, a remote location, or even at several offices will rise dramatically. This no-limits, locational freedom will enhance the flexibility benefit for workers and employers alike.

■ THE LOYALTY INITIATIVE

How can your business start to develop the programs you need?

In Chapter 5, we showed a model to improve customer loyalty. A parallel model can be used to build employee loyalty based on three principles formed from lessons about what works for companies that have been successful in developing long-term employee relationships.

1. *Focus on specific segments.* Too often when companies decide to combat turnover, they implement a policy or program that applies across the board. Such responses typically are a waste of money because even if they are motivating to some, they are available for everyone, including mediocre performers who have little impact on corporate performance.

2. *Emphasize building loyalty, not reducing churn or turnover.* The goal is to find out what works in keeping valued employees—not stopgap measures to save employees who might be about to leave. For example, spending to (publicly) reward key employees at 5-, 10-, 15-, and 20-year anniversaries—with the value of the reward depending on their value (as with customer rewards)—has a better yield than last-minute bribes, which rarely keep employees anyway and diminish respect for the business (because it wasn't offered in due course). Typically, building loyalty entails a solid mentoring system in addition to many of the lessons listed previously.

3. *Systematically prioritize efforts based on ROI.* As strong as initiatives may be initially, most programs wear out, and motivational factors change over time. Continuing success at loyalty requires continuous assessment and a willingness to adapt as needed.

Once the direction is set, the means to develop an effective process can begin. The typical steps of the work are displayed in Figure 8.2, which naturally mirrors the process to engender loyalty among valuable customers.

Because beginning a journey is often the hardest part, we might elaborate on the diagnostic phase. The initial activities are designed to ensure that the effort capitalizes on what is already known. Usually, companies have a great deal of knowledge about the issues at hand, but rarely is it codified in a useful way. Thus, the first step is to vacuum up relevant data and information and then interview managers of all key functions about their experience and hypotheses and about any data they (or their reports) have accumulated—be it surveys, spreadsheets, or the like.

The emphasis is to define the key attributes of the kind(s) of customer(s) and employee(s) that the business

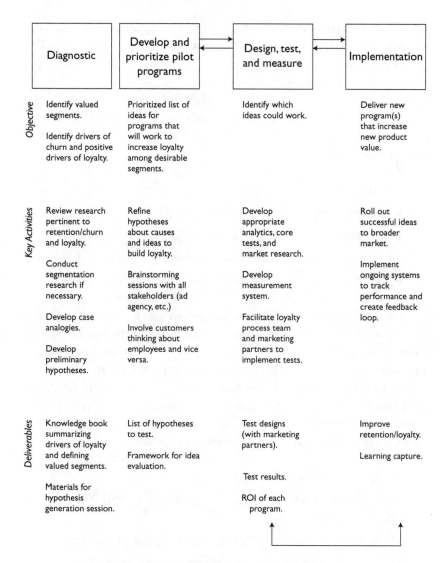

Figure 8.2 Loyalty Program Process.

Source: Rob Duboff and Carla Heaton, "Employee Loyalty: A Key Link to Value Growth," *Strategy & Leadership* (January/February 1998): 8–13.

wants to retain over the long term. Then, among these segments, the drivers of loyalty must be determined. Finally, the critical incidents—the key encounters between customers and employees, the "moments of mutual truth"—must be uncovered so that ultimately the business can prioritize, train, and monitor the growth of loyalty at the component part level. Examples of these impactful, mutual moments include:

➤ Checking in at a hotel.

➤ A ticketing problem at the airport.

➤ Waiting in line at a theme park.

➤ Signing up for a new communications service.

➤ Any service or product malfunction.

Each of these encounters has an impact on both the customer and the employee. The impact is heightened proportionately by the number of people in queue, the time of day, and the degree to which the customer feels important.

Critical incidents that relate only to the employee must be identified so that ultimately the business can prioritize, train, and then monitor the growth of loyalty at the component part level. Examples of these include:

➤ Orientation on entry.

➤ Perception of fairness in promotion and compensation decisions.

➤ Training opportunities to increase employability.

Each of these encounters has an impact on the employee. Understanding which moments have the most impact allows companies to focus their fire accordingly. If the drivers and the moments are not known and documented, then fresh research is needed.

Once the information is assimilated, it should be codified (on-line or in print) and organized in a useful way, capable of being updated in a knowledge-book format.

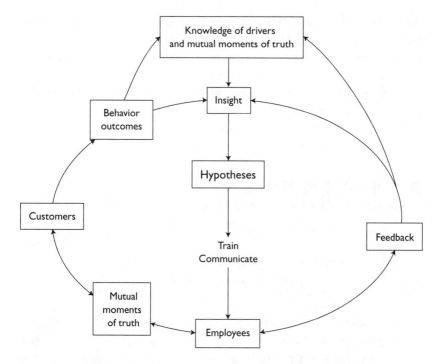

Figure 8.3 Improving Customer-Employee Loyalty.

Source: Rob Duboff and Carla Heaton, "Employee Loyalty: A Key Link to Value Growth," *Strategy & Leadership* (January/February 1998): 8–13.

These data, information, and executive interviews form a solid basis for hypothesis generation that fuels the remaining steps in the process, which essentially follow scientific precepts and a continuing interaction between the insight generating, communication to employees and customers and feedback loops (depicted in Figure 8.3).

Although learning the long-term impact obviously takes time, the key is to continually monitor results, learning what works and what doesn't. Such measurement must focus on the segments of concern, and the assessments must be both behavioral and attitudinal or emotional. The incremental competitive advantage awaits those who can do both.

Imagine what you could accomplish with the input of marketing research to help you develop a recruitment profile for high-performing employees, locate the most productive ways to recruit, identify best practices in human resources procedures, change your corporate culture to increase employee satisfaction, and develop ongoing communications efforts to sustain employee commitment and ensure employee loyalty—and along with it, customer retention and loyalty and corporate profitability.

■ EMPLOYEE PERFORMANCE AND LOYALTY DIAGNOSTIC

To measure the worth of efforts you are taking to secure and retain top talent in key areas of your business, ask yourself if you have fully utilized marketing research. Specifically:

➤ Are you as knowledgeable about your key employee segments as about your key customer segments? Are you using research tools to address employees to the extent you are for customers?

➤ Has marketing research helped your business identify and refine the profile of a valuable employee?

➤ Has marketing research identified and refined the factors that help create and maintain loyalty of these valuable employees?

➤ Has marketing research developed each of the appropriate tools to measure performance on these factors? Has marketing research identified any gaps and how to eliminate them?

➤ Has marketing research measured the effectiveness of communication to employees? Has marketing research identified any gaps and how to eliminate them?

➤ Does marketing research have an effective exit interview program and process in conjunction with HR?

➤ Has marketing research identified and refined the marketing and recruiting drivers that lead to effective recruitment?

➤ Is key competitors' experience in recruitment being tracked? Is the analysis pursued on a channel-by-channel basis?

➤ Has market research identified any gaps and how to eliminate them?

➤ Has marketing research identified potential or emerging trends that may impact potential recruits?

➤ Has marketing research identified and refined issues that may emerge and could impact the loyalty of valuable employees?

➤ Has market research started to address the impact of the Internet and Intranet technology on all the employee issues? Has a monitoring process been established?

◼ NOTES

1. *Fortune,* January 12, 1998.

2. Brian Friedman, James Hatch, and David Walker, *Delivering on the Promise: How to Attract, Manage and Retain Human Capital* (New York: The Free Press, 1998).

3. Jonathan Low and Anthony Siesfeld, "Measures That Matter," 1998, an Ernst & Young study.

4. *Fortune,* October 13, 1997.

5. Anthony Rucci, Steven Kim, and Richard Quinn, "The Employee-Customer Profit-Chain at Sears," *Harvard Business Review,* (January/February 1998): 82–88.

6. Mark Huselid, "The Impact of HR Management Practices on Turnover, Productivity and Corporate Financial Performance," *Academy of Management Journal,* Volume 38, No. 3, 1995, pp. 635–672.

7. Edward Gubman, *The Talent Solution* (New York: McGraw-Hill, 1998), 306–307.

8. Ibid., 308.

9. Jeffrey Pfeffer, *The Human Equation: Building Profit by Putting People First* (Cambridge, MA: HBS Press, 1990) 55, 177.

10. Jonathan Low and Anthony Siesfeld, "Measures That Matter."

11. Peter Cappelli, *The New Deal at Work* (Cambridge, MA: HBS Press, 1999).

12. "Downsizing: A Downer," *Forecast,* March 1999, p. 5.

13. American Management Association, *1994 AMA Survey on Downsizing Summary of Key Findings* (New York: AMA, 1994).

14. Frederick Reichheld, *The Loyalty Effect* (Cambridge, MA: HBS Press, 1996).

15. Peter Drucker, "Management and the World's Work," *Harvard Business Review* (September/October 1998): 65–76.

16. Carla S. O'Dell, Nilly Essaides, Nilly Ostro, and C. Jackson Grayson, *If Only We Knew What We Know* (New York: Free Press, 1998).

17. "Attraction and Retention. Some Employer Perspectives," William M. Mercer, internal document, April 1998.

18. *Financial Times,* July 9, 1999.

19. Leonard L. Berry, *Discovering the Soul of Service* (New York: Free Press, 1999).

20. Robert Duboff and Lori Underhill Sherer, "Customized Customer Loyalty," *Marketing Management* 6, no. 2 (summer 1997): 20.

*C*hapter

Researching the Future Internet

We do not see things as they are, we see things as we are.
—The Talmud

Death can come quickly to a market trader: It is difficult to recognize that you're in a crisis and react to it when your business appears extremely healthy.

—Bill Gates, more recently

The Internet is the greatest story yet of Strategic Anticipation®. Its promise still deals mostly with the future; businesses that now generate quarterly losses but enjoy remarkable market capitalization could only be about the future. Which future? Those who anticipate reasonably well will reap the benefits of value migration to the new wired world; those who don't will suffer legendary losses.

The Internet today still represents only a primitive precursor of something we have yet to experience. A wired world with very inexpensive, addressable, two-way communication serves only as the foundation. As the media, services, and other businesses build on that foundation, everything will change. Don't let this cause you paralytic anxiety. Rather, allow it to spur excited inquiry.

What will the Internet, its offspring, and the new markets they engender be like? Let's use the principles of Strategic Anticipation® to develop a reasonable vision of the Internet a few years ahead.

As we discussed in Chapter 1, to effectively map the future, we must consider four key elements: futures, customers, economics, and alignment. Our goal is not to predict but to identify potential opportunity.

■ FUTURES

Let's look beyond today's Internet capabilities and assess some broad trends that promise improved business and consumer benefits. Bandwidth, which for many years has been the greatest barrier to Internet development, is expanding. High-speed access via digital fiber-optic network or satellite, supported by advanced digital compression technology, will become commonplace. This much more vibrant technical palette will drive development of new jaw-dropping environments using enhanced multimedia such as three-dimensional and virtual reality simulation, full-motion video and animation, and stereo sound. These enhancements will bring to life the Internet's greatest capability: real-time communication and feedback. This individually targeted, high-impact, two-way communication medium resides in, or among, computers, neighboring those ever-growing consumer databases. We've already witnessed the first phase of the marriage between the Internet and consumer databases. Its offspring both delight and frighten the U.S. public. When Amazon.com greets you as an old friend and suggests books of interest, we are delighted. When we hear about volumes of varied personal data being accumulated and cross-referenced on each of us, delight turns to fright. And fright leads to public outcry! A closed-loop consumer information system could be a dream come true for marketers and researchers; but first we must use it to provide meaningful benefits to consumers while zealously guarding their privacy.

At the same time, advancements in television technology are running parallel to Internet development. TV screens have grown wider and thinner to the point that watching your favorite TV shows on a 57-inch wall screen is no longer the dream of futuristic novelists. High-definition digital television offers the choice of cinema-like pictures, endless channel capacity, or a little bit of both. Intelligent set-top boxes, or TV sets themselves, will deliver some of the capabilities associated with the Internet, but the integration of these next-generation TVs with the Internet itself may be the most awesome possibility of all.

■ CUSTOMERS

As Internet penetration expands worldwide, the on-line population will more closely mirror the general population. No longer a universe of nerds, these are your customers, wired and ready for contact! Although global reach ranks as one of the greatest opportunities of the Internet, development varies across regions. For example, Jupiter Communications forecasts 67.6 million households on-line in the United States by 2003, which translates into a 63.4 percent penetration rate. That's up from 44.9 million households, or 44 percent, in early 1999. For Europe, where the Internet gap with the United States is closing, Jupiter predicts 47.3 million households on-line in 2003. That's a penetration rate of slightly more than 30 percent, an increase of 14.1 percentage points for the same period (see Figure 9.1). Expect wide variations among European countries as well. Jupiter Communications predicts higher-than-average increases in Germany, the United Kingdom, and Scandinavian countries (see Figure 9.2).

These forecasts encompass Internet access from both traditional PC and nontraditional devices. Set-top television boxes, game-player consoles, enhanced telephones, and personal digital assistants (PDAs), in addition to inexpensive network computers designed for instant Internet access, are

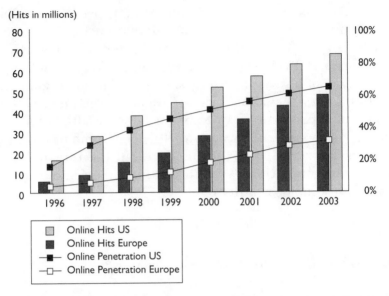

Figure 9.1 Comparison of On-line Hits and On-Line Penetration for both U.S. and European Households, 1996–2003.

Source: Reprinted with permission from Jupiter Communications. www.jup.com, July 1999.

creating a more diverse audience both in terms of age and household income demographics. Each may constitute very different consumer segments. How these technologies are applied will segment the market further, reflecting a great variety of needs and satisfactions. Wired versus wireless, full-featured computers versus specialized devices, entertainment versus information, business versus personal, access at home versus work—the variety will be kaleidoscopic. Some will succeed, but only some.

Consumers guard the gate. Which new services and delivery platforms will they buy? The more critical question may be, Which ones will be loved enough to be purchased at high margin? It's impossible to test consumer acceptance of goods and services that do not yet exist, but we can reasonably anticipate what will differentiate winners from losers. Market research can help us understand what drives consumer

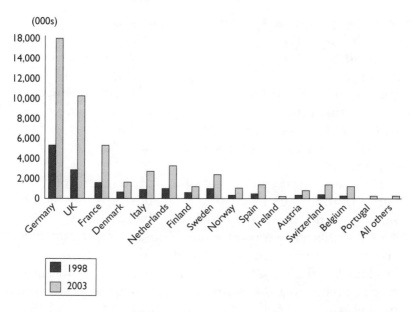

Figure 9.2 On-line Households in Europe, 1998 and 2003.

Source: Reprinted with permission from Jupiter Communications.
www.jup.com, July 1999.

purchases and usage behavior toward today's products and services. Let's look at three types of drivers: cost of entry, relevant differentiators, and unmet needs. *Cost of entry* refers to attributes that are simply required. Food must taste good; toys must be safe. Although a product or service receives no extra credit for these, it cannot succeed in business without them. *Relevant differentiators* are attributes linked to buyer values that set your product apart from others in ways that are meaningful enough for consumers to select yours over others, even at a higher price. *Unmet needs* are those attributes consumers wish (consciously or not) that the available brands offered but don't. They could become relevant differentiators for a new brand or the basis of an entirely new product or service.

As prospective e-businesses plan for the future—or as off-line businesses assess on-line options—they need to ask themselves key questions: What business do we want to be

in? Whose business do we have to take and expand to succeed? The next step is to question current and potential consumers of those businesses: What drives you to your current
brand(s)? What's missing that we can offer and that would
make enough of a difference for you to switch? Although we
can't test the future, we can develop a deep understanding of
the driving forces underlying the present market configura-
tion to reasonably anticipate the future. Market research
holds the gatekeeper's key.

Two examples come immediately to mind. One of the relevant differentiators in the brokerage business has been discounting. The market historically has been segmented
between full-service and discount brokers. On-line brokers
like E*Trade recognized that driver and ran with it, bypass-
ing traditional discount brokers. Recognizing the significance of this Strategic Anticipation®, Schwab quickly followed
suit. On-line brokers still need to meet the cost of entry
requirements, such as the certainty that your trade will be
executed promptly and accurately. As these businesses
evolve and grow, the search continues to identify unmet
needs that can be serviced interactively. Studying lead users
would be an excellent way to identify these needs. Those that
find them first, execute well, and communicate boldly can
expect to segment the market further, winning the most
profitable customers as the value migrates with them.

Book retailing provides the second example. Brick-and-
mortar booksellers had segmented into the small mall shops,
such as B. Dalton, which carries limited but popular titles,
while larger Borders and Barnes & Noble stores offer wider
selection with a reader-friendly atmosphere. Selection is a
relevant differentiator that can be totally fulfilled on-line.
Amazon.com did just that.

■ ECONOMICS

On-line commerce will continue to fuel Internet expansion.
E-commerce sales may have been as high as $8 billion for

1998, and some forecasts predict up to $1 trillion in Internet sales by 2003. The marketplace has spoken, erasing any prior fears that consumers would shun on-line credit card transactions. The more businesses use the Internet and World Wide Web to market and sell products, the more consumers take advantage of it. Recent studies estimate that 60 percent of the Internet user population now shops on-line. At the same time, an even greater population exists for infomercial, home shopping, and catalog purchasing, and they are waiting for a good enough reason to move on-line.

Many companies now are investing to build an on-line consumer franchise that will enable them to reap the benefits of this soon-to-be megaharvest. Businesses that barely existed a decade ago, such as Amazon.com, eBay, Yahoo!, and E*Trade are now major brands and almost household names. America Online, once considered the archrival to the Internet, has surfed its way to success. Microsoft, for example, generated 133.4 million banner ad impressions the week ending July 18, 1999, and reached 29.5 percent of home Internet users, according to the Nielsen/NetRatings. Amazon.com was second, with 69.8 million impressions reaching 23.8 percent of home Internet users in the same week. Once these penetration figures are multiplied by a much larger on-line population base and each household increases its on-line purchase rate, the economies of scale will be staggering.

Market research can measure the size of these audiences, but more importantly it can help us understand their characteristics and dynamics. Is your site attracting the types of visitors that will help you meet your business objectives? What aspects or features of your site attract them? What's your repeat visit rate, your average visit duration, and your total reach of your target group in a month? On-line ratings services can answer these questions for you, but your insightful analysis of their answers can guide you to a strategy that builds and retains the right consumer franchise on which to build a growing, profitable e-business.

E-commerce may have stolen the show for now, but on-line advertising revenues continue to grow, reaching $2 billion for 1998. Many businesses deliver superior customer service on-line, globally, 24/7, at a fraction of the cost of a telephone center. A few have begun to address the real opportunity of relationship marketing. Rising postal, paper, and labor costs created a barrier to ongoing dialogue between brands and their consumers. The Internet, therefore, offers a far superior and affordable communication channel. Not every business can sell directly on-line, but every business must bond with its most profitable consumers.

Even though Ernst & Young believes that ultimately the most value will be derived from economic transfers (business-to-business) on-line, customer interfaces (be it advertising, information, or transactions) will likely all be powerful forces on-line, and quite possibly the on-line impact will overshadow the off-line arena for all three soon. So research will be used here to address many of the same issues that face e-commerce, with an important addition—determining the effectiveness of your marketing communications. Traditional research tools of copy testing and tracking already have migrated to the Web and closely mimic their traditional counterparts. This creates a bridge between old and new media. But the Web offers something more—the passive monitoring of actual behavior after exposure. If you want your advertising to influence consumers' actions on-line, you can monitor the outcome by setting a cookie on the browser. Public attitudes toward cookies are changing. Not long ago they were feared as agents of Big Brother, surreptitiously snooping on your every move. Today, many users recognize them for what they are—agents of convenience. Nevertheless, it is essential that researchers ensure the privacy of their respondents. This trust cannot be broken.

■ ALIGNMENT

Right now there's a 50 percent chance that your business has a Web site. Many are either conducting on-line transactions now or are working towards that goal. Commerce is a key unifying force for Web-related business development.

Although large companies paved the way for on-line commerce, small businesses are entering the marketplace at an amazing rate. A 1999 study by IDC, a Framingham, Massachusetts–based market research firm, reported that 1.2 million small businesses with fewer than one hundred employees had Web pages at the end of 1998, more than double the number of pages in 1997. And the number of small businesses is expected to double once again—to 2.1 million on-line—by the turn of the century. The once-in-a-lifetime opportunity to unseat an industry leader—the David versus Goliath factor—is a powerful magnet. Yahoo!, Amazon.com, and E*Trade, among others, have overtaken established rivals. Who's next?

■ A NEW VISION

So what can we extrapolate from these four elements? We could foresee a marriage between television and the Internet, one that creates a powerful platform for exposure and transactions. The Internet we're likely to be using in the near future will probably resemble—or even be a part of—your television set. The Internet, in turn, will become a conduit into the home and provide a level of consumer convenience well beyond anything we see today as more and more consumers embrace TV-based shopping. But this is just one scenario!

As we strategically anticipate the future of marketing in the next generation of the Internet, we foresee a large number of scenarios. But first we should note that there might be more to this medium than consumer marketing. The future of television transmission, telephony, radio, and other media may all lie with the Internet. Business-to-business applications on-line are already huge. These need to be considered as potential resource competitors or resource underwriters. For simplicity, for now we will limit our scope to consumer marketing (but the same logic can obtain for business marketing as well).

We can anticipate at least four delivery platforms—television, the PC, the PDA, and the protean potential of smart household appliances. It's easy to anticipate entertainment appearing on television, information on PCs, brief reminders on PDAs, and appliances diagnosing and repairing themselves as they phone into technical support. Platforms and applications actually may cross in ways we cannot begin to imagine. Consider just six potential applications: entertainment, information, communication, transactions, notification, and activation. Now cross them with the four delivery platforms. Will we see entertainment on television, PCs, PDAs, or appliances? Just imagine! The first two already exist. Games on PDAs seem likely. The *Today Show* on your toaster? Unlikely. But let's play the game out to consider the 24 possible combinations of platforms and applications; how many are likely, and which will be big businesses? But wait, there's more! Don't forget the consumers; how many different types might there be? We can count on at least nine likely segments—couch potatoes, surfers, chatters, e-mailers, researchers, need-to-know-nows, recreational shoppers, smart shoppers, and computer geeks. Multiplying segments by applications and platforms yields well over two hundred possible new businesses. The Internet offers an outstanding playing field for Strategic Anticipation®!

■ RESEARCHING THE FUTURE

The Internet provides unique capabilities for Strategic Anticipation®. Panels, for example, are very efficiently constructed on-line. A group of experts from around the world can readily collaborate on scenarios using bulletin boards, chat, or simple e-mail. Delphi on-line may transmute into a substantially superior technique. Those most engaged could rapidly trade ideas, providing enhanced perspective for those less involved. The Internet is a natural setting for Delphi; it began as a means for scientists around the world to communicate with each other toward a similar end.

Lead-user techniques have at least two Internet applications. Lead users can be both identified and recruited for panels on-line, which will facilitate their communication with the business. More importantly, it will enable structured or unstructured communication among themselves to accelerate the evolution of their usage. In this setting the lead user and expert panel look quite similar, while the options for information gathering become quite rich, including:

➤ Internet-based conferences.

➤ Chat-based on-line focus groups.

➤ E-mail query and response.

➤ E-mail- or Web-based surveys.

➤ Collaborative scenario building.

➤ Delphi.

With the Internet as a vehicle, we can expect significant reductions in cost, effort, and cycle time, which makes both Delphi and lead-user techniques much more useful tools for decision makers. We hope to see them applied more commonly, pointing the way to profitable new businesses.

■ RESEARCHING THE FUTURE OF THE INTERNET

Now let's turn the mirror on itself. Lead-user inquiry is an ideal instrument for understanding how use of the Internet may proceed. One telecommunications company is studying those customers who are already making the bulk of their long-distance calls via the Internet. Learning their reactions, motivations, and frustrations will enable this company to develop an offering to keep these heavy users in their customer base and their company in the long-distance business. History offers some harsh lessons. Telegraph companies weren't interested in the telephone, but their customers were! Long-distance companies can't ignore the Internet. Sprint and MCI already carry much of the Internet traffic. AT&T recently bet big on cable television—an even bigger pipeline into the home. Studying lead users could teach them how to capture even more of the value migration, be it through branded on-line service or bundling on-line, telephone, television, or in-home equipment or carriage. Most of the largest corporations in the United States are betting heavily on one or more of these scenarios. Their lead users can help them win.

■ THE FUTURE OF E-COMMERCE

Today's e-commerce businesses have several commonalties. Using the principles of Strategic Anticipation®, we should consider futures, consumers, economics, and alignment. Much of the near future's technology is already in hand; we just have to anticipate *how* it will be applied. Bandwidth will increase, and with it the visual appeal of Internet communications, providing far greater persuasive power than currently available. The types of products typically sold on-line today require no convincing—computers, books, CDs, and even drugs and nutritional supplements can be purchased by title or model number. Selling automobiles may prove more challenging.

The convergence of the Internet and the television heightens impulse buying. Think of a viewer clicking on an article of clothing or a piece of furniture featured in the entertainment program they are watching. The potential for music, videos, and books to be sold much like T-shirts at a concert is so obvious it's barely worth mentioning. Sponsorships may return in a big way, this time selling their licensed wares during the programming.

Highly (artificially) intelligent data mining of massive consumer databases may enable a specific product to be recommended to each shopper with complete confidence in their total satisfaction with it. Wasn't it those legendary liberal return policies that overcame consumer fear and skepticism to launch catalog shopping into mass success? Couldn't an equally powerful legend be constructed around smart shopping? "The computer picked out my new sofa, and it's perfect for me!"

The economics of e-commerce are simple. Substitute the cost of home delivery for the cost of retail distribution. It's a no-brainer for products with low delivery cost and high retail markups, especially those with tremendous variety for which the inventory costs of carrying a large selection become onerous—books, CDs, airline tickets, drugs, and the like. As more such products fill the home delivery pipeline, we might anticipate volume-driven home-delivery price reductions. These, in turn, will change the economics further, bringing more products into the e-commerce orbit. Where will this process end? That's a great question for a lead-user study—how far will they go?

The competitive economics of e-commerce paint a less rosy scenario. Neoclassical economic theory tells us that under perfect competition, prices are continually cut under marketplace pressure until profits are minimized. If the migration of retail business from brick-and-mortar to virtual stores represents the first phase of e-commerce, the fierce future of perfect on-line competition threatens to be the second phase. How might this unfold? How might it be averted? A Delphi study among on-line retail gurus might enable us to anticipate the moves of the game to find an outcome acceptable to all and a road that leads there.

Consumers, as always, hold the key. We may build it, but if they don't come, we have a disaster! What are the benefits that will move their business on-line? These will certainly vary by product category and consumer segment. Which segments in which categories will be large enough and profitable enough for investment? What benefits will be the price of entry, and which promise to provide a brand with the relevant differentiation required for exceptional profit margins? Studying today's lead users may offer some clues; following lead users over time, however, will prove very instructive. Commitment to continuous learning and business revisioning separates the profitable leaders from the struggling followers.

Aligning the processes that provide benefits to consumers and economic value to businesses is no different, in concept, on the Internet. The unconstrained possibilities are so huge, the capital requirements relatively cheap, and the maneuverability of a virtual business so great that failure seems almost impossible. This is a very dangerous illusion! More now than ever, a scenario-planning approach is essential. The maneuverability that makes you comfortable also provides stealth to your competitors—especially those whom you don't realize are already coming up behind you! Technological or economic foundations can vaporize overnight. You need to prepare for almost anything. Scenarios enable you to consider the possibilities and prepare for them in advance.

■ THE FUTURE OF MARKETING COMMUNICATION

Large investments are being made today, particularly in one scenario—interactive television convergence. Viewers are expected to actively interact with their televisions by selecting both programming and advertising. The highly refined targeting of such ads and the high level of viewer involvement will provide a marketing communications vehicle of such effectiveness that traditional television will pale before it. This intelligent, digital system will track all of its contacts with you, learn more about you, and over time develop a trusted and more influential relationship—a virtual friend, if you will. The interactive entertainment business strategy makes similar assumptions in which viewers actively select their programming, play games, change camera angles, do their own instant replays, and more. If this fantastic new medium fails to raise typical viewers from their couch potato stupor or loses their attention as they race through all sorts of activities while the television portrays a talking lamp, fortunes will be lost.

The technology is willing. The economics are improving. Will the consumer cooperate in a way that aligns their needs with what businesses need to earn profits? That is a question for market research that parallels the program described for e-commerce.

■ THE FUTURE OF EMPLOYEE COMMUNICATION

Chapter 8 described the opportunities of tuning in to your employees with reliable research methods. Suffice it to say that the Intranet, the inside-the-company twin of the Internet, is an extremely efficient vehicle for dialogue with employees. Surveys can be executed, with all of the benefits of on-line research to be described in the following sections. Collaborative projects such as Delphi and scenario planning can be managed at low cost and high speed. Employee communications can be handled by the same channel.

■ THE FUTURE OF RESEARCH

The Internet is beginning to revolutionize market research itself. Its ability to quickly and efficiently obtain insights into the attitudes, opinions, and behaviors of consumers will enhance or—in many cases—cannibalize traditional research techniques such as mail and telephone surveys and focus groups. E-commerce sites allow market researchers to gain these insights at the point of purchase and directly integrate them with the inquiry and purchase behavior data automatically captured by the Web site's server log. Relationship marketing promises to blur the lines between research and direct marketing, testing our ethical judgment in the process. Every on-line dialogue with a customer will be data. As e-commerce and relationship marketing grow, so will the customer databases. Advanced analytical techniques such as neural networks and genetic models will enable us to navigate this deluge of data to identify the key consumer insights. Doing business in a wired world will provide a depth of consumer understanding that will make today's marketing strategies seem primitive.

Market researchers must quickly grasp the Internet and take full advantage of its strategic benefits. On-line research offers such promise by its ability to provide what is generally considered impossible: a technique that is faster, cheaper, and better!

➤ Faster

Speed is the first characteristic that pops into most people's minds when weighing the benefits of on-line research, and for good reason. Imagine the potential of having at your disposal almost immediate, continuous feedback with customers and consumers. Survey research has often been used differently from behavioral research techniques—such as television ratings or scanner data—because of time delays inherent in its collection. But with real-time consumer feedback, on-line market research can more effectively support your business objectives by providing, for example, key information on awareness, attitudes, and intention on an overnight basis or real-time consumer segmentation. Consider the value such resources would add to your ability to maneuver in today's dynamic and competitive marketplace!

➤ Cheaper

Actually, not all costs will be cheaper. But you can reduce costs for the field data collection portion of a project and achieve far greater sample sizes than ever before! Larger and more sharply targeted samples become feasible. Therefore, more specific, focused, and useful data become affordable.

➤ Better

The Internet offers many of the best features of current research techniques. On-line research can incorporate error checking and logical flow control (also known as *skip patterns*) in much the same way as telephone-based research, along with the convenience of a self-administered mail questionnaire. And given the fact that researchers and respondents are wired together, responses, reminders, and follow-ups are much easier for everyone concerned. On-line research can deliver test stimuli to the respondents far more efficiently than mail. Of even greater potential—we believe, once bandwidth catches up—is the opportunity to use the Web's multimedia capabilities to provide audio and visual stimuli. Use your choice of music or voice-over sounds with graphics, photographs, animation, and full-motion video to motivate the respondent through the questionnaire and turn your survey instrument into more of a game (a FUN experience) than a questionnaire (a BORING chore or—if it looks like a test—even a SCARY task!).

Put all these benefits together, and they create an entirely new use for survey research. Consumer awareness, attitudes, and preferences can be monitored continuously. These added benefits will transform the way in which survey data is used to support business decisions, but more important is the potential for on-line research to solve the data quality problems that challenge us more and more each day.

The Internet could not have come at a better time for market research. The quality of telephone research now faces severe scrutiny as refusal rates to telephone surveys have increased during the past decade—from 40 percent in 1988 to 46 percent in 1997. Although efforts are being made to turn the tide of declining respondent cooperation, other factors come into play. For example, some who rely on research have grown dissatisfied in recent years, citing extremely lengthy time frames and high costs for data collection. Traditional market research methods may not answer questions fast enough or efficiently enough to be relevant at a time when the pace of business decision making keeps accelerating.

On-line research can help resolve these challenges. As research technology progresses, market researchers have the opportunity to reinvent how they work. And those who lead will benefit from the transition from wood pulp, clip boards, and phone calls to a digital setting of household connectivity and consumer convenience.

How big will the on-line market research industry grow to become? Some predict that between 25 and 30 percent of all research will be conducted over the Internet by 2001. That would represent over a billion dollars. It's no surprise that research companies are investing heavily on this new vision of the future.

■ THE NEXT GENERATION OF MARKET RESEARCH

As with any new technology, initial application focuses on simple translations of tasks previously accomplished with earlier technology. The real breakthroughs come some time later, after enough familiarity has evolved for a radically new vision to appear. Consider two such possibilities for on-line research. First, it enables total integration of attitudinal and behavioral data. The latter tells us *what;* the former tells us *why.* Putting these two pieces together more fully, you may unlock the riddle of understanding consumer behavior and therefore manage it more effectively. The second is that the data is always there. If something happens—a new competitor emerges or your market share drops—you don't need to design, field, analyze, and interpret a new research study. You already have the data in your hands to tell you what's going on. The result: Management reaction time is slashed.

Looking a little further into the crystal ball, we also see the potential for passive attitudinal data. This would be an oxymoron today because to get attitudes, you have to ask questions. In the wired world, however, everything is logged in a database somewhere; the questions you ask (as well as the content you seek) may tell us more than we could ever learn from the questions you answer.

■ CAVEAT RESEARCH EMPTOR!

Recent side-by-side comparisons of on-line and traditional surveys indicate that they would result in the same business decision. It's critical to emphasize that matching sample characteristics is still key to achieving comparability. In fact, a few issues remain unresolved as this point in time:

➤ Is the on-line universe representative of your target population?

➤ Can on-line research predict the behavior of your target population?

➤ Do we have a sound sampling frame? Keep in mind that the development of random-digit dialing was a key factor in the evolution of telephone research. Do we have the analog for on-line research at this point? Not yet.

➤ Do we understand response-time bias—the systematic differences between early and late responders?

➤ Do we know enough about the nonresponse bias that we find on-line?

➤ Do respondents report as truthfully on-line as they do when being interviewed by phone?

These are a few of the questions that must be answered before we can be confident that an adequate methodology has been developed to allow us to enjoy the benefits of on-line research. As on-line penetration grows, however, these issues will be resolved. The challenge for market research now is to determine when it is right for each type of study.

PROJECT LANDMARK

As one ground-breaking study revealed, no consistent or defining differences in attitudes and behaviors were found among two Internet samples and the general population. Project Landmark is a comprehensive study conducted by Market Facts and fielded through the mail to determine if the Internet could provide a valid data collection alternative for mainstream consumer goods and services. Two samples were drawn from the Market Facts consumer mail panel (CMP), which consists of more than five hundred fifty thousand prerecruited

(Continued)

(*Continued*)

households that have agreed to participate in research projects. The panel has been in existence since 1947 and has participated in varying types of research, from mail and telephone surveys to in-person focus and groups and, most recently, on-line studies.

Internet access represented the key differentiating factor between the two samples. The general population sample drawn for this study was selected randomly from the CMP without regard for Internet access. The Internet population was randomly pulled from a subset of the CMP that had been previously screened for Internet access. Both groups were balanced on five key demographic characteristics: household size, household income, age of respondent, population density, and geographic location. To ensure that the impact of the Internet was isolated on attitudes and behaviors, a third sample was added and also balanced to the general population on two additional characteristics: education and occupation. By adding these two additional factors, the study was able to isolate the impact of the Internet relative to any differences attributable to these added characteristics.

Project Landmark's research uncovered no consistent or defining differences in attitudes or behaviors between the two Internet samples and the general population. What differences did exist were directional and limited to the areas of technology, media habits, research participation, and credit card ownership.

Not surprisingly, on-line users are more receptive to technology, but not just with the Web. Attitudes and behaviors regarding technology expressed by the on-line community apparently existed before they began accessing the Internet. That is to say, their decision to surf the Web did not suddenly create a more favorable attitude toward technology and made them rush out to the nearest high-tech store. Adopting the Web was a logical extension.

Differences in media consumption and habits were expected, given the fact that previous research indicated that the Internet population watches less TV and relies more on the Web for their information needs than the general population. They're more likely to read business and travel-related publications and nationally recognized newspapers, which is consistent with their desire to obtain information and their greater inclination to travel. Therefore, the Internet audience can serve as a key prognosticator of future media behavior. Media habits will continue to shift as Web acceptance approaches critical mass. Gaining an understanding of these trends will certainly help your business to strategically anticipate future media efforts and direction.

On-line users, particularly males, are more receptive to participating in marketing research and more likely to participate in research studies, which is a key finding for the research community. This group—younger males in particular—traditionally has been difficult to research. The Internet as a data collection tool will likely increase response rates among this group.

It's no surprise to find higher levels of credit card ownership among on-line users. After all, the ability to open and maintain an on-line account requires submission of a credit card number.

Once you get past technology and information gathering, on-line users live their lives very much the same way as the general population. The Internet itself does not appear to impact a user's basic beliefs, attitudes, or behaviors. But consistent distinctive attitudes toward technology, innovation, and ethnocentrism did surface.

The on-line population believes technology now has and will continue to have a positive impact on their lives. They feel that technology gives them an edge for the future, and they respect those who achieve computer literacy. The general population takes a different view, particularly in their opinion that technology hinders social skills and their belief that you don't need to be able to use a computer today. Regarding innovation, on-line users were more likely to describe themselves as "tinkerers" (that is, those with a desire to tinker with something they can't figure out, as opposed to asking for help) than the general population. In the area of ethnocentrism, on-line users proved less fervid about buying U.S. made products than their general population counterparts.

OPINION POLLS

As the Internet universe veers toward the mainstream, Harris Black International found that on-line research can indeed predict population behavior. In 1998, the company attempted

(*Continued*)

(*Continued*)

to forecast the outcome for gubernatorial and senatorial races in 14 states by using both its traditionally successful telephone survey methodology and comparing its results with those of an on-line survey. As part of the Harris Election 1998 Experiment, researchers invited members of its Harris Poll Online (including nearly three million members at the time) to visit a password-protected Web site and participate in two 10-minute surveys. With 24/7 availability, researchers found that on-line members took part in the pioneering effort at all hours of the day.

The result: The Harris Election 1998 Experiment correctly predicted the winner in 21 of 22 races. The average error of projections for the 44 main candidates (2 candidates in each of the 22 races) came out slightly less than 4 percentage points, which they reported is nearly identical to the average error for telephone polls for similar elections.

The Harris Election 1998 Experiment established that on-line surveys, drawing from a base of almost 3.9 million Internet users, could produce remarkably accurate predictions of voter behavior and compared favorably in most areas with the results from telephone, mail, and in-person interviews. Moreover, it brought more validation to the concept of using the Internet for mounting nationally representative research.

QUAKER OATS

To determine the feasibility of converting a tracking study of Rice Cakes from shopping mall–based to Internet-based research, Quaker Oats conducted a side-by-side comparative study. How did the data compare? Both methodologies delivered very similar data regarding measured levels of total brand awareness, total ad awareness, overall liking, purchase interest, and attribute ratings. Some differences became evident, however, between the on-line and off-line methodologies.

Quaker, which was performing its tenth wave of an awareness, attitude, and usage (AAU) tracker that had historically been conducted via mall intercept using a central location test (CLT), used dual, simultaneous (mall and on-line) methodologies, both of which used shelf shots and print and TV ads as visual stimuli. The study had two primary objectives:

1. Maintain trendability, and thus usability, of all tracking measures.

2. Measure comparability of the two to determine what, if any, differences emerged between the two methodologies.

The off-line study was a mall intercept via CLT screening for female, primary grocery shoppers who also purchase rice in four geographically dispersed markets that had been used before in previous waves. The on-line version took place on Opinion Place—a specialized research site that offers a wide range of research methodologies in a secure environment within the America Online (AOL) proprietary network. The site (AOL keyword: Opinion Place), which was developed by Digital Marketing Services, a joint venture of AOL and The M/A/R/C Group, attracts between twenty thousand to thirty thousand AOL members a week.

On-line promotions invited potential respondents to visit Opinion Place at their convenience to see if they qualified for the study. When AOL members enter Opinion Place, they are directed to a screening questionnaire. Before they begin it, however, they are randomly assigned to one of the surveys currently being conducted. Users have no knowledge of the types of surveys that are being conducted or any control over which survey to which they are assigned.

After finishing the brief screening questionnaire, the system analyzes whether respondents qualify for the survey to which they were previously assigned. If they do qualify, respondents are directed to that survey. If not, Opinion Place checks to see if they qualify for one or more of the other current research studies.

The Quaker study involved more complex programming in order to capture, and actively refer to, unaided awareness data. Qualified respondents (screened for the same qualifications as those in the CLT study) were redirected from AOL to the study located at < http://www.opinion-web.com > (The M/A/R/C Group's Web-based survey domain), which provided the needed programming.

(Continued)

(*Continued*)

Several issues came to light during development of this study. Researchers had to manage the differences between a self-administered, on-line questionnaire and an interviewer-administered CLT questionnaire to ensure trendability of the collected data. Rewording the questionnaire to a self-administered format added some complexity to the question-naire development process.

Graphics capabilities had an impact on the kind of visual stimuli used. For example, the shelf shot used to spur awareness differed between the two studies. Mall respondents saw a complete photograph of brands in the category; on-line respondents saw four separate shelves, which were then presented one at a time, with the names of the brands listed below, due to restrictions on graphics resolutions and download times.

Presentation of TV ads for evaluation were fairly similar. In the mall, a photo board was handed to the respondent. In the on-line study, the photo board pictures and text were presented using an animated graphics format that automatically advanced each frame of the photo board after a predetermined time.

How did the data compare? Both methodologies delivered very similar data. Measured levels of total brand awareness, total ad awareness, overall liking, purchase interest, and attribute ratings were not significantly different, but some results varied. For example, on-line unaided brand awareness was less specific in the on-line study than in the mall study as shown in Table A9.1 and could be attributed to the lack of personal probes normally provided by a live interviewer.

Table A9.1 Unaided Brand Awareness (by Flavor and Size)

	Mall (%)	On-line (%)
Flavor unspecified	0	17
Size unspecified	8	35

Source: The M/A/R/C Group.
Donna Wydra, "Online Tracking; A New Frontier," in *Towards Validation Online Research Day, An ARF Emerging Issue Workshop* (New York: Advertising Research Foundation, 1999) p. 35.

Variations in presentation could also be responsible. Mall respondents saw an 8″ × 10″ photographic shelf shot, while on-line respondents viewed one shelf set at a time. The result: On-line respondents viewed larger package sizes on each shelf.

A third area where data differences between the methodologies emerged was in television ad and brand recognition scores. Although overall claimed recognition levels were similar, the mall data included more incorrect responses, whereas the on-line data contained more "don't know" answers.

The Quaker study offers some valuable lessons for market research regarding an on-line platform:

➤ Moving off-line to on-line requires substantial initial time investment on both the front and back ends of the project. Make sure you factor in enough time on the front end to get the survey up and running to ensure trendability, incorporate differences between the on-line and off-line environments, and pretest the questionnaire. Allow adequate time on the back end as well for analysis. In addition to the standard tracking analysis, you need to analyze differences between on-line and off-line results. And if the data sets need to be combined (for example, to gain adequate base sizes), you must consider the implications of combining the data.

➤ Although the on-line environment is similar to the off-line one in many ways, differences are inherent. The Quaker study showed comparable incidence levels and interview length but also noticeable differences in terms of interviewer influence. Interviewer presence can be both a positive in terms of more detail owing to verbal probes and a negative in that more incorrect responses were in place of "do know" answers. Therefore, desired level of response detail and topic sensitivity should be consciously evaluated and built into the study design. Use on-line programming and logic to prompt more specifically. In this case, researchers could have included specific fields for flavor and size in the brand awareness questions.

DISCOVERY COMMUNICATIONS

In an effort to grow its home video business—as well as its profitability—Discovery Communications (DCI) developed a concept-testing system to identify high-potential title concepts prior to marketplace introduction. DCI had developed a library containing more than one hundred videocassette titles spanning such topics as history, nature, science, and technology as well as how-to videos for both adults and children. Although some of these videos had appeared on Discovery networks, others were developed directly to video.

The first phase of concept testing featured a study using titles including documentary, how-to, and family video titles that were already in the market. Two methodologies were used:

1. A three-phase approach that included mail screening followed by a concept mail-out and then a telephone interview.

2. A self-administered survey conducted on Opinion Place.

Both methods relied on the same questionnaire and were conducted among DCI's core video target of consumers ages 18 and older who had purchased an educational, documentary, or how-to video in the past 12 months. Each concept was rated on purchase intent, likeability, price/value, uniqueness, and a simulated purchase opportunity.

The mail portion of the study began with the distribution of 80,000 screening surveys, which resulted in 50,000 returned. Concepts then were sent out to 900 of DCI's core target. Each respondent received an envelope containing 5 of the 25 video concepts. The 25 concepts were divided into 5 sets of 5 concepts, and the order of evaluation was rotated within each set. Approximately three days following the concept mail-out, respondents were contacted by telephone for the concept interview. After preliminary video purchase behavior information was gathered, respondents verified the rotation number printed on their sealed envelope. Then they opened the envelope and placed the contents face down on a flat surface. A letter between *A* and *E* was printed on the back of each concept, and respondents were given a randomly selected letter and asked to read the corresponding concept. Then they rated the concept on purchase intent, likeability, price/value, uniqueness, and a simulated purchase opportunity. The random selection and rating was repeated for each concept. Interviews were completed with 405 core target consumers.

The on-line portion used a blanket screening "Town Fair Quiz" among Opinion Place visitors to identify potential video buyers. The same screening questions were used, and respondents who met the screening criteria of having purchased an educational documentary or how-to video during the past 12 months were then invited to participate. Those who agreed received an invitational e-mail sent anywhere between two days to two weeks from the qualification date for the concept test, but it was a blinded e-mail invitation so that potential respondents were not aware of the survey subject until they logged on to it. When they entered the survey, preliminary video purchase behavior information was gathered, after which 5 of the 25 video concepts were presented. Text for the concepts was displayed one at a time on the respondent's computer screens. After reading the concept, they answered the same questions regarding likeability, price/value, uniqueness, and a simulated purchase opportunity. As in the mail study, concepts were divided into 5 rotations with 5 concepts per rotation. Concepts within each rotation were randomly rotated to minimize first-order bias. To compensate respondents for their time—and therefore enhance cooperation—on-line respondents were given an incentive for completing the survey. Because all were AOL members, the incentive was either 1 hour and 20 minutes of free time for those on AOL's light-usage plan or $2.50 off the next monthly bill for members on the heavy-usage plan. Interviews were completed with 518 core target consumers

Although females account for most video purchases (89 percent), DCI balanced both samples to include near equal proportions of male and female respondents because males represent a key target for the company's documentary videos as well as for Discovery programming. About half of each sample had purchased videos by direct channels and the other half at retail outlets.

So what did DCI discover? The two different methodologies generated very different winning titles. For 7 out of 25 titles, the difference between the two purchase potential scores was 10 points or greater. In addition, Opinion Place generated

(*Continued*)

(*Continued*)

higher scores, averaging 6 points higher. More important, the rankings of the scores were substantially different. Of particular note was the fact that DCI's best-selling title—which researchers anticipated would generate the highest purchase potential scores from both groups—did in fact rank number 1 among mail respondents but only number 10 with Opinion Place respondents.

As expected, females tend to have higher purchase potential scores than males. Opinion Place females gave an average purchase potential score of 22.2 percent, while males averaged 18.9 percent. Mail survey females had an average score of 15.1 percent; males gave an average of 13 percent. Gender appeared to have a greater impact on title preference among mail respondents than Opinion Place respondents.

The only significant demographic difference between the two sample populations regarded age: Opinion Place respondents were younger. Weighting the data to balance the age, however, did not generate similar scores between the two groups.

Given the differing results, DCI decided to use the mail panel for future video concept testing to more accurately reflect the general video buying population. However, the company plans to continue using Opinion Place when appropriate for studies involving men or on-line users.

A cautionary tale!

■ DIAGNOSTIC

Do you know:

> ➤ How your profitable customers are using the Internet?
> ➤ How many of your customers or potential customers are using the Internet?
>   —What are they doing/using?
>   —What are the trends?
>   —Whom are they loyal to on-line?

➤ What are the drivers of growth?

➤ Why are they on-line?

➤ What attracts and detracts your customers to/from e-commerce?

➤ What are your competitors doing, and how can you outsmart them?

➤ If you are now on-line:

—What are the usage patterns? What share of your most valuable customers off-line do you capture online? Why?

—How can you materially improve your relevant differentiating customer benefits via the Internet? What significant unmet needs can you now meet?

—How should you reach/communicate/transact with your customers on-line? What are their requirements and preferences?

—Are you using the latest ways to monitor your customers on-line while complying with ethical requirements?

—Do you personally read a sample of e-mails from your best customers?

—Are you monitoring key drivers of usage? Do you know the drivers?

➤ Regarding conduct of research online:

—How is the on-line population you need to learn from different from their unwired counterparts? Are these differences relevant to your interests?

—Do respondents answer the types of questions you need to ask differently on-line than they do using your current methodology?

—Does the information provided by the earliest responders differ from that of the later responders? How much longer must you wait for these differences to wash out? How quickly is it safe to act on on-line survey information?

—What are the benefits of on-line research to your business model? How can you maximize their bottom line impact? Could improved information flow, via the Internet, improve your business model?

■ APPENDIX: ETHICAL GUIDELINES FOR THE CONDUCT OF ON-LINE RESEARCH

The Advertising Research Foundation (ARF), working with the European Society For Market and Opinion Research (ESOMAR), has developed the guidelines excerpted here to protect the interests both of Internet respondents and of the users of Internet research findings. The full document is available from the ARF.[1]

➤ Cooperation Must Be Voluntary

The privacy of Internet respondents must be sacred, and their cooperation must at all times be voluntary. No personal information that is additional to that already available from other sources should be sought from, or about, respondents without their prior knowledge and consent.

When obtaining the necessary agreement from respondents, researchers cannot mislead them regarding the nature of the research or how the findings will be used. We understand that occasions arise when the purpose of the research cannot be fully disclosed to respondents at the beginning of the interview in order to prevent biased responses. But researchers must avoid deceptive statements that could annoy or even harm respondents, such as deceiving individuals regarding the usual length of the interview or failing to alert them to the possibility of being re-interviewed at a later date. Be up-front regarding any costs they may incur, when appropriate, (on-line time, for example) for their cooperation in the survey. Respondents are entitled at any stage of the interview—or after the fact—to request that part or all of the record of their interview be destroyed or deleted. And researchers must conform to such requests where reasonable.

➤ Disclose Your Identity

Respondents must be told the identity of the researcher carrying out the project and given the address at which they can contact the researcher without difficulty if they decide at a later date.

➤ Safeguard Respondents' Rights to Anonymity

Unless they have given their informed consent to the contrary, anonymity must always be preserved. When respondents permit data to be passed on in a form that personally identifies them, researchers must ensure the information is used strictly for research purposes. Personal information cannot be used for nonresearch purposes, such as direct marketing, list building, credit rating, fund-raising, or other marketing activities relating to those individual respondents.

➤ Data Security

Take appropriate precautions to protect the security of sensitive data and be reasonably sure that any confidential information provided to them by clients or others is protected against unauthorized access. For example, make sure that sensitive data housed on computer networks are adequately protected by a firewall.

► Reliability and Validity

Those who use market research, as well as the general public, cannot be misled in any way regarding the reliability and validity of Internet research findings. It's essential that researchers adhere to the following:

> ► Follow scientifically sound sampling methods consistent with the purpose of the research.

> ► Publish a clear and readable statement of the sample universe definition used in a given survey, the research approach adopted, the response rate achieved, and the method of calculating this wherever possible.

> ► Publish any appropriate reservations about the possible lack of projectability or other limitations of the research findings that result from nonresponse or other factors.

Keep in mind that any research about the Internet (penetration, user population, etc.) that uses other data collection methods, such as telephone or mail, must also clearly state any sampling or similar limitations.

► Interviewing Minors

Observe all relevant laws specifically relating to minors, although we acknowledge that identifying minors on the Internet cannot be done on the Internet with any major degree of certainty at this point. Obtain permission from a responsible adult before interviewing a minor under the age of 14. Avoid questions on topics generally regarded as sensitive wherever possible, but always handle every case with extreme care.

► Unsolicited E-Mail

Minimize unsolicited e-mail and avoid any inconvenience or irritation such electronic mail may cause the recipient by clearly stating its purpose in the first sentence and making the entire message as brief as possible. Wherever possible, give respondents the ability to exclude themselves from further mailings relating to the research project as well as from any subsequent research resulting directly from it.

■ NOTES

1. Available from the ARF in *Towards Validation Online Research Day, An ARF Emerging Issue* Workshop, (New York: Advertising Research Foundation, 1999).

Is Your Market Researcher Up to the Challenge?

Statistics are no substitute for judgment.
—Henry Clay

Data are not information, information is not meaning.
—Theodore Levitt

Now that you have a clear understanding of Strategic Anticipation® and why it should play a major role in your strategic business-planning process, a critical question remains: Are your market researchers up to the challenge?

Based on recent reports from several leading consulting firms, probably not.

➤ Although many companies today practice just-in-time manufacturing, they often conduct just-in-case marketing. Between 1982 and 1993, manufacturers dramatically reduced their inventories from 2 times monthly sales to around 1.4 times monthly sales. During the same time period, retail and wholesale inventories increased. Companies are failing to leverage their efficient demand-driven production systems by coupling them with similar marketing systems. Instead, they continue to practice forecast-driven marketing. Once these forecasts are enshrined in format targets and budgets, companies deploy their marketing arsenals to achieve those goals, too often at the expense of profitability and the long-term health of the business.

➤ Companies continue to engage in wasteful and even harmful sales promotions. According to *Forbes,* packaged goods manufacturers spent $6.1 billion on more than 300 billion coupons in 1993. Only 1.8 percent of those coupons were redeemed, and of those, 80 percent were used by shoppers who would have purchased the brand anyway. Of the remaining 20 percent, many were redeemed by pure deal shoppers who are not likely to purchase the brand without a large incentive.

➤ Management focuses too much of its marketing arsenals on acquiring new customers. In most companies, retaining customers often is the responsibility of another department or, even worse, no one's responsibility. In some industries—long-distance telecommunications, for example—customer churn has become a major drain on marketing resources and company profitability.

In this chapter, we will look at the best model- and decision-making processes that support principles of Strategic Anticipation® and ensure that your company maintains a continual future-oriented focus.

The key for any successful market research department lies in the ability of its members to sharpen their future-oriented decision-making skills. This begins with identifying and understanding the forces that shape the future and the extent to which they can be predicted. In turn, this requires understanding which events can be predicted and which cannot as well as the probability of accurately forecasting future events.

Uncertainty needs to be understood and taken into account regarding all future-oriented decisions. Such uncertainty can be effectively managed when research departments function at a level of risk consistent with your business culture and take appropriate actions or elaborate on strategies that can soften the impact of negative surprises or events that deviate from initial predictions and strategic plans.

Decision makers must realize that biases and limitations affect their judgment. Therefore, methods to avoid or minimize the negative consequences of such biases and limitations must be factored into the process. An understanding of what contributes to success—as well as those that avoid failure—need to be understood and exploited. Make sure your researchers comprehend the advantages and limitations of planning as a way of preparing to deal with future events, in addition to acceptance of the implications when the future turns out different from what was originally planned.

Realistic and effective approaches to formulating strategies—both competitive and noncompetitive—must be devised and practiced. Researchers need to constantly seek out creative new ways of solving existing problems and generating original ideas. In addition, managers must realize the value of management theories and how such theories can support them in better management of their business. Be it forecasting, planning, formulating strategies, or making major decisions, they also need to fully understand the inherent limits of managerial theories, not to mention the mistakes made in the past. That way, they can avoid similar mistakes in the future.

■ THE ELEMENTS OF PLANNING

Planning for future events can be outlined as a six-step process. Planning will surely fail if one of the steps is omitted or not properly managed. But we must be honest here. Completing all six planning steps does not guarantee success. A variety of other factors (faulty forecasting, environmental changes, competitive actions or reactions, accidents, and so on) may cause failure. Ford Motor Company's Edsel car—introduced in 1957—remains a classic example for researchers today. At that time, the thinking, rationale, market research, design characteristics, testing, and competitive analysis conducted for that automobile launch were indeed impressive. Market research studies had actually started 10 years earlier. Extensive interviews were made to uncover consumer preferences, and top-notch designers were recruited to develop a distinctive style to a size considered prefect for what the consumers wanted at that time. Building the car required lavish resources; promotion and advertising required ate up even more cash. In the end, Ford suffered an estimated $200 million loss, the equivalent of close to a billion dollars by today's economic standards. As noted earlier, continuous research and proper focus could have made a deference.

So let's look at the six planning steps you need to include:

➤ Understand the Need to Plan

Any planning attempt starts with the realization that something needs to be done ahead of time and that action is required to achieve some desired goal. Critical tasks prior to reaching any decision are: understand the situation at hand, consider the problems that could arise when nothing is done, explore the uncertainties, examine the constraints (human, financial, capacity, and material) and the possible benefits, and study the various possibilities for planning and the best approach.

➤ Formulate Alternatives

Once you have established the need for planning, careful study is required to identify all the striking aspects of the task being considered while determining various planning alternatives. Generating alternatives is key, and it requires knowledge about the planning situation under consideration, creativity to generate cutting-edge and potentially successful alternatives, and realism. By *realism,* we mean that identified alternatives must be pragmatic and feasible given current organizational, human, financial, and other constraints. The end result of this planning stage—which likely will involve a fair amount of deliberation—is the ability to formulate a number of planning alternatives that are then presented to management for further consideration. Usually a committee comprising managers assisted by staffpeople takes on this responsibility of studying the most appropriate way to approach planning and the formulate alternatives. Key ingredients include the knowledge, creativity, and realism needed to come up with clever and practical alternatives.

➤ Select the Best Alternative

Senior management must evaluate all available alternatives so that the best among them can be selected. In a world characterized by certainty, selection of best alternatives may seem trivial. But let's face it. In today's business and economic conditions, uncertainty in forecasting, evolving environmental conditions, competitive actions and reactions, and unforeseen events all can destroy the best-laid plans and bring unexpected results or even failure (remember the Edsel!). Selecting the best alternatives, therefore, is a subjective process in which you must weigh the benefits and costs in relation to future uncertainty and the potential risks involved. Such evaluation depends a great deal on managers' subjective preferences, their vision of the future, and their willingness to take risks. When determining the best alternatives, management must realize that as the dollar value of the plans being envisioned grows, the longer the planning horizon becomes as well as the potential benefits and the possible risks if something goes wrong. Planning requires commitments and can result in losses when the future turns out different from original expectations. Planning for short-term, repetitive situations usually is more straightforward than planning for the mid-term (budgeting) or long-term (capital expansion, new product introduction), especially when short-term situations can be quantified and a single measurable objective can be specified and subsequently optimized in the search for the best solution. For mid-term and long-term planning, evaluation becomes much more difficult because trade-offs between short- and long-term benefits are impossible, uncertainty cannot be quantified, and consumer preferences may change. In such cases, determining the essential features of planning, deciding on the main problems confronting the planners, and coming up with appropriate objectives are critical aspects that inevitably influence the perception and ultimate selection of available alternatives. If the essential features, problems, and objectives cannot be correctly identified, planning may disintegrate into an analytical exercise on how to deal with the wrong alternatives or how to evaluate unimportant alternatives using tons of numbers and several computer models. Such cases usually create a perfectly applied analytic selection process that creates zero value.

➤ Implement the Best Alternative

Planning requires concrete action that includes commitment of resources, overcoming resistance to change, and identifying specific tasks that must be completed within certain time parameters. A great deal of coordination and considerable human relations skills often are needed to successfully implement the selected planning alternative.

The person in charge of implementation must be able to get things done and solve a wide array of problems that inevitably surface during any implementation effort, particularly when large or complex tasks are involved or when implementation is carried out for the first time. For repetitive planning tasks, implementation can be formalized in a way so that it can be applied on a routine basis each time planning is required. Moreover, for the first few times, extra effort can be concentrated on refining the plans and making the process of implementation more efficient. It may even be possible to implement both the new planning procedure involving the best alternative and another alternative (if one had been considered as a rival to the best one selected). That way, you can compare the results and confirm the value of the best alternative. In the same way, the new planning procedure can be compared with the ongoing approach to planning—if one exists—to iron out any wrinkles during the transition.

➤ Monitor and Control Results

It's a rare event indeed when actual outcomes mirror those originally predicted during the planning process. Inaccurate forecasts, competitive moves, unforeseen events, unanticipated difficulties, lack of adequate resources, changing environmental conditions, new or underestimated constraints, unforeseen resistance to implementing the plans, and many other factors can affect implementation and result in deviation between plans and reality. Effective monitoring can quickly uncover such deviations. Establish the reasons why they are happening. That way you can take corrective action. Monitoring actual results, establishing causes, and taking corrective action are indispensable planning/implementation activities, more difficult in practice than academic books on the subject of planning seem to imply. In many planning situations, feedback is neither frequent nor precise (consider, for instance, the evaluation of long-term investments or entering new markets). Moreover, the causes of deviations are not obvious, as results below expectations can be attributed to many factors.

➤ Pursuit versus Abandonment of Plans and Planning

Many plans never come to fruition despite the amount of effort made or the number of adjustments or modifications are taken. Similarly, planning processes (e.g., budgeting and production scheduling) can become inappropriate, ineffective, or even obsolete. Fundamental changes in the environment or the market place, serious errors in implementation, unrealistic assumptions about the future, or ill-conceived plans or planning procedures can result in the need to abandon existing plans or planning processes. A correct assessment of the situation at hand, coupled with timely and effective action, is not always easy. Management may believe that investing additional effort and resources to continue a little while longer may rectify the situation and bring about the long-expected benefits. Numerous examples exist of human optimism—of seeing the proverbial light at the end of the tunnel and not wanting to give up after large amounts of money and effort have been spent. On the other hand, premature abandonment can bring about huge opportunity losses when persistence and some additional effort could have brought success and profits. For instance, several companies decided to abandon their entry into the computer market after suffering mounting losses and strong competition. They discovered later that microchips and microprocessors were required for their basic manufacturing activities, which would force them to pay much higher prices to acquire new companies capable of providing the needed expertise than if they had kept their initial computer operations. Consider Xerox. In 1968 the company acquired Scientific Data Systems (SDS), a computer company, for $900 million. It also created a research center in Palo Alto, which built the first personal computer (Alto) in 1973. Xerox abandoned its computer operations seven years later and took a $1.3 billion write-off. To make matters worse, Xerox never capitalized on the development of the personal computer constructed by its Palo Alto center. But Steve Wozniak and Steve Jobs, founders of Apple Computer, did. Had Xerox continued devoting resources for a few more years, it would have achieved an unbeatable lead over IBM and other microcomputer manufacturers. If Apple—which had little financial support, no marketing organization, and minimal engineering expertise—did so well, Xerox could have wrapped up the microcomputer market had it not given up prematurely just before microcomputers became a multibillion-dollar market. But Xerox gave up, and that decision cost the company an opportunity to be a major (if not the most important) player in the fast-growing microcomputer market. New efforts by Xerox to reenter the microcomputer market in the 1970s failed since the opportunity had passed. Worse yet, suggestions that the new personal computer should be used to develop a word processor were not followed, which further aggravated Xerox's opportunity losses.

Other key ingredients for successful planning include the following:

> ➤ *Know the difference between tactics and strategy.* Develop your strategic marketing plan first, placing greater emphasis on scanning the external environment. Identify early the forces emanating from it and develop appropriate strategic responses that involve all levels of management.

> ➤ *Have the marketing function work closely with operations.* Put marketing planning as close as possible to the consumer. Whenever practical, have both the marketing and sales departments report to the same person, who would not normally be the chief executive officer.

> ➤ *Know the difference between the marketing function and the marketing concept.* Marketing is a management process in which the resources of the entire organization are applied in an effort to satisfy the needs of selected customer groups and achieve business objectives. First and foremost, marketing is an attitude of mind, not a series of functional activities.

> ➤ *Develop in-depth analysis.* Devise a checklist of questions customized according to the level in the organiza-

tion and agreed upon by all levels. Use these questions as the basis for your organization's management information systems. Encourage managers to incorporate the tools of marketing into their audits, such as product life cycles and product portfolios.

➤ *Understand the difference between process and output.* Information is the foundation on which a marketing plan is built. Internal and external information creates intelligence, and your marketing plan, in turn, uses that intelligence to outline your organization's competitive advantage, that is, how managers perceive their own position in their markets relative to their competitors. State objectives to be achieved within a designated period of time, strategies to achieve those objectives, required resources, and anticipated results.

➤ *Make sure those responsible for market research have the knowledge and skills for the job.* Communication and interpersonal skills are key, but more importantly, these individuals need to know how to use the tools of marketing (see "The Tools Market Researchers Need to Succeed" at the end of this chapter).

➤ *Devise a systematic approach to marketing planning.* Having a set of written procedures and a common format for marketing planning will ensure that all key issues are systematically considered, pulls together the essential elements of strategic planning for every strategic business unit (SBU) in a consistent manner, and helps corporate management compare diverse businesses and understand the overall condition of and prospects for the organization.

➤ *Prioritize objectives.* Make sure all objectives are prioritized according to their impact on the organization and their urgency and that resources are allocated accordingly. The key role of senior management is to concentrate lower-level management attention on factors that are both high leverage and actionable in order to get the essential jobs done effectively.

■ PRINCIPLES FOR A WORLD-CLASS MARKET RESEARCH MODEL

You can develop the best market research department when you apply the following guidelines:

➤ Have a well-defined market research group that is organizationally distinct and led by a senior manager who is head of market research. Research staff are accountable to both the market research group and the business units.

➤ Consider the market research group as a center of excellence, with top-quality people recruited for specific research skills.

➤ Assign dedicated research professionals within the market research group to each business unit. These reps become part of the business unit team and focus on satisfaction of internal customers. These dedicated research professionals are sometimes located together in a central group and sometimes located within the business units.

➤ Make business units responsible for research budgets. In some cases, the market research department can be responsible for some discretionary budget.

➤ Have internal customers sponsor all research projects.

➤ Develop research plans, budgets, and prioritization during the annual planning process. Make sure both researchers and end users take part in the planning process.

➤ Ensure that the research culture is action oriented and focused on business issues.

➤ Create a structured network through which research staff maintain contact with regular staff meetings to exchange ideas on new techniques, coordinate cross-business unit issues, and swap notes on vendors.

➤ Communicate research material internally via presentations, not just by distributing hard copy through interoffice mail.

■ THE BEST PROCESS

World-class companies have devised formal processes for conducting, analyzing, and using market research that contributes to a constant cycle of learning. The following model ensures proper identification of key drivers, which are periodically updated; provides for continuous monitoring versus expectations; promotes consistent steering; and ultimately results in continuous improvement.

1. *Strategy formulation.* The central research group works alongside strategy/business planning so that all research has clear strategic objectives. Independent research groups may contribute to sensitive areas of strategy, for example, by providing objective analysis when two business units are developing competing products.

2. *Product initiation.* Although only business units hold budgets for research, the research rep often initiates a study either at the annual planning session or ad hoc during the year.

3. *Problem formulation.* Research reps should be fully involved in structuring hypotheses with line management and should network with other research staff to avoid duplication.

4. *Research design and methodology formulation.* The research rep is the expert who takes responsibility on the business unit team for design, which is formulated in conjunction with an outside supplier.

5. *Data collection.* Outsourced, but the research rep and appropriate line management would attend focus groups.

6. *Analysis and interpretation.* The external agency provides initial interpretation, but the research rep develops the analysis in line with wider business issues and internalizes the learning.

7. *Communication of results.* Always done through the presentation and explanation of findings, usually by

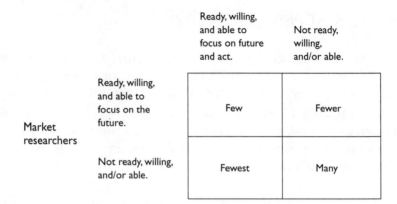

Figure 10.1 Business Decision Makers.

the research rep. Knowledge is shared with the research group and with other business units, if appropriate.

8. *Implementation.* All research is action oriented and focuses on a business decision. The research rep needs to monitor and evaluate during the implementation phase, performing further work as necessary.

All of these elements must work together in an ongoing cycle as indicated by Figure 10.1.

■ VALUE HIERARCHY FOR MARKET RESEARCH

The value that market research brings to the organization can be viewed as a triangle segmented by four key business tools: data, information, knowledge, and wisdom (see Figure 10.2).

➤ Data

Serving at the base of this hierarchical triangle, data is developed using custom research and ongoing tracking and mea-

Figure 10.2 Value Hierarchy for Market Research.

surement research. The result is a status report that provides a historical look at what is going on in the marketplace.

➤ Information

Internal market research consultants, as well as project databases and on-line extracts, combine to give you response analysis, a look at why things are happening and your first glimpse into the future.

➤ Knowledge

Using cross-study synthesis, decision support models, and buyer decision models, you now create an integrated response simulation. At this point, you actually begin to create possible futures by determining the meaning behind the insights provided by your data and information segments as well as development of "what if we" scenarios.

➤ Wisdom

All efforts lead to this outcome. By now you have fully integrated the three previous segments to develop an action plan based on what your customer segment experts now can determine are the best available decisions.

■ BEST PRACTICES

Building and maintaining a yearly knowledge book will allow you to synthesize and memorialize key learning that will help your business to better understand critical drivers, including key customer satisfaction and loyalty, and develop successful marketing strategies.

Knowledge is the fuel that runs your business. In the new value chain—which begins with the customer and ends with your organization—knowledge represents the key raw material that keeps your system going. Knowledge can be ignored and disorganized. If you're like most businesses, knowledge hoarding is the biggest obstacle to utilizing your intellectual capital. Only 12 percent of respondents polled in a recent Ernst & Young survey described their company as above average at transferring existing knowledge across their own internal borders. A whopping 47 percent admitted to poor performance in this vital area. At its best, market information can be organized to almost laser-like proportions by which both suppliers and customers profit. It all depends on how you look at knowledge and your ability to create and use it.

Knowledge patterns will proliferate as the economy moves from manufacturing of goods to application of useful ideas. Several major knowledge patterns currently exist, but many companies are not ready to take advantage of them because they failed to anticipate or plan for them, that is, they don't fit into traditional strategic models. But your business can profit from knowledge patterns once you gain an in-depth understanding of the current patterns and use them to anticipate the profusion of new patterns that will emerge in the near future. Let's look at three major knowledge patterns that have emerged to date.

➤ Product-to-Customer Knowledge Pattern

In the product-to-customer knowledge pattern, profit-oriented suppliers convert a flow of product transactions into a profound and systematized knowledge of customers' preferences, price sensitivity, and buying behavior. This knowledge can produce new profit streams in many different ways: category management, precision merchandising, or dramatic increases in the innovation success rate.

Category Management

As we discussed in Chapter 7, grocery store shelves are literally crammed with products, complicated by the multitude of new products introduced to the market. Retail real estate—not the product itself—has become the real profit source. Product expertise allows manufactures to create and capture that knowledge, which they then convert to a new, knowledge-based offering for retailers: category management.

A mismatch between what's on the shelves and what customers want leads to lost sales and customer frustration. In each product category, the manufacturers know (or could know) more about customer preferences, price sensitivity, and buying behavior than the retailers do, and they can work to correct any mismatch. More manufacturers are offering to manage the entire category, not just their own products, for retailers. Superior knowledge of customer behavior gives manufacturers the ability to generate significantly higher gross margin per square foot by skillfully manipulating manufacturers' brands, house brands, generics, and quantities of stock to produce the greatest return on shelf space.

The value lies in the unique customer knowledge that manufacturers use to create the maximum returns for the grocer.

Precision Merchandising

It's a problem retailers continually face: How do you balance demand and availability? Excess inventory results in greater carrying costs; insufficient inventory means having needed products out of stock, resulting in lost gross margin.

The product-to-customer knowledge pattern allows companies to remedy this problem not just by store but by region. Wal-Mart's huge transactions flow by region has allowed it to develop predictive algorithms that help model demand patterns with heretofore unimagined precision. This customer knowledge at a macro level helps to avoid both stockouts and excess inventory on a region-by-region basis. Precision merchandising takes the guesswork out of merchandising.

Consider a location-by-location example of precision merchandising being developed by Coca-Cola. The application of telemetry technology will enable soft-drink manufacturers such as Coca-Cola to monitor the in-stock status of each individual vending machine. Greater profitability will be realized from reductions in both stockouts and service calls, thanks to actual knowledge of customer purchasing behavior.

Innovation Success Rate

The product-to-customer knowledge pattern also has a role for industrial companies. In this case, the product becomes a commodity, and the supplier gains deep insights regarding customer's usage systems to the point where it can create a precise model of the customer's true economics. GE, for example, developed highly sophisticated models of the technical and economic performance of its products (locomotives, jet engines) in the context of the customers' usage systems. GE uses this information to define and drive its product and service innovations that matter most to each customer. It has shifted its focus from the product itself to how the product works for the customer.

One specialty chemical company took the idea of customer modeling to the next level. Like GE, it developed proprietary models of its products' economic and technical value added to the customer. But it has also developed a model of the customers' political hierarchy and decision-making process. The company—which succeeds by selling innovative materials and fabrication methods to the automotive industry—knows that it's political value, not just economic value added, that matters. Economic innovation will fall flat when it means significant career risk for the decision makers.

The company's "politics *and* economics decision-making" model (developed on a plant-by-plant basis) allows it to introduce innovations only where there is a high probability of acceptance, given the prevailing political climate. Although its competitors have the technical abilities to create economic value added, they lack the political knowledge of the customer that could result in high success rates for new product introductions.

➤ Operations-to-Knowledge Pattern

There used to be great profitability in owning fixed assets and running operations based on those assets. Consider airlines, hotels, bookstores, steel mills, computer manufacturers, and many others. Some are still profitable, but many have lost profit or fail to return the cost of capital. Overcapacity, customer power, and competitive intensity have driven profits away. When profits fade from basic asset-intensive operations, there are numerous opportunities to create profit in new ways: build a unique knowledge position, fill a niche that has room for just one player, or create services built on knowledge so scarce that it makes these services valuable to buyers and sellers alike.

Only a few players so far have been able to develop these new profit-making activities, based on the knowledge and experience they gain from running their operations. In some cases, outsiders capitalized on the operations-to-knowledge pattern and often generate more profit than the industries from which their information is derived. Both are provided by players from outside the base industry. Airlines and TV networks find it difficult to make money, while the *Official Airlines Guide* and *TV Guide* make handsome profits.

The selling of contract services represents one of the most pervasive forms of the operations-to-knowledge pattern. Marriott, for example, divested itself of all hotel ownership to concentrate on providing management services both in previously owned properties as well as new hotels where managers asked Marriott to run their operations for them. Barnes & Noble's expertise in running bookstores allowed it to compete successfully for contracts to run college bookstores. Although the institutions retain the assets, Barnes & Noble profits from ownership of the management contracts.

Each of these companies changed despite the fact that their original business models remained profitable. In other cases, the operations-to-knowledge pattern was adopted in crisis. Case in point: Japanese steel makers siphoned value away from U.S. steel mills in the 1970s only to see their own value decline during the next decade. Value was shifting from ownership of capacity to knowledge-based value. Unlike their U.S. predecessors, Japanese steelmakers capitalized on this shift from operations to knowledge. They sold proprietary processes and process expertise to steel makers around the world. They also sold plant design and engineering services to new steel installations in Latin America, Korea, and other markets. They generated enormous profit margins from these knowledge-based services while steelmaking margins were dropping to zero. By doing so, they extended the returns on their economic activity by a decade longer than would have been possible in a pure asset-ownership-and-operations business model.

The biggest obstacle to taking advantage of the operations-to-knowledge pattern is a mental block that causes organizations to believe "We're a manufacturer" or "We're a hospital," as opposed to thinking "We're a business organization whose job is to create customer benefits and wealth through the constant search for new sources of profitability." Clearly, it no longer makes sense to think of the world in terms of "products" or "services." Instead, think "productized" services and "serviced" products, as Chris Meyer and Stan Davis suggest in their book *Blur*.[1]

➤ Knowledge-to-Product Pattern

The shift from value based on tangibles to value based on knowledge is beginning to permeate the economy. But there is an important movement in the other direction, as experience, expertise, and knowledge are transformed into products. In many business situations, knowledge is valuable but inaccessible. Trapped in the labor-intensive economics of professional service firms or in fragmented databases, it is hard to access and hard to apply. An embryonic but increasingly frequent pattern is one in which knowledge is converted into a product in a way that creates benefits for customers through convenient, cost-effective access and suppliers through the opportunity for much higher rates of value growth.

Consider the following examples of companies that leveraged the knowledge-to-product pattern:

➤ SAP, the German software manufacturer, produces software systems designed to help companies link their internal business processes. In the past, companies had to develop internal systems and often purchased large quantities of systems integration services to reach the same results.

SAP converted knowledge of these internal processes and challenges into a product that allows companies to address business process linkage issues more effectively and at a lower cost.

➤ SDRC (Structural Dynamics Research Corporation) was an engineering consulting firm that transformed its engineering expertise into a computer-aided design/ computer-aided manufacture (CAD/CAM) program that allowed customers to do nondestructive testing of new product designs and, as a result, shorten their time to market.

➤ PeopleSoft used its knowledge of human resource processes and procedures to develop software products and platforms for HR applications that allowed customers to manage their HR processes more efficiently and, at the same time, enabled PeopleSoft to experience dramatic value growth.

■ DIAGNOSTIC–STRATEGIC ASSESSMENT OF RETURN ON INVESTMENT FOR A MARKETING RESEARCH DEPARTMENT

1. Quantify the contribution of new products and services developed with the advance involvement and approval of the marketing research department (MRD).
2. Measure the growth in total lifetime value of targeted customers (for example, those in segments shown to be profitable) from programs developed with the advanced involvement and approval of the MRD.
3. Calculate the savings of programs, products, or services that were not pursued or were stopped on the basis of MRD work.
4. Calculate total market research costs (MRC) of work paid, both internal and external.

To calculate return on investment (ROI), first determine the total net present value (NPV) of the figures developed in steps 1, 2, and 3. Then divide that number by the total market research costs developed in step 4. Multiple the resulting number by 100.

The formula looks like this:

$$ROI = \frac{NPV\ (1\ +\ 2\ +\ 3)\ \times\ 100}{MRC\ (4)}$$

THE TOOLS MARKET RESEARCHERS NEED TO SUCCEED

INFORMATION

➤ How to get it.
➤ How to use it.

POSITIONING

➤ Market segmentation.
➤ Planning systems.
➤ Competitive strategies.

PRODUCT LIFE CYCLE ANALYSIS

➤ Gap analysis.

PORTFOLIO MANAGEMENT

➤ Product portfolio matrix.
➤ Directional policy matrix.

(Continued)

(Continued)

MANAGEMENT OF THE FOUR *P*S

➤ Product.

➤ Price.

➤ Place.

➤ Promotion.

TYPICAL RECOMMENDATIONS TO IMPROVE A RESEARCH DEPARTMENT

➤ If not overcoming turf to integrate, lock in a communication exchange between researchers.

   —Quarterly meetings.

   —Daily/weekly e-mails.

   —Midlevel linkage.

➤ De-average all research product for internal clients.

   —Recreate all routine report formats/contents for each key user (automate where possible).

   —Cross-pollinate by informing one group about the implications and activities of others.

➤ De-average all research studies of external consumers.

   —Focus on the future profitable segments.

➤ Create a futures team.

   —Technology.

   —Competition.

   —Research techniques.

➤ Build on-line knowledge books.

➤ Initiate 360 reviews within department and customer satisfaction process for internal clients.

EXAMPLE OF RESEARCH DEPARTMENT CHARTER

Quality information for better decision-making

➤ Develop, acquire, and provide accurate, reliable, and useful information for effective, strategic decision making.

> ➤ Conceptualize and quantify decisions to maximize profitable customers and valuable employees.
>
> ➤ Business development: Measure to manage and manage to grow.
>
>   —Understand and anticipate behavior.
>
>   —Identify opportunities (and risks) for growth.

■ NOTES

1. Stan Davis and Christopher Meyer, *Blur: The Speed of Change in the Connected Economy* (Cambridge, MA: Perseus Books, 1998).

Conclusion

At the beginning of this book, we told you that we had a point of view and that we were writing only for those willing to think about the future and accept that it will likely be different than today. More importantly, we hope it is now clear that you must be willing to do something about the difference—to act in anticipation of what might happen.

So for us, truths 1 and 2 are that the future will be different from the past and present (so no more straight-line forecasts) and that effective leadership requires Strategic Anticipation®.

Our third point is that market research can be a major contributor to enabling anticipation. We've tried to illustrate how research and researchers can provide knowledge and insight that will help decision makers understand and think about scenarios and options for the future and, just as importantly, how customers, competitors, channels, and employees might behave. In the best cases, research can validly estimate how people will react to various actions the business might take. Throughout the planning process, we believe, research should interact with leadership and finance people to ensure that the economic implications are perceived. (As we noted, too often even very good research loses its possible utility because it is not linked to economic reality. Most prevalent is probably new product work that yields recommendations based only on relative demand for features and channels without balancing the relative costs of producing those features and distribution.)

Finally, there needs to be linkage of the future research with how the business is aligned, though admittedly, we did not delve into this issue other than to acknowledge that future strategy cannot be made in an organizational vacuum. You can only move where your people and processes can go, and they can only get there with effective guidance.

Having written all this, we must now acknowledge the fourth truth.

Although we provided many positive examples of use of tools and truly future-focused businesses, we don't really know of many major businesses today in which market researchers are an integral part of a leadership team practicing Strategic Anticipation®.

Our belief is that most researchers are not researching the future, and even fewer decision makers are pushing them to do so. Our hope is that the information conveyed in this book will help change this balance, that decision makers will demand more from their researchers, and that the researchers will meet the challenge.

In fact, let's take another look at Figure 10.1:

Market researchers		Ready, willing, and able to focus on future and act.	Not ready, willing, and/or able.
	Ready, willing, and able to focus on the future.	Few	Fewer
	Not ready, willing, and/or able.	Fewest	Many

Business Decision Makers.

Index